D1432726

SILVER BURDETT & GINN
SOCIAL STUDIES

New Jersey
Yesterday and Today

THE GREAT SEAL OF THE STATE OF NEW JERSEY

LIBERTY AND PROSPERITY

1776

GRADE-LEVEL CONTRIBUTORS

Sandra F. Ginsburg-Hirsch, Teacher,
Hillside School, Closter, New Jersey

Sister Mary Inez, Teacher,
St. Steven's School, Kearny, New Jersey

Kenneth F. MacDonald, Teacher,
Silver Bay School, Toms River, New Jersey

Thelma B. Williams, Teacher,
Sussex Avenue School, Morristown, New Jersey

SILVER BURDETT & GINN
SOCIAL STUDIES

New Jersey Yesterday and Today

ELAINE FAY,
Former Director of Education,
New Jersey Historical Society, Newark, New Jersey

CHARLES A. STANSFIELD, JR.,
Professor of Geography,
Glassboro State College, Glassboro, New Jersey

CONSULTANTS

HERBERT C. KRAFT,
Professor of Anthropology and Director of the
Archaeological Research Center and University Museum,
Seton Hall University, South Orange, New Jersey

BARBARA M. TUCKER,
Assistant Professor of History,
Rutgers, The State University, New Brunswick, New Jersey

SILVER BURDETT & GINN

MORRISTOWN, NJ • NEEDHAM, MA
Atlanta, GA • Cincinnati, OH • Dallas, TX • Menlo Park, CA • Northfield, IL

ISBN 0-382-08305-9

CONTENTS

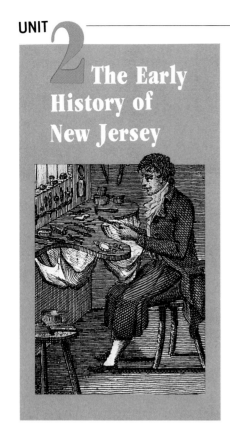

2 The Early History of New Jersey

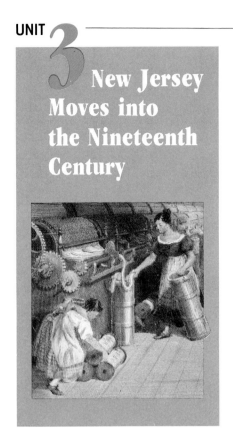

New Jersey — Our Home

This year will be an exciting year for you. You will be learning all about your home state, New Jersey. The land of New Jersey has wonderful variety. In this unit you will learn about the beautiful land of New Jersey — its farmland, seashore, mountains, and forests.

You will also learn about the people of New Jersey — who they are, where they live, and what they do. You will learn why and how the land is useful to New Jerseyans.

Farming helps to keep New Jersey green. New Jersey farmers grow fruits and vegetables and raise animals.
■ **What farming activity is shown in this photograph?**

The seashore, mountains, and forests of New Jersey are enjoyed
by New Jerseyans and by people from out of state.
■ Does the land near where you live look like any of these places?

Because New Jerseyans are proud of their state, they have chosen symbols that tell about New Jersey. A symbol is something that stands for, or tells about, something else. The state bird and state flower are symbols of New Jersey. Let's look at these and other symbols of our state.

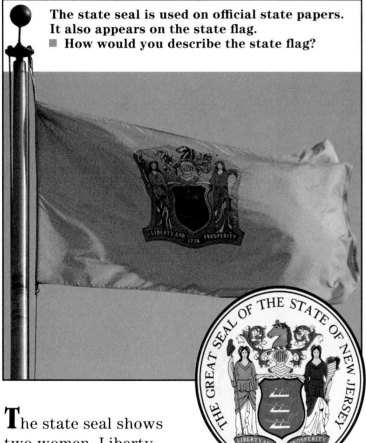

The state seal is used on official state papers. It also appears on the state flag.
■ **How would you describe the state flag?**

The eastern goldfinch is New Jersey's state bird. The goldfinch lives in our state all year round. It can be seen in fields and meadows, where it feeds and nests near the ground. The male bird is bright yellow and has a black forehead in the summer. The female is a grayish-yellow color. The wings and tails of both are black with white markings.

The state seal shows two women. Liberty stands on the left. Ceres, the goddess of agriculture, or farming, stands on the right. The horn of plenty held by Ceres, the horse's head, and the three plows shown below it are all symbols of New Jersey's agriculture. Farming was important when the state seal was designed. It is still important to our state today. The state motto is "Liberty and Prosperity." The date 1776 is the year New Jersey and other states broke away from Great Britain to form our country.

The eastern goldfinch is our state bird.
■ **Is this goldfinch a male or a female?**

The leaves of the red oak are green in the spring and summer.
■ **Do you know what the nut of the red oak is called?**

Among the many kinds of trees that grow in the forests of our state is the red oak. The red oak is New Jersey's state tree. The red oak is one of the fastest-growing kinds of oak trees. Because of this, it is often chosen for planting along streets and avenues. But whether seen in the city or the country-side, the rich red color of its leaves in the fall is a beautiful sight.

Our state flower is the purple violet. The purple violet is one of many kinds of violets. Violets grow in the wild. They are also grown in gardens. The small flowers of the violet bloom in the spring. The purple vio-let grows throughout New Jersey. This kind of violet is also known by another name— "Jersey Gem." Do you know what a gem is?

The purple violet can be found all over New Jersey.
■ **How would you describe the flowers and leaves of the purple violet?**

There are many times when you will find maps helpful. If you can read a map, chances are you will not get lost. You might even find interesting places to visit by using maps. Maps show you where things are. They help you find out how to go from one place to another. They also can tell you how far places are from one another.

Pat and her friends are looking at a map of Six Flags Great Adventure. They have just finished riding Rolling Thunder. They are trying to find the way to the hamburger stand where they are going to meet Pat's parents for lunch. They are hungry and do not want to get lost.

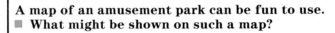
A map of an amusement park can be fun to use.
■ What might be shown on such a map?

Tony and Maria like to shop with their mother at Cherry Hill Mall. The map of the mall helps the three of them save steps and time on their shopping trips. Tony is using the map of the mall to find out where a sports shop is. Maria has a puppy. She wants to buy a book about training dogs. She will find the bookstore that is closest to the sports shop.

The mall map shows all the stores in the mall.
■ Where in a mall is such a map found?

14

Marilyn draws her route on the chart. Then she notes the landmarks on her route. In flight she checks off each landmark as she sees it.
■ Why, do you think, does she check off each landmark as she sees it in flight?

Some people use maps every day in their jobs. Marilyn flys a small plane on her job. Before a flight, she plans her trip with a special map called an aeronautical (ar ə nôt′ i kəl) chart. The chart looks somewhat like a road map. It has landmarks, such as bridges, highways, towns, and rivers. The chart also shows airline routes and landing fields.

Many kinds of sports events and concerts are held at the Meadowlands Sports and Recreation Complex in East Rutherford. It is the home of the New Jersey Generals, New York Giants, and New York Jets football teams; the New Jersey Nets basketball team; and the New Jersey Devils hockey team. Christopher and his friends are using a stadium seating map at the Meadowlands to find their seats. They do not want to miss the kick-off.

The children are checking the seating plan.
■ How do their tickets help them?

These are just a few examples of ways that people can use maps. In Unit 1 you will begin to use many different kinds of maps. These maps will teach you a great deal about New Jersey — your home state.

1 Your Community and You

Studying History Around You

Why do we study history?

VOCABULARY

geography	government
history	transportation
ancestor	commute
community	

What Is History? This school year you will be studying the **geography** and **history** of New Jersey. Geography is the study of the earth and how people use it. History is the story of what happened in the past. (Words in heavy type are in the Glossary, which begins on page 269.)

Your **ancestors** are part of history. An ancestor is a member of your family who lived long ago. Your parents' lives are part of history, too. The events that take place in your lifetime will also be part of history. An event is an important happening.

The Past Is Important Learning about the past helps us to understand the way things are today. When we

This photograph shows Millburn's Main Street early in this century. Compare it with the photograph of the community's Main Street today.
■ What things are the same?
■ What things are different?

know why something has changed, it makes more sense to us. We also study history because we are curious about the way people lived in the past. We want to know where they lived, what they ate, and what they did for fun. Finally, learning about history helps us to avoid making the mistakes of the past as we plan for the future.

Where You Live The place where you live is important because it has a history all its own. The place where you live is called a **community.** A community may be a town or a city. It may even be one part of a town or city. What is the name of the community in which you live?

Every community is different. Some are large, and others are small. One community may be 200 years old. Another may have started just 10 years ago. But all communities have some things in common. All communities have places where people live. Communities also have stores, schools, and places of worship. Most communities also have some kind of **government.** A government is a group of men and women who make laws and see that the laws are carried out. Communities are good places to learn about history.

How Communities Begin and Grow Some of the communities in New Jersey began many years ago. Often

17

they were started at a special location. Many early communities, such as Trenton and Paterson, were located near a river or a waterfall. This water was important because it helped to give power to waterwheels in mills. Grain was ground in gristmills to make flour, and logs were cut into lumber at sawmills.

Some communities, such as Vineland, began where there was rich farmland for growing crops. The communities of Newark and Elizabeth grew up near busy roads and trails. Many communities by roads and trails and by rivers or the ocean became **transportation** centers. Transportation is the moving of people and goods from one place to another. Transportation connects a place with many other places.

Today, location is still an important reason why communities begin and grow. Many new communities are located near highways or railroads. Others are located near river or sea ports. A port is a place where ships can load and unload goods.

Communities also grow because of the jobs they offer. Many New Jersey communities, like Morristown, Paramus, and Clifton, have large companies with many jobs. Some people live in one community but work in a different one. They must **commute** to and from work. *Commute* means "to travel back and forth regularly." Most people commute by bus, train, or car.

This old mill is located in Clinton.
■ What does it tell you about how the community of Clinton started?

There are two other reasons why communities begin and grow. One reason is that communities offer many goods and services. Goods are supplies that people need to live, and services are things that are done for people. Another reason is that some communities are located in a beautiful place near a lake, a beach, or the mountains. In New Jersey, communities like Hopatcong and Cape May began for this reason.

CHECKUP
1. What is history?
2. Why is the past important?
3. List four reasons why communities grow.

4. **Thinking Critically** In what kinds of places do people in a community live?

Looking at Your Community

What is local history?

VOCABULARY

| local history | historical |
| monument | marker |

Looking Around You The community you live in is one of the best places to begin your study of history. The history of a community is called **local history.** The beginnings of a community, the people who have lived there, important events that have happened there, and even old buildings make up local history. To learn about community history, find answers to these questions.

1. Who were the first people to live here? Why did they come here?

2. Why is this community located where it is?

3. Why did this community grow?

After you have learned something about your community's beginnings, take a good look around you. Most of us live in a place but never really explore it. Where do people live in your community? What kinds of buildings are there?

Sometimes, buildings can be your first clues in finding out about local history. Why a building was built and who built it are good questions to start you on your search. You can start with just about any building, from your own house to the grocery store down the street. Here are

A one-room schoolhouse over 100 years ago, this building is now a branch of the Paramus Library.
■ How can you tell that the building was once a schoolhouse?

19

some questions to ask about buildings in your community.

1. When was this building built?
2. Why was this building built?
3. How is it used today?

When you have answered these questions, you will understand how the building has helped your community to grow. By studying buildings, you may learn where people in the past lived in your community, where they went for entertainment, what kinds of jobs your community once offered, and how your community has changed over the years.

Monuments, Markers, and Main Street A **monument** is something that is built to honor a person or event. A monument can be a building, a sculpture, or a tower. A sculpture is a work of art that is usually made of stone or wood. A tower is a building that is very much taller than it is wide. Are there any monuments in your community? You can learn about local history by studying monuments. They can tell you about an important person who lived in your community or a special event that took place there. What do monuments in your community tell about?

Historical markers also tell about the past. Historical markers are signs that show where old and important buildings are located,

Historical markers and monuments are all shapes and sizes.
■ How do the monuments shown here differ?
■ What do the markers tell you about New Jersey's past?

Thomas Nast drew cartoons about events and people of the late 1800s. He was also known for his drawings of Santa Claus. Nast once lived in this house in Morristown.
■ **Why, do you think, is his house important to the community?**

where a battle was fought, or where some other event took place. Sometimes a historical marker will tell about an important meeting that took place in a building or a famous person who once lived there. New Jersey has many historical markers.

Now you know that monuments and historical markers tell about *special* people, events, and buildings. But where can you go to learn more about the everyday history of your community? To Main Street! Main Street is a fun place to learn about local history. Main Street is the most important street in your community. By exploring Main Street, you can learn what was important to people

living in your community in the past and what is important today. How many food stores are on your community's Main Street? Does it have a movie theater, barbershop, or drug store? Are there any clothing shops, bookshops, or travel agencies? How long have these places been here? From monuments to markers to Main Street, your community is a special place, with a history like that of no other community.

Learning from Names Every community has a name. Names often tell us about the history or the geography of a place. How did your community get its name?

This theater in Red Bank was named after Count Basie. The well-known musician and band leader was born in the town of Red Bank.
■ What kinds of events do people enjoy at the Count Basie Theater?

Every street also has a name. Sometimes streets are named for people who have been important to the community. In Princeton, for example, Witherspoon Street was named for John Witherspoon. Witherspoon was a minister and the president of the College of New Jersey, which is now Princeton University. Can you think of streets in your community that are named for people? Who were those people?

Buildings in a community can have names, too. A building may be named for the person who owns it or for the people who helped to build it by giving money. It may also be named for a famous person. The Clara Maass Medical Center in Belleville, for example, is named for the New Jersey nurse who helped doctors find out more about the disease malaria. Think of the names of some buildings in your community. Find out how they got their names.

CHECKUP
1. What does local history include?
2. What is a historical marker?
3. What can you learn from names of places in a community?

4. **Thinking Critically** If you could build a monument in your community, what person or event would you choose to honor?

Finding Out About the Past

What are some historical sources?

Newspapers Looking around you is the first step in learning about local history. The second step is to study **historical sources.** A historical source is something or someone that tells us about the past. Monuments, markers, and old buildings can be historical sources. But there are many other kinds of sources. For example, old newspapers are another important kind of historical source. They explain what happened in the past. Advertisements in old newspapers can give you clues about life in the past. They can tell you what kinds of goods people could buy and how much goods cost. Can you think of another kind of advertisement in an old newspaper that would tell you how people lived?

Historical Documents Another kind of historical source is a **historical document.** A historical document is a written record from the past. Letters are one kind of historical document. By reading old letters, you can find out what people thought about and how they lived. Sometimes old letters will even tell you about past events in a community.

Another kind of historical document is an **account book.** An account book is a record kept by a store. It tells what goods were sold and how much they cost.

This advertisement for a grocery store in Englewood tells a great deal about life in the 1940s.
■ What items can still be found in stores?
■ How are prices different today?

23

The government of each community also keeps records. There are records of births, deaths, and marriages. By looking at community records, you can also find out who owned a piece of land or a certain house. You can learn about the kinds of services the community had. Did the community have a police or fire department? When were roads built?

The Camera's Eye   Almost everyone enjoys looking at old photographs. We especially like to see what we looked like when we were very young. We also like to look at photographs of our family. Photographs are good historical sources because they can show how people dressed in the past, what houses looked like, and even what Main Street was like. You can compare old pictures to more recent ones to see how much things have changed.

Of course, before the camera came along, people drew and painted pictures of people, places, and things. Old drawings and paintings are also good historical sources. They can tell you about even earlier times than photographs.

Artifacts and Archaeology   What do old glass bottles, a coin made 100 years ago, and an Indian clay pipe all have in common? They are **artifacts** (är′ tə fakts). An artifact is an object that was made and used by people in the past. Where are artifacts found?

Old photographs can tell you many things about the past.
■ What community service is this?
■ How is this community service different today?

24

Old toys such as these are artifacts.
■ **How do these toys from the past compare with toys that you have?**

Some artifacts, like old clothing and toys, can be found in the attics or basements of people's homes. Others have been buried in the earth because they were used so long ago. The science of digging up artifacts and studying them is called **archaeology** (är kē äl′ ə jē). You can learn about history by looking at artifacts and trying to find out how old they are, who made them, and how they were used.

Oral History People can be good historical sources, too. Talking with people who remember the past is a good way to learn about history. This is called **oral history.** Parents, grandparents, and people who have lived in your community a long time can share their memories of the past with you. Here are some questions you might ask:

1. How long have you lived in this community?
2. What was it like to live here many years ago?
3. Has this community changed much since you have lived here?

If you want to learn about the past from others, you must be a good listener.
■ **In what ways is a tape recorder a useful tool for oral history?**

CHECKUP

1. What is a historical source?
2. Name four kinds of historical sources and compare them.
3. What can you learn about history by studying artifacts?
4. **Thinking Critically** What could you tell somebody about the history of your community since you have lived there?

25

Your Family and the Community

How can you explore the history of your family?

VOCABULARY

genealogy

Your Family's History Every family, like every community, has a history. A written history of a family is a **genealogy** (jē nē äl′ ə jē). A genealogy is a record of the births, deaths, and marriages in a family. Does your family have a written history?

Even if your family does not have a genealogy, you can still become an expert on your family's past. You will need to ask questions, study historical documents, look at family artifacts, and dig out old family photographs. Studying family history is a lot like studying local history.

Growing a Family Tree A family tree is a list of all your family members, starting with you and working backwards in time. You can start a family tree by asking the following questions.

1. When and where was I born?
2. What was my mother's last name before she married?
3. When and where were my parents born?
4. What are the names of my grandparents?

You may not know this family, but you can tell something about them from this photograph.
- How old, do you think, were different members of the family?
- How, do you think, were they related to each other?

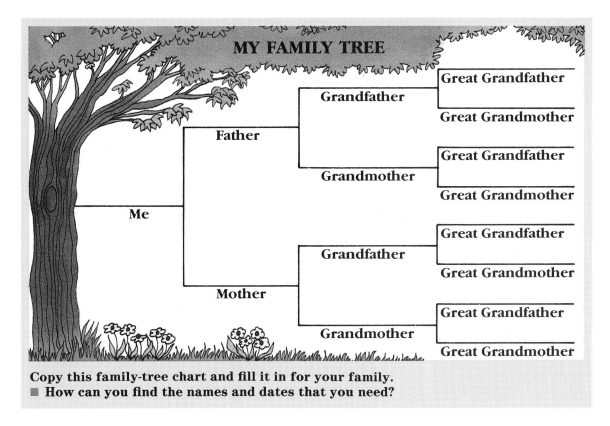

MY FAMILY TREE

Me

Father

Mother

Grandfather

Grandmother

Grandfather

Grandmother

Great Grandfather

Great Grandmother

Great Grandfather

Great Grandmother

Great Grandfather

Great Grandmother

Great Grandfather

Great Grandmother

Copy this family-tree chart and fill it in for your family.
■ **How can you find the names and dates that you need?**

When you have found the answers to these questions, you can then interview aunts, uncles, cousins, and anyone else in your family who can help you grow your family tree. You can keep your information on a chart like the one above.

Digging Deeper into Your Family's History   After you have interviewed all your family members, dig out some family records. They will help you fill in the missing pieces. Births, marriages, and deaths may have been recorded. Your family may have saved historical documents, like newspapers, diaries, or letters. The family photo album will also help you. To find out about how your ancestors lived and what they thought about, you can talk with family members and use oral history.

Family and Community   As you learn about your family's history, you will learn how your family contributed to your community. The history of your family is part of the history of your community. It is also part of the history of our state and country.

CHECKUP

1. What is a genealogy?
2. List three historical sources that help you to study the history of your family.
3. **Thinking Critically**   What can you learn about your ancestors from old photos?

Saving Our History

How is local history preserved?

Local Historians People who work at finding out about a community's history are **local historians.** They use historical documents, photographs, family histories, and artifacts to **research** local history. *Research* means "to search for facts about something." After careful researching, a local historian might write a book about a community's history. Has a book been written about your community's past?

Historical Societies and Museums One way to save community history is to **preserve** artifacts and old documents and books. *Preserve* means "to keep safe and unchanged." History is preserved by historical societies and museums. A historical society is a group of people who are interested in history. These people gather and keep historical sources and artifacts that are important to local or state history. A museum is a place where artifacts are preserved and displayed so that people can study them. Is there a historical society or museum in your community? What kinds of programs does it offer?

Elaine Fay, one of the authors of this book, works at the New Jersey Historical Society in Newark.
■ **What different kinds of sources can you find in the photograph of the library at the New Jersey Historical Society?**

These children are visiting the birthplace of Grover Cleveland in Caldwell. Cleveland was the only person born in New Jersey who became President of the United States.
■ **Who, do you think, takes care of this historic house?**

Libraries A library nearby may have several books about your community. It may also have old newspapers, photographs, historical documents, and maps.

Preserving Old Buildings Many old buildings are worth preserving. But often these old buildings are torn down to make space for newer or bigger buildings. When an old building is destroyed, the history of that building and of part of the community is destroyed, too. Today, many people in communities all over New Jersey are helping to save old buildings that are important to local history. Some of these old buildings are **historic houses.** A historic house is one that

looks the way it did many years ago. The house may have been the home of a famous person. It may have been the place where an important event took place. The Camden home of the poet Walt Whitman is a historic house. Whitman lived there from 1884 to 1892. The house still holds his furniture and belongings and is open to the public.

CHECKUP

1. What do local historians do?
2. How do historical societies and museums help to save history?
3. **Thinking Critically** If an old building was going to be torn down in your community, what could you and others do to try to save it?

Using the Parts of This Book

CONTENTS

This book has many special parts to help you learn about New Jersey. The first of these parts is the Contents. It shows you how the book is divided into units and chapters. Turn to the Contents pages at the front of the book. Answer the following questions:

1. What is the name of Unit 2?
2. What are the names of the chapters in Unit 2?
3. On what page does Chapter 13 begin?

INDEX

Another helpful part of this book is the Index. It shows you the numbers of the pages on which various topics are discussed. The topics are arranged alphabetically. Turn to the Index, which starts on page 283. Answer these questions:

1. Which pages would you turn to if you wanted to read about farming in New Jersey? About industry?
2. On what pages would you find information about glaciers? About Atlantic City? About railroads?

GLOSSARY

The Glossary is another important part of this book. The Glossary, arranged alphabetically like the Index, defines all the key social studies words. These are the words found in the box at the beginning of each lesson. Turn to the Glossary on page 269. Answer these questions:

1. What is a natural resource?
2. What is population density?
3. What is climate?
4. What is a moraine?

GAZETTEER

Another part of this book that is arranged alphabetically is the Gazetteer. It contains information about many places —cities, rivers, and other geographic features. The page number at the end of each definition directs you to a map that shows where the place is. Turn to the Gazetteer, which starts on page 265. Answer these questions:

1. Where is Camden located?
2. How high is High Point?
3. What is the Delaware Water Gap?

GRAPH APPENDIX AND ATLAS

The Graph Appendix and the Atlas are two more parts of this book that will help you. The Graph Appendix provides you with information in the form of graphs. Turn to the graphs on page 278. What kinds of information do they give you?

The Atlas is a special collection of maps. Turn to the Atlas, which starts on page 260. Name the maps that you find in the Atlas.

CHAPTER 1 REVIEW

MAIN IDEAS

1. History is the story of what happened in the past.
2. We study history to understand the way things are today, to learn about how people lived in the past, and to avoid making the mistakes of the past.
3. The history of a community is called local history.
4. Some historical sources are monuments; historical markers; old buildings; old newspapers; historical documents such as letters, account books, and government records; old photographs, drawings, and paintings; artifacts; and people with memories and information to share.
5. You can explore your family's history by talking to family members, studying family records and historical documents, and making a family tree.
6. Local history is preserved by local historians, historical societies, museums, libraries, and people in communities.

VOCABULARY REVIEW

On a separate sheet of paper, write the word or words that best complete each sentence below.

1. A community is (**a**) things people have in common, (**b**) the place where people live, (**c**) a park.
2. A monument is (**a**) a book about the past, (**b**) an important event in the past, (**c**) something that is built to honor a person or event.
3. Old newspapers, artifacts, and documents are (**a**) used for studying science, (**b**) books about history, (**c**) historical sources.
4. An account book is (**a**) a written record of goods belonging to a person, (**b**) a record of goods and prices kept by a store, (**c**) a record of family events and members.
5. A local historian is a person who (**a**) works in a library, (**b**) tears down old buildings, (**c**) works at finding out about a community's history.

CHAPTER CHECKUP

1. How are communities alike and how do they differ?
2. Why is it important to preserve old buildings and put up historical markers?
3. What is a historical society?
4. **Thinking Critically** What could a person in the future learn about your life and times by studying a photograph of you?
5. **Thinking Critically** How does your family's history help you to learn more about your community's past?

APPLYING KNOWLEDGE

Do a project on the history of your school. You might start by finding out when your school was built, what it used to look like, and how it has changed. Try to find old photographs of your school building or the original plans for building your school. Next, interview teachers, parents, and your school principal to find out what it was like to go to your school 5, 10, or even 25 years ago. How has going to school changed? Do you think that going to school now is better? Why or why not?

2 Tools for Learning About New Jersey

Learning About the Earth

How is a globe like the earth?

VOCABULARY

astronaut	ocean
sphere	continent
globe	map

Where Do You Live? How would you answer if someone asked you where you live? Would you give the name of the street on which you live? Or would you simply say that you live on the earth? Of course, both answers would be correct. Your street is part of the earth. You do live on the earth. The earth is your home. In fact, the earth is the home of all people. Only **astronauts,** or people who travel in outer space, can leave the earth for a long stretch of time. And even they must return.

High Above the Earth Have you ever wished that you could be in a spaceship high above the earth?

Both the photograph taken from space and the globe show the earth.
■ What do the different colors in the photograph taken from space show?

About 20 years ago, this was only a dream. But today we can go to the moon. We can fly away from the earth and look at it from outer space. Photographs of the earth can be taken from space. Look at the photograph on the left. It was taken from a spaceship far above the earth.

The earth is a **sphere.** That means it is round like a ball. If you look at a ball, you can see only half of it at a time. In the same way, you can see only half of the earth at one time.

A Model of the Earth   As the picture shows, the earth is made up of land and water. The picture of the **globe** on page 32 will help you to see more clearly the difference between land and water. A globe is a model of the earth. It shows the shapes of the earth's land and water.

Oceans and Continents   About two thirds of the earth is made up of water. The largest bodies of water are called **oceans.** There are four oceans. They are the Atlantic, Pacific, Indian, and Arctic oceans.

Only about one third of the earth is land. This land is divided into **continents.** A continent is a very large body of land. There are seven continents. They are Asia, Australia, Africa, Europe, Antarctica, South America, and North America. Asia is the largest continent. Australia is the smallest. The **map** below shows the oceans and continents. A map is a special kind of drawing.

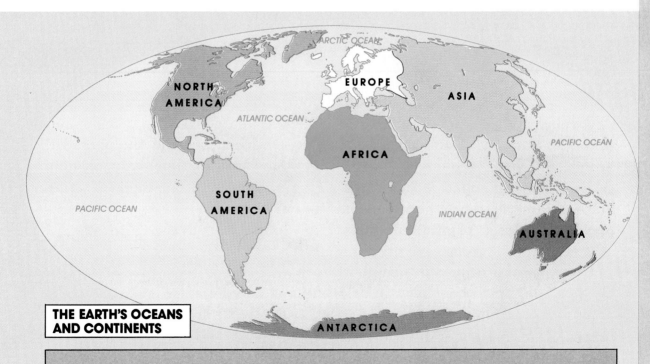

THE EARTH'S OCEANS AND CONTINENTS

The photographs and the map show that the surface of the earth is made up of land and water.
■ Can you name the earth's seven continents and four oceans?

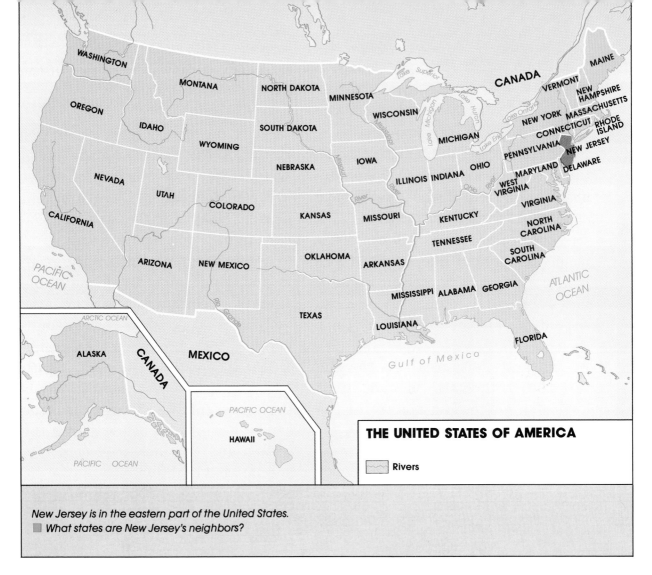

New Jersey is in the eastern part of the United States.
■ *What states are New Jersey's neighbors?*

Countries For us the most important continent is most likely North America. Do you know why? There are more than 170 countries on the earth's land. Our country, the United States of America, is on the continent of North America. The United States is the second largest country in North America. Only our neighbor Canada is larger.

States Our country is divided into 50 parts. Each part is called a state. You live in New Jersey. This year you are going to learn more about your state. You will learn about the history and geography of New Jersey. This chapter and the next will give you information that will help you in your study of the geography of our state.

CHECKUP
1. What is a globe?
2. Name the four oceans.
3. What is a continent?
4. How many states are there in the United States?

5. **Thinking Critically** What, do you think, would you be able to see on the earth from outer space?

Finding Your Way on a Map

What do boundary lines and a compass rose tell about places on a map?

VOCABULARY

boundary	west
border	North Pole
north	South Pole
south	compass rose
east	

Boundary Lines There are many tools that will help you to learn about your state. Maps are among the most important tools you can use. Look at the map at the bottom of this page. What does the map show? When might someone use a map like the one on this page? Have you ever used a map of this kind?

A **boundary** is a line that separates one state or country from another. States and countries **border,** or touch, one another at the boundary. Sometimes the boundary is called the border. The map on page 40 shows the states that border New Jersey. It shows the boundaries between the states. The Delaware River is one of New Jersey's boundaries. What state is across the Delaware River from New Jersey? What state lies across Delaware Bay from New Jersey? What other state shares a boundary with our state?

Perhaps you have visited this amusement park.
- **What places would you visit?**
- **Where would you go to eat?**

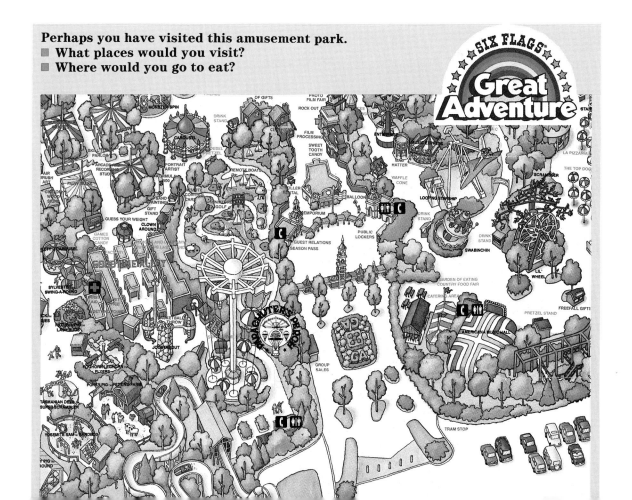

SIX FLAGS
Great Adventure

The Language of Maps Have you ever been lost? Have you ever wanted to go somewhere but did not know how to get there? Have you ever been in an amusement park, looking for a special ride? Or have you ever been at a zoo, looking for the animals you most wanted to see? If so, maps could have been a big help to you. Maps show you where things are. They also can tell you how far places are from one another. Maps can give you important and interesting facts. To find these facts on maps, you must learn the language of maps. It is a simple language.

Directions Before learning where things are on a map, you must learn about directions. There are many ways to tell where something is. You could say that something is *up* or *down*. You might say it is *above* or *below*. You might also say it is to the *left* or to the *right*. Or it might be *in* something else or *on* something else. You have probably used these direction words many times. There are four other special direction words you should learn. They describe the main directions on a map. They are **north, south, east,** and **west.**

North is the direction toward the **North Pole.** The North Pole is the most northern place on the earth. The boy in the picture below is pointing to the North Pole on a globe. Look at the second picture on this page. The girl in this picture is pointing to the **South Pole.** The South Pole is the

The North Pole and the South Pole are opposite each other.
- **Which pole is the boy pointing to?**
- **Which pole is the girl pointing to?**

If you face north, east is on your right. West is on your left.
■ **What direction is behind you?**

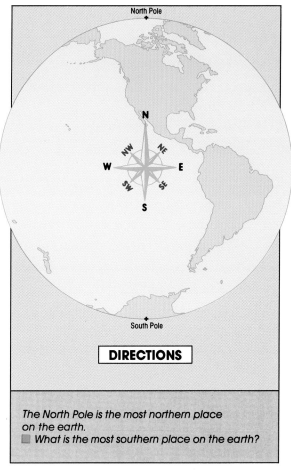

DIRECTIONS

The North Pole is the most northern place on the earth.
■ *What is the most southern place on the earth?*

most southern place on the earth. It is at the opposite end of the earth from the North Pole. South is the direction toward the South Pole. North and south are opposite one another.

East and west are the other two main directions. They too are opposite one another. If you face north, east will be on your right. West will be on your left.

Sometimes a drawing like the one on the map above is used to show where north, south, east, and west are on a map. This drawing is called a **compass rose.** The letters *N*, *E*, *S*, and *W* stand for north, east, south,

and west. Sometimes we need to find places that are in between two of the four main directions. The other letters show where these in-between directions are. *NE* stands for northeast. Northeast is between north and east. What do you think the other letters stand for? Find the in-between directions on the map.

CHECKUP
1. How can maps help you?
2. Name the four main directions.
3. What is a compass rose?
4. **Thinking Critically** Why do states and countries have boundaries?

Using Latitude and Longitude

How can you locate places on a map?

VOCABULARY

Equator	Prime Meridian
hemisphere	grid
latitude	estimate
longitude	

The Equator Halfway between the North Pole and the South Pole is a special line. It circles the entire earth. This line is called the **Equator.** A half of the earth is called a **hemisphere** (hem′ ə sfir). The land and water north of the Equator is called the Northern Hemisphere. The land and water south of the Equator is called the Southern Hemisphere. The continent on which we live is in the Northern Hemisphere. Find both the Northern Hemisphere and our continent on the map below.

Latitude The Equator is a line of **latitude.** All the lines that run *across* the map are called lines of latitude. Those between the Equator and the North Pole are called lines of north latitude. Those between the Equator and the South Pole are called lines of south latitude.

The Equator is numbered 0°. It is the most important line of latitude. All of the other lines of latitude measure distances north or south of the Equator. These distances are measured in degrees. The symbol for de-

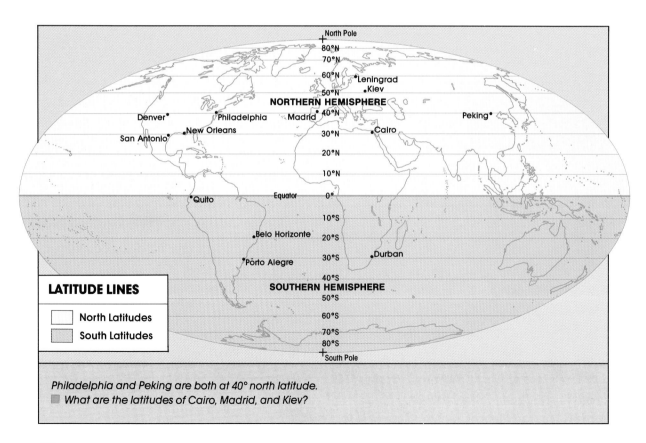

Philadelphia and Peking are both at 40° north latitude.
▪ *What are the latitudes of Cairo, Madrid, and Kiev?*

38

grees is °. Latitude lines make it easier to find places on a map.

Longitude Lines of **longitude** are another set of lines drawn on maps. These lines run from the North Pole to the South Pole. There is one special longitude line. It is called the **Prime Meridian** (prīm mə rid′ ē ən). It is numbered 0°. All of the other longitude lines measure distances east or west of the Prime Meridian. The Prime Meridian passes through Greenwich, England.

The Prime Meridian divides the earth in half from east to west. The land and water that lies west of the Prime Meridian is called the Western Hemisphere. The land and water that lies east of the Prime Meridian is called the Eastern Hemisphere.

Look at the map below. Put your finger on the line marked 30°E. Move it until you come to Leningrad. You will see that Leningrad is found at 30° east longitude. Look back at the map on page 38. You will see that Leningrad is also found at 60° north latitude. To tell someone where Leningrad is, you would say that it is at 60° north latitude and 30° east longitude. Can you find another city that is shown on both maps? Philadelphia is also shown on both maps. How would you tell someone where Philadelphia is found? Turn to the map on pages 260–261. Find the latitude and longitude of Oslo, Norway.

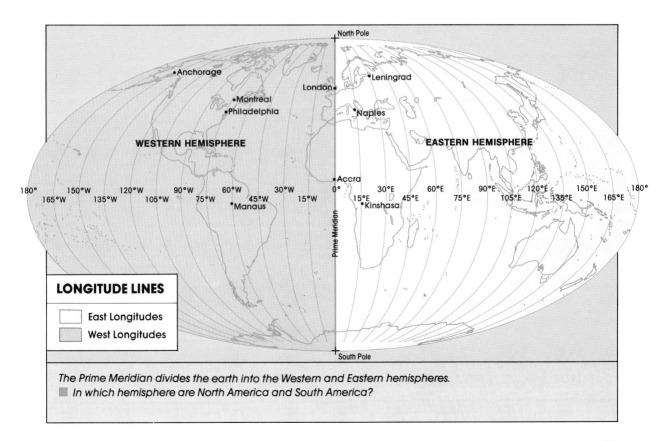

LONGITUDE LINES
☐ East Longitudes
▨ West Longitudes

The Prime Meridian divides the earth into the Western and Eastern hemispheres.
■ *In which hemisphere are North America and South America?*

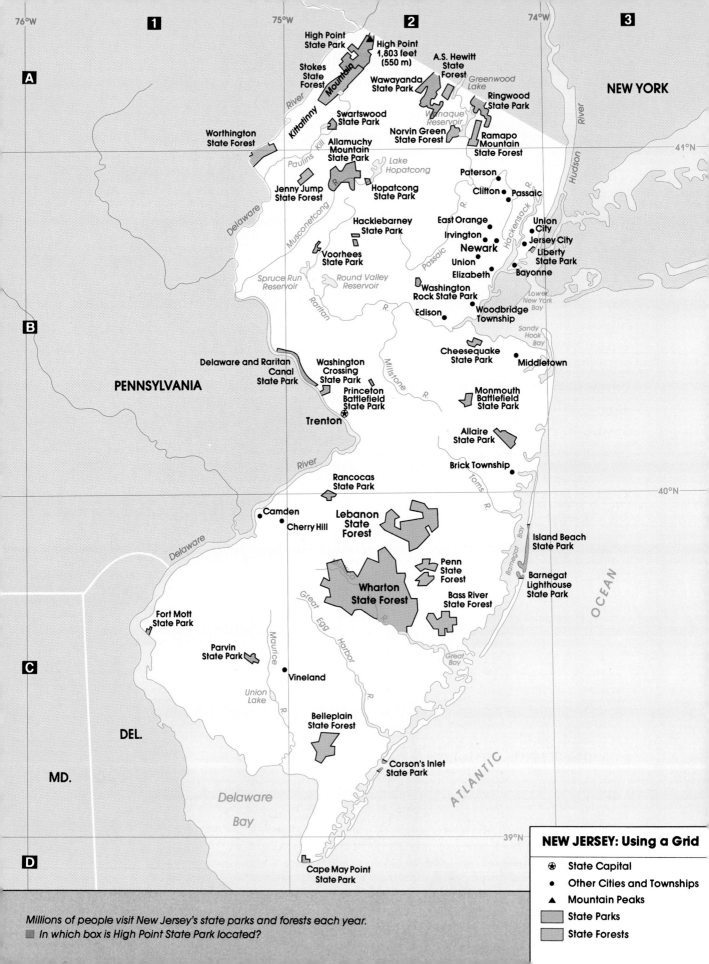

76°W   **1**   75°W   **2**   74°W   **3**

A

High Point
State Park

Stokes
State
Forest

High Point
1,803 feet
(550 m)

A.S. Hewitt
State
Forest

Greenwood
Lake

NEW YORK

Wawayanda
State Park

Ringwood
State Park

Kittatinny

Worthington
State Forest

River

Swartswood
State Park

Wanaque
Reservoir

Norvin Green
State Forest

Ramapo
Mountain
State Forest

Hudson

River

41°N

Paulins
Kill

Allamuchy
Mountain
State Park

Lake
Hopatcong

Paterson

Clifton

Passaic

Jenny Jump
State Forest

Delaware

Musconetcong

Hopatcong
State Park

R.

East Orange

Hackensack

Union
City

Jersey City

Hacklebarney
State Park

Irvington

Newark

Liberty
State Park

Voorhees
State Park

Spruce Run
Reservoir

Round Valley
Reservoir

Raritan

Passaic

Union

Elizabeth

Bayonne

Washington
Rock State Park

Lower
New York
Bay

R.

Edison

Woodbridge
Township

Sandy
Hook
Bay

B

PENNSYLVANIA

Delaware and Raritan
Canal

Washington
Crossing
State Park

Millstone

Cheesequake
State Park

Middletown

Princeton
Battlefield
State Park

R.

Monmouth
Battlefield
State Park

Trenton

Allaire
State Park

River

Toms

Brick Township

Rancocas
State Park

40°N

Camden

Cherry Hill

Lebanon
State
Forest

Island Beach
State Park

Barnegat

Bay

Penn
State
Forest

Wharton
State Forest

Bass River
State Forest

Barnegat
Lighthouse
State Park

Fort Mott
State Park

Delaware

OCEAN

Maurice

Parvin
State Park

Great

Egg

Harbor

Great
Bay

DEL.

Vineland

Union
Lake

R.

C

MD.

Belleplain
State Forest

R.

ATLANTIC

Corson's Inlet
State Park

39°N

Delaware

Bay

Cape May Point
State Park

D

NEW JERSEY: Using a Grid

✸   State Capital

●   Other Cities and Townships

▲   Mountain Peaks

   State Parks

   State Forests

Millions of people visit New Jersey's state parks and forests each year.
  In which box is High Point State Park located?

Using a Grid If you know the latitude and longitude of a place, you can find it on a map by using the **grid.** A grid is a system of crossing lines that form boxes. Crossing latitude and longitude lines are a grid.

Sometimes the places you are looking for are not found exactly at the point where the two lines cross. When this happens, you have to **estimate,** or figure out *about,* where those places are. Look at the map of New Jersey on page 40. You will see that Camden is very close to 40° north latitude. It also is located very close to 75° west longitude. Now find Trenton. Trenton is not found exactly on any line of latitude or longitude. Therefore you have to estimate its latitude and longitude. Trenton is between 40° north latitude and 41° north latitude. It is nearer to 40° north latitude. So you would be close enough if you said that Trenton is at 40° north latitude. It is also between 74° west longitude and 75° west longitude. It is closer to 75° west longitude. So you would be close enough if you said that it is at 75° west longitude. Figure out the latitude and longitude for Newark and Elizabeth.

Notice that the crossing lines of latitude and longitude form boxes. At the top of the map, you will see the numbers 1, 2, and 3. Along the left-hand side of the map, you will see the letters *A, B, C,* and *D.* Put a finger on the *B.* Put a finger of your other hand on the 2. Now move both fingers, one across and one down, until they meet. You have now found box B-2. You will see that Elizabeth, Jersey City, and Paterson are all in box B-2. This is another way of finding places on a map. Road maps often have letter-number grids to help you find places. What state parks are found in box C-2?

This lighthouse in Barnegat State Park is sometimes called Old Barney.
■ **What do people enjoy doing here?**

CHECKUP

1. What do latitude lines measure?
2. What do longitude lines measure?
3. What is a grid?
4. **Thinking Critically** Does a compass rose or a grid locate places on a map more exactly?

Symbols and Scale

How are real places and things shown on a map?

VOCABULARY

symbol   scale
key

Symbols A map can show where any place or thing on the earth is found. Maps use **symbols** to stand for real things and places. The part of the map that tells what the symbols stand for is called the **key.**

There are many symbols that can stand for the real things and places on earth. The table on the next page shows only a few of the symbols that might be used on a map. The table also shows a photograph of the real place or thing that each symbol stands for. Below each symbol is its name. What other real places and things are shown on maps?

Scale Maps cannot show places and things in their real size. To do that, you would need a piece of paper as large as the place being mapped. So maps are drawn to **scale.** This means that the places and distances shown on maps are many times smaller than their real size on the earth.

A certain number of inches on a map stands for a certain number of feet or miles on the earth. When we show size or distance this way, we say the map is drawn to scale. The map scale in the key box tells the real size or the real distance from one place to another.

Scale is also used to make copies of people or things. Have you ever played with dolls or model trains or model airplanes? Then you have a good idea of what scale is. The dolls you may have played with were

THE METRIC SYSTEM

On page 45 you will find the words *1 inch stands for about 50 miles. (One centimeter stands for about 32 kilometers.)* Centimeters and kilometers are units of measure in the metric system.

The metric system is a way of measuring area, distance, weight, capacity, and temperature. This system is used in all major countries except the United States. Plans are being made to "go metric" in the United States also.

To get you ready for the change to the metric system, both American and metric measurements are given in this book. Each measurement used in our country is followed by the metric measurement that is about equal to it. Miles are changed to kilometers (km), inches to centimeters (cm), feet or yards to meters (m), acres to hectares (ha), pounds to kilograms (kg), and degrees Fahrenheit (°F) to degrees Celsius (°C).

MAP SYMBOLS

REAL PLACE OR THING

SYMBOL

SYMBOL

SYMBOL

SYMBOL

NAME

Railroad

NAME

Road

NAME

City

NAME

Trees

REAL PLACE OR THING

SYMBOL

SYMBOL

SYMBOL

SYMBOL

NAME

Airport

NAME

River

NAME

House

NAME

Dairy Farming

much smaller than real people. The models you may have built were much smaller than real trains or airplanes. Many model airplanes are built to a scale of 50 to 1. This means that if you built a 1-foot-long model, you would know that the length of the real airplane was 50 times 1 foot, or 50 feet.

Make believe you are in an airplane flying over a football field. The football field would probably look like the drawing below. This drawing was made to a scale in which 1 inch stands for 20 yards. The drawing is 6 inches long. So the total length of a real football field is 120 yards, or 6 groups of 20 yards (20 + 20 + 20 + 20 + 20 + 20 = 120). How wide is a real football field?

There are many kinds of models. This girl is putting a model of a rocket together.
■ Is the model the same size as a real rocket?

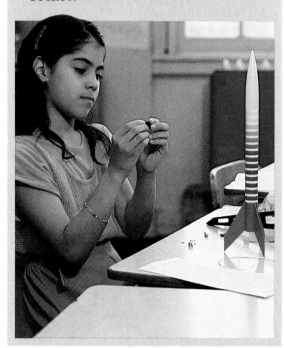

This is a drawing of a football field. It has been drawn to scale. Each inch on the drawing stands for 20 yards.
■ What do the numbers on the drawing stand for?
■ How many yards is it from the end of the field to the middle?
■ How many yards is it between each line on the field?

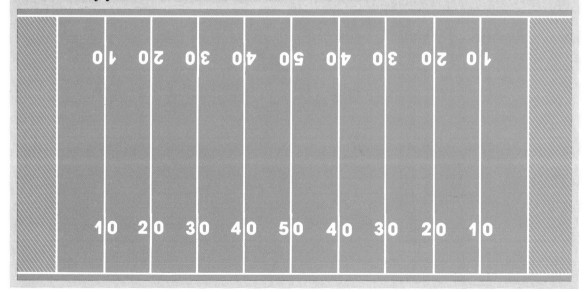

New Jersey and Scale The scale line on a map shows how much an inch (or centimeter) on the map stands for in real distance on the earth. A map can be drawn to many different scales. All three maps below show New Jersey. Each map is drawn to a different scale.

Put a ruler under the scale line of the map on the left. You will see that 1 inch stands for about 50 miles. (One centimeter stands for about 32 kilometers.) On this map, how many inches (cm) is it in a straight line from Newark to Atlantic City? Your answer should be about 2 inches (5 cm). To find out how many miles (km) it is from Newark to Atlantic City, you multiply 2 × 50 (5 × 32).

Go through the same steps with the two other maps. The number of inches (cm) to miles (km) changes. However, when you use the scale to figure miles (km), the distance between Newark and Atlantic City stays the same.

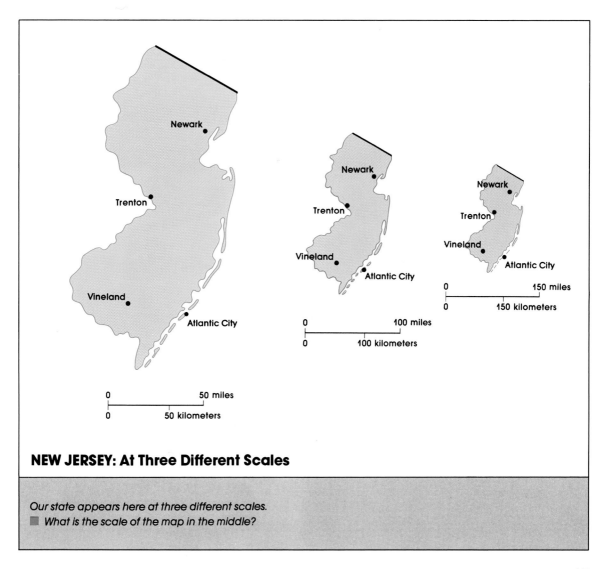

NEW JERSEY: At Three Different Scales

Our state appears here at three different scales.
■ *What is the scale of the map in the middle?*

The photograph and the map show the same airport. As you can see, the map colors stand for real things.
◻ How many runways are there?
◻ What are the flat buildings near the center of the photograph?

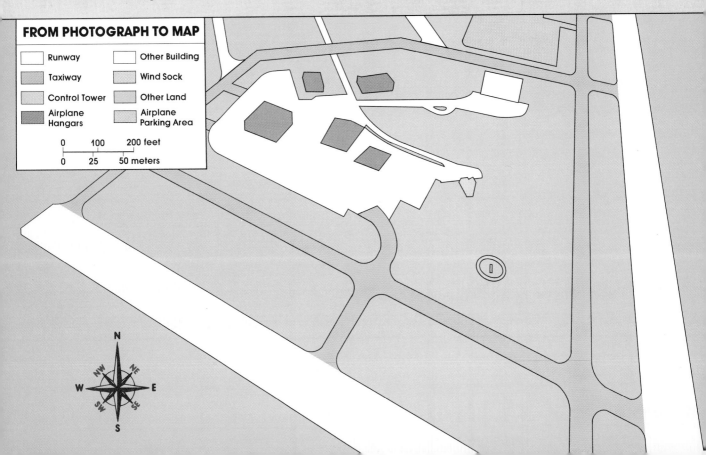

FROM PHOTOGRAPH TO MAP

◻ Runway
◻ Taxiway
◻ Control Tower
◻ Airplane Hangars
◻ Other Building
◻ Wind Sock
◻ Other Land
◻ Airplane Parking Area

```
0      100      200 feet
0   25       50 meters
```

This photograph of the stadium at the Meadowlands Sports and Recreation Complex was also taken from an airplane.
■ **What different things can you see in the photograph?**

A Bird's-eye View You have learned that symbols, scale, directions, and a grid system are some of the things that make maps special. Another is that a map shows how the earth looks from straight overhead. A map is a bird's-eye view of a part of the earth. A map shows what a bird would see if it looked straight down on the earth from high in the sky. You would see what the bird sees if you were in an airplane looking down on the earth. The higher the airplane flies, the more of the earth you would see. If you went up high enough, you could see about one half of the earth.

The photographs on these pages were taken from an airplane. The map on page 46 shows the same place as in the photograph above it. Find some shapes in the photograph. Find those same shapes on the map. Find a color on the map. Look at the key to find what it stands for. Each color stands for a real place or thing.

CHECKUP
1. Why do maps need symbols?
2. Why are maps drawn to scale?
3. **Thinking Critically** What shapes and symbols would you use to show a bird's-eye view of your school and the area around it?

47

Using a Map Grid

WHAT IS A MAP GRID?

You have learned that some maps have a grid, or system of lines that form boxes as they cross one another. The boxes are numbered across the top of the map. They are also lettered down the side of the map. You can use the letters and numbers to find places on a map.

SKILLS PRACTICE

Use the map grid below. Name the city or town that is located in each of the boxes formed by the following letters and numbers.

1. A-2
2. D-1
3. B-4
4. A-6
5. C-4

For examples 6 through 10, decide which letter-number location below matches the activity you could do there.

6. Camping
7. Mountain climbing
8. Watching airplanes take off and land
9. Picking corn
10. Watching popcorn being made
    a. D-2
    b. A-6
    c. A-1
    d. D-4
    e. A-3

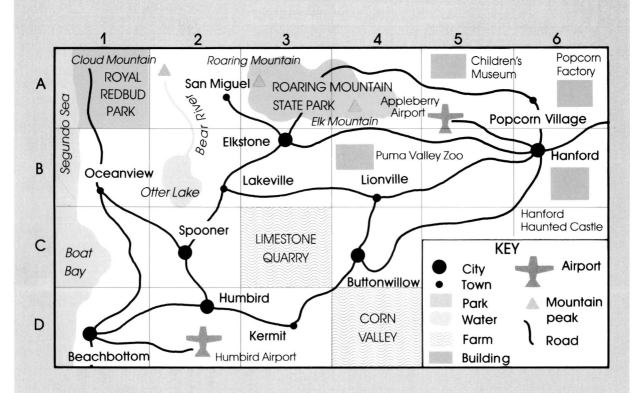

CHAPTER 2 REVIEW

MAIN IDEAS

1. A globe is a sphere like the earth and shows the shapes of the earth's land and water.
2. There are four oceans (Atlantic, Pacific, Indian, and Arctic) and seven continents (Asia, Australia, Africa, Europe, Antarctica, South America, and North America) on the earth.
3. Boundary lines show where one state or country ends and another begins. A compass rose helps to tell in what direction places are.
4. Lines of latitude and longitude can be used to locate places on a map.
5. Symbols on maps stand for real places and things. The scale of a map helps to show places and distances many times smaller than their real size.

VOCABULARY REVIEW

On a separate sheet of paper, match these words with the definitions.

  a. sphere   **f.** boundary
  b. globe   **g.** Equator
  c. continent   **h.** Prime Meridian
  d. astronaut   **i.** grid
  e. hemisphere **j.** symbol

1. A line that separates one state or country from another
2. The longitude line numbered 0°
3. The latitude line numbered 0°
4. A round shape like a ball
5. A person who travels in outer space
6. A model of the earth
7. A shape on a map that stands for a real place or thing
8. A half of the earth
9. One of the seven very large bodies of land on the earth
10. Crossing lines that form boxes

CHAPTER CHECKUP

1. On what continent is the United States found?
2. What is the most northern place on the earth? The most southern place on the earth?
3. What are the names of the lines drawn on maps that help us to find places?
4. How does a map show what the symbols mean?
5. **Thinking Critically** Describe a time in your life when a map was or would have been a very important tool.
6. **Thinking Critically** Why is the direction finder on a map called a compass rose?
7. **Thinking Critically** Is a map that is not drawn to scale of any use to a traveler?

APPLYING KNOWLEDGE

1. Use a world map to find each city at the latitudes and longitudes below. Write the name of each city and the continent on which it is found.
   a. 34°S and 58°W
   b. 30°N and 31°E
   c. 51°N and 0°
   d. 31°N and 122°E
   What do the city at 51°N and 0° and the place Greenwich, England, have in common?
2. Bring a road map with a grid to class. Make a list of cities on the map. Ask a classmate to find those cities without using the grid. Then have your classmate use the index and the grid on the map to find the cities. Have a classmate test you in the same way. What difference does using the grid make?

3 The Geography of New Jersey

Tools of Geography

What kinds of maps and other tools help us learn about New Jersey?

VOCABULARY

patent	county
population density	graph

Small, But Important Of the 50 United States, New Jersey is smaller in area than most. Only four states — Rhode Island, Delaware, Connecticut, and Hawaii — are smaller. But New Jersey's small size has never held it back. There are many reasons to be proud of New Jersey. Our state is first in many things.

What do light bulbs, submarines, pencils, and air conditioning have in common? They were all invented in New Jersey. Many great scientists and inventors have lived and worked in New Jersey. Albert Einstein discovered the secrets of atomic energy while living in Princeton. Atomic energy is power that comes from

This photo collage includes some New Jersey firsts. Also shown is an industry in which our state is a leader today.
■ What does each photograph show?

changes in an atom. Thomas Edison invented the electric light and the phonograph in Menlo Park. Samuel Morse and Alfred Vail tried the world's first telegraph in Morristown. Samuel Colt made the world's first revolver in Paterson. A revolver is a handgun that can be fired many times without being reloaded.

New Jerseyans are still inventing things. In a recent year, over 2,000 New Jerseyans got **patents** on their inventions. A patent is a paper that gives only the person who invented a thing the right to make, use, or sell the invention.

New Jersey is first in our country in highway safety. Our state has the safest roads to travel. New Jersey had the country's first traffic circle and first drive-in movie. Atlantic City is the most popular place to visit in the United States. More people visit Atlantic City than Disney World! The first game of organized baseball was played in Hoboken. Princeton and Rutgers played the first college football game at Rutgers, in New Brunswick.

New Jersey is an exciting place where many things have happened and continue to happen first. It is a good place to live and work. It is a good place to play, too. That is why so many people live in New Jersey.

Geography, The Study of People

Over 7 million people live in our state. There are more than 238 million people in the United States. This means that about one out of every 34 people in the United States lives in New Jersey. New Jersey is the ninth most populated state in our country. Only eight states have more people. They are California, New York, Texas, Pennsylvania, Illinois, Florida, Ohio, and Michigan. All eight of these states are larger in area than New Jersey. As you know, New Jersey is the fifth smallest state.

There is much for you to learn about the people of New Jersey. The study of people is one of the most important parts of geography.

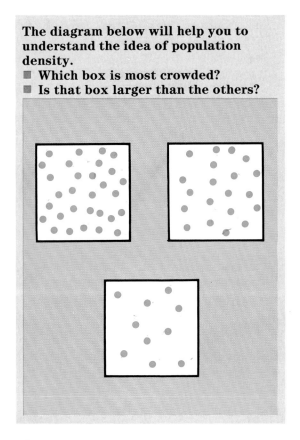

The diagram below will help you to understand the idea of population density.
- **Which box is most crowded?**
- **Is that box larger than the others?**

Population Density

The map on the opposite page shows the **population density** of New Jersey. Population density is how crowded a place is. Although eight states have more people than New Jersey, our state has the highest population density of all 50 states. This means that New Jersey has more people per square mile than any other state. To find the population density of a place, we divide the number of people who live there by the size of the land. New Jersey has 7,515,000 people. They live in a state that has only 7,468 square miles (19,342 sq km) of land. If we divide 7,515,000 by 7,468, the answer is about 1,006. So New Jersey has about 1,006 people per square mile (389 per sq km). Of course, each square mile of New Jersey does not have exactly 1,006 people. Some parts of our state have many more people per square mile. Other parts have fewer people. The map shows this. What parts of our state are most crowded? What parts of our state are least crowded?

Cities

The map on page 53 also shows the cities and townships in New Jersey with 50,000 or more people. Look at the list on the map. The cities and townships are grouped by the number of people they have. How many have 200,000 or more people? How many have between 100,000 and 199,999 people? How many have between 50,000 and 99,999 people?

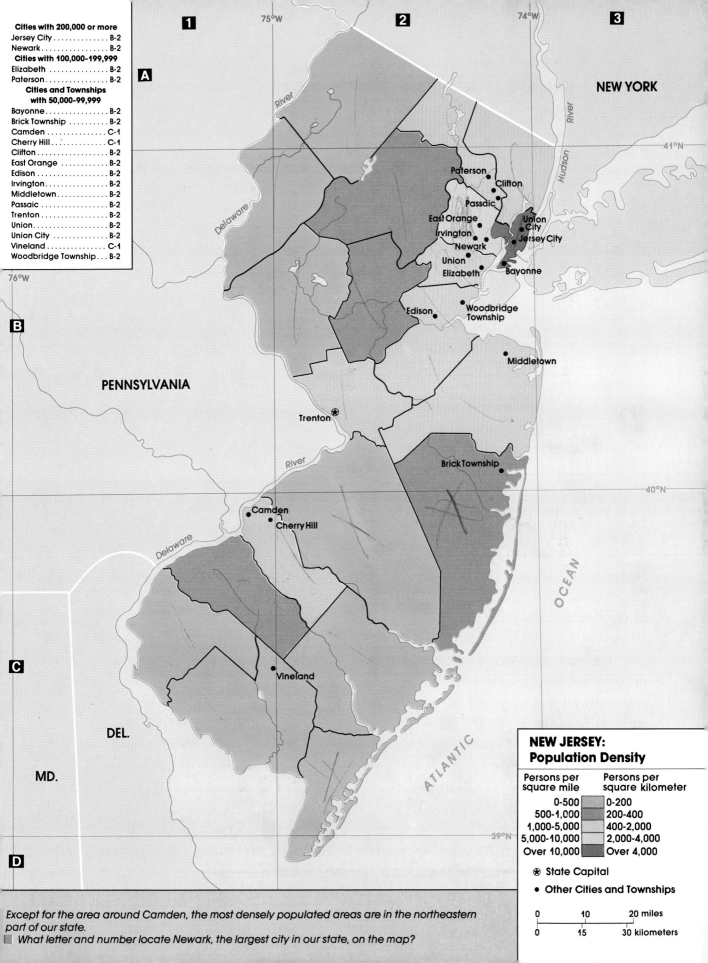

NEW YORK

PENNSYLVANIA

Paterson
Clifton
Passaic
East Orange
Union City
Irvington
Jersey City
Newark
Union
Elizabeth
Bayonne
Edison
Woodbridge Township
Middletown
Trenton
Brick Township
Camden
Cherry Hill
Vineland

DEL.

MD.

Delaware River
Hudson River

ATLANTIC OCEAN

**NEW JERSEY:
Population Density**

Persons per square mile	Persons per square kilometer
0-500	0-200
500-1,000	200-400
1,000-5,000	400-2,000
5,000-10,000	2,000-4,000
Over 10,000	Over 4,000

⊛ State Capital

● Other Cities and Townships

0   10   20 miles
0   15   30 kilometers

Except for the area around Camden, the most densely populated areas are in the northeastern part of our state.
  What letter and number locate Newark, the largest city in our state, on the map?

Counties New Jersey's cities and other communities are located within the state's **counties.** A county is a part of a state. New Jersey is divided into 21 counties. The map on the opposite page shows where each county is located. What is the name of your county? Find your county on the map.

Reading a Table Look at the table on page 280. It shows the names of all the counties in New Jersey. Look at the headings across the top of the table. What other facts are shown in the table?

A table is an easy way to organize facts. It can show some of the same things that a map can. A table can also show some facts that a map generally does not show. Let's compare the table on page 280 with the counties map on page 55.

On the map it is easy to see that Burlington County and Ocean County are the two largest counties in our state. But the map does not show you exactly how large the two counties are. You can find this information in the table on page 280. The table shows you that the area of Burlington County is 808 square miles (2,093 sq km). The area of Ocean County is 641 square miles (1,660 sq km). This shows that Burlington County is the largest county in the state of New Jersey.

Look at the map again. It is hard to tell which is the smallest county in

This county courthouse is in Elizabeth. The Latin word over the door is *Justitia.*
■ **What do you think *Justitia* means?**

New Jersey. That is because there are a few small counties in the same part of the map. If you look at the table, it is easy to see what the smallest county is. There are 21 counties in New Jersey. The smallest county would be twenty-first in area. Find 21 under the heading *Area Rank.* You can see that Hudson County is the smallest county in the state. Its area is 46 square miles (119 sq km). Find it on the map.

Find your county in the table. What does the table tell you about your county?

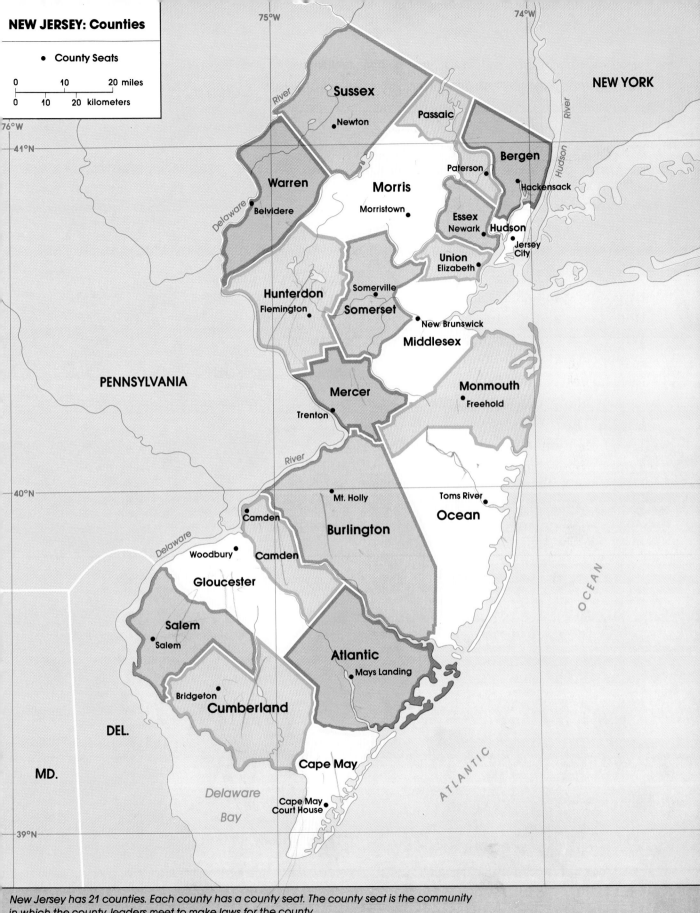

NEW JERSEY: Counties

- • County Seats

0   10   20 miles

0 10 20 kilometers

NEW YORK

76°W

41°N

75°W

74°W

Sussex
  • Newton

Passaic
  • Paterson

Bergen
  • Hackensack

River

Warren
  • Belvidere

Morris
  • Morristown

Essex
Newark •

Hudson
  • Jersey City

Delaware

Union
Elizabeth •

Hunterdon
  • Flemington

• Somerville

Somerset
  • New Brunswick

Middlesex

PENNSYLVANIA

Mercer
  • Trenton

Monmouth
  • Freehold

River

40°N

• Mt. Holly

• Toms River

• Camden

Ocean

Burlington

Delaware

• Woodbury   • Camden

Gloucester

Salem
  • Salem

Atlantic
  • Mays Landing

• Bridgeton

Cumberland

DEL.

Cape May

MD.

Delaware Bay

Cape May
Court House •

ATLANTIC

OCEAN

Hudson River

39°N

New Jersey has 21 counties. Each county has a county seat. The county seat is the community
in which the county leaders meet to make laws for the county.
  In which county do you live?
  What is the name of your county seat?

Drawings to Compare Things You have been learning about our state through words, pictures, maps, and tables. Now let's learn by reading **graphs.** A graph, like a map, is a kind of drawing. It uses pictures, circles, bars, or lines to compare things.

Pictographs There are four different kinds of graphs. The simplest is called a pictograph. It uses small pictures or symbols to show information. Look at the pictograph below. What is its title? Notice that each symbol stands for 30,000 people. The five largest cities in our state are shown along the side of the graph. Look at the row for Newark. It shows 10 whole symbols and ½ of another symbol. Since each symbol stands for 30,000 people, 10½ symbols stand for 315,000 people. The pictograph can only give you an idea of the population of Newark and the other cities. It cannot show the exact number of people. About how many people live in Jersey City? In Paterson? In Elizabeth? In Trenton?

Pie Graphs The drawing below is called a pie graph. If you have ever cut a piece of pie, you know how a pie graph works. It is used to show the parts of a whole. The whole circle stands for all the people in New Jersey. The pieces of the pie stand for the different groups of people in our state. What groups are shown on the graph? Which is the smallest group? Which are the two largest groups?

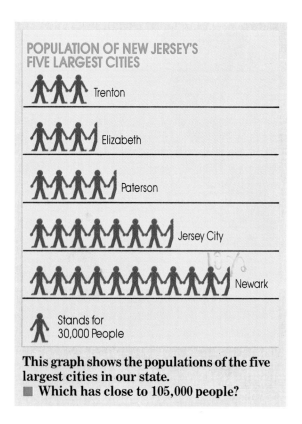

POPULATION OF NEW JERSEY'S FIVE LARGEST CITIES

Trenton
Elizabeth
Paterson
Jersey City
Newark

Stands for 30,000 People

This graph shows the populations of the five largest cities in our state.
■ Which has close to 105,000 people?

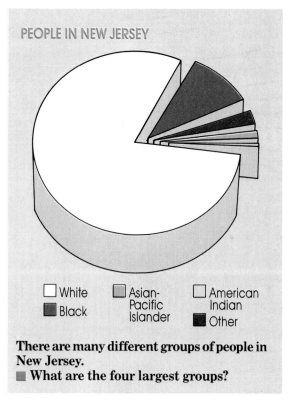

PEOPLE IN NEW JERSEY

☐ White ☐ Asian-Pacific Islander ☐ American Indian
■ Black ■ Other

There are many different groups of people in New Jersey.
■ What are the four largest groups?

56

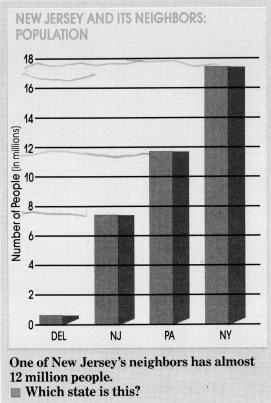

NEW JERSEY AND ITS NEIGHBORS: POPULATION

One of New Jersey's neighbors has almost 12 million people.
■ Which state is this?

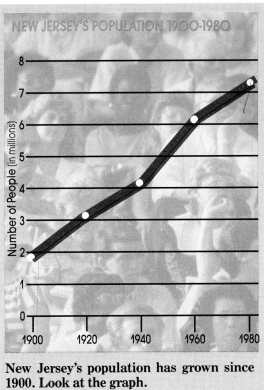

NEW JERSEY'S POPULATION 1900-1980

New Jersey's population has grown since 1900. Look at the graph.
■ When did it grow the fastest?

Bar Graphs One of the most useful kinds of graphs is a bar graph. Look at the one above. New Jersey and its neighbors are each shown by a bar. Their names are given on the bottom of the graph. Which state has the tallest bar? This means that it has the most people. Put your finger on the top of the bar for New York. Now move your finger to the left. The numbers along the left show how many people there are in each state. The state of New York has more than 17½ million people. How does the population of New Jersey compare to that of New York? How many people live in Pennsylvania? Does Pennsylvania have more people than our state?

Line Graphs A line graph is another kind of graph. It is generally used to show how things change over a period of time. The line graph above shows the change in New Jersey's population between 1900 and 1980. How many people were living in New Jersey in 1920?

CHECKUP
1. Where does New Jersey rank in area among the 50 states?
2. Which of the 50 states has the highest population density?
3. Name four kinds of graphs and explain how they are different.
4. **Thinking Critically** Why, do you think, are Essex and Hudson counties the most crowded places in our state?

New Jersey's Natural Resources

What are four important natural resources in New Jersey?

VOCABULARY

natural resource	agriculture
mineral	nursery
ore	reservoir
fuel	

Recognizing Resources New Jersey has many **natural resources.** A natural resource is something provided by nature that is useful to people. People use natural resources to meet needs and wants. **Minerals,** forests, soil, and water are all natural resources. Minerals are things found in the earth that are neither plant nor animal. Minerals such as iron and stone are used to build things. Forests provide wood for building and for making paper and other wood products. Forests are also good places to go camping. Soil is one of the most important resources for farming. Water is also needed for growing things. It is used for drinking, bathing, and sports, too.

Minerals One of the minerals found in our state is iron **ore.** An ore is a mineral that is mined because it contains something that can be used, such as a metal like iron. At one time our state was one of the largest producers of iron ore in America. Today some iron ore is still mined in Morris County, when the price is right. If the price of the metal is high, the ore

Stone, sand, and gravel are important New Jersey minerals. This mining location is near Paterson.
■ Find Paterson on the map on page 40.

is mined. If the price is too low, though, people may decide not to mine the ore. Some New Jersey mines start and stop depending on the price of iron.

Many rare minerals have been found near Franklin in Sussex County. *Rare* means "not common or often found." More than 200 different minerals have been found at Franklin! Some are found nowhere else. Many of these minerals can be seen in a museum in Franklin. For many years, Franklin was also an important source of zinc ore. The metal zinc is used to coat iron and steel and to make paint and rubber.

58

The most important minerals in our state are very ordinary. They are stone, sand, and gravel. Gravel is small loose pieces of rock. Stone found in New Jersey includes basalt (bə sôlt′), limestone, granite (gran′ ət), and sandstone. Most of the stone is found in the northern counties of our state.

Southern New Jersey has some fine glass sands. When melted in very hot furnaces with other minerals, these sands become glass. Perhaps some of the bottles and jars in your refrigerator were made in New Jersey. Other sands are mixed with gravel and chunks of rock to make concrete for building.

There is oil and natural gas about 80 to 100 miles (129 to 161 km) off the coast of New Jersey. Both oil and natural gas can be used as **fuels.** A fuel is something that can be burned to produce heat or power. These mineral resources off the New Jersey coast are not being drilled yet. Someday they may be very valuable to our state and country.

Forests New Jersey's forests have always been a great resource. New Jersey still has a lot of forestland. More than a third of our state is forest. In fact, there is almost twice as much land in forest in our state as there is in farms. Some of the forests

SOME NEW JERSEY FOREST PRODUCTS

Posts and Poles

Firewood

Landscape Wood Chips

Christmas Trees

This chart shows only four New Jersey forest products.
■ **What other uses of New Jersey wood might be shown here?**

59

in New Jersey are state forests. The state protects these forests. Find the state forests on the map on page 40. Camping, fishing, hunting for sport, and hiking are important uses of forests. Have you ever gone hiking or camping in a state forest?

Soil Soil is the top layer of earth. It is crumbled rock and mineral pieces. It also includes rotting plants. Without soil, **agriculture** would not be possible. Agriculture is another word for farming. Farming is growing crops and raising animals. Agriculture is important to New Jersey. Today over 9,500 farmers work over 1 million acres (405,000 ha) of land in our state. Many of the foods produced in New Jersey are sold in the nearby big cities of New York and Philadelphia. During the summer you will see many kinds of New Jersey-grown foods at stores and roadside stands.

Over 50 kinds of vegetables are grown in our state. Corn and tomatoes grown in New Jersey are among the most delicious in the nation. Many fruits are also grown here. New Jersey is the second largest producer of blueberries, the third largest producer of cranberries, and the fifth largest producer of peaches in the United States. Other products of New Jersey agriculture are hay and grain for feeding farm animals. Dairy cows, beef cattle, horses, and chickens are raised in our state.

Perhaps you have bought vegetables and fruit at a roadside stand.
■ What New Jersey farm products are on sale here?

Flowers, such as roses and orchids, and other plants are grown here in greenhouses and **nurseries.** A nursery is a place where plants are grown for sale. It is easy to understand why New Jersey is called the Garden State.

Water New Jersey has a large number of rivers. The Delaware and the Hudson are our state's most important rivers. The Delaware River

Canoeing is a popular sport among New Jerseyans. These people are canoeing in the Pinelands.
■ **What water sport do you enjoy?**

There are over 800 lakes and ponds in New Jersey. The largest of these is Lake Hopatcong in Morris County. Most of the others are also in the northern part of our state. They include Budd, Culvers, and Greenwood lakes and Green Pond. Swimming and boating are popular in New Jersey lakes and ponds. New Jerseyans also enjoy fishing in fresh water in the state.

Reservoirs (rez′ ər vwärz) in our state provide water for many needs. A reservoir is a place where water can be collected and stored for use. Water from reservoirs can be used for drinking, cooking, bathing, and cleaning. Water is also needed in many industries in our state. It is used to make things such as soup in the soup-canning industry. It is also used for power.

The Atlantic Ocean off New Jersey provides fish and other seafood. Some New Jerseyans fish for a living, catching lobster, flounder, bluefish, and other fish. Clams, oysters, and other shellfish are also brought in. Other New Jerseyans just fish for fun. The seaside is also a place to relax and to enjoy water activities.

forms New Jersey's western boundary. The Hudson forms its eastern boundary. Important ports on both rivers make our state a major water-transportation center. The Raritan River is the longest river completely within our state. It flows for 75 miles (121 km) from Somerset County to Raritan Bay and has a number of branches. Use the map on page 40 to find these three rivers and others in our state.

CHECKUP ▮
1. What is a natural resource?
2. Name three New Jersey fruits.
3. How is water in our state used?

4. **Thinking Critically** Explain why it is important to take care of our state's natural resources.

New Jersey's Climate

What is the climate of our state like?

VOCABULARY

weather	temperature
climate	growing season
precipitation	

Weather Everybody talks about the **weather.** Weather is the way the air is at a certain time. Rain, snow, heat, and cold are all parts of weather. The weather is important to all of us. The weather can change from day to day. It can even change from hour to hour. People often listen to or watch weather reports two or three times a day. People need to

---

These newspaper maps tell about the weather on November 6, 1985.
■ Did any precipitation fall in the state that day?

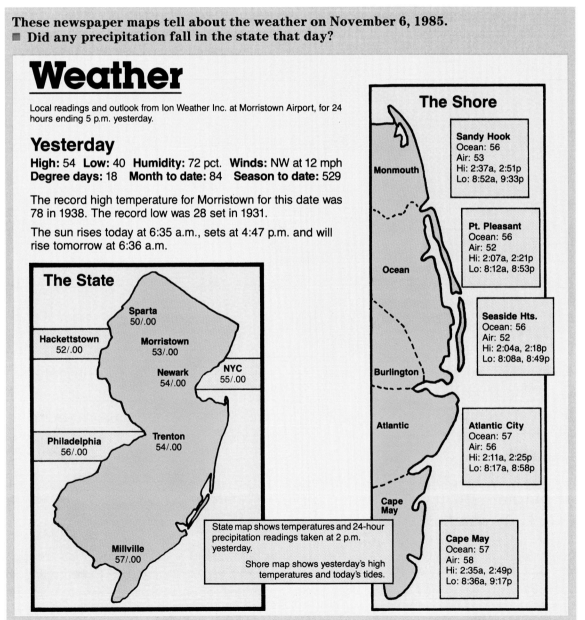

Weather

Local readings and outlook from Ion Weather Inc. at Morristown Airport, for 24 hours ending 5 p.m. yesterday.

Yesterday

High: 54 **Low:** 40 **Humidity:** 72 pct. **Winds:** NW at 12 mph
Degree days: 18 **Month to date:** 84 **Season to date:** 529

The record high temperature for Morristown for this date was 78 in 1938. The record low was 28 set in 1931.

The sun rises today at 6:35 a.m., sets at 4:47 p.m. and will rise tomorrow at 6:36 a.m.

The State

Sparta
50/.00

Hackettstown
52/.00

Morristown
53/.00

Newark
54/.00

NYC
55/.00

Philadelphia
56/.00

Trenton
54/.00

Millville
57/.00

State map shows temperatures and 24-hour precipitation readings taken at 2 p.m. yesterday.

Shore map shows yesterday's high temperatures and today's tides.

The Shore

Monmouth

Ocean

Burlington

Atlantic

Cape May

Sandy Hook
Ocean: 56
Air: 53
Hi: 2:37a, 2:51p
Lo: 8:52a, 9:33p

Pt. Pleasant
Ocean: 56
Air: 52
Hi: 2:07a, 2:21p
Lo: 8:12a, 8:53p

Seaside Hts.
Ocean: 56
Air: 52
Hi: 2:04a, 2:18p
Lo: 8:08a, 8:49p

Atlantic City
Ocean: 57
Air: 56
Hi: 2:11a, 2:25p
Lo: 8:17a, 8:58p

Cape May
Ocean: 57
Air: 58
Hi: 2:35a, 2:49p
Lo: 8:36a, 9:17p

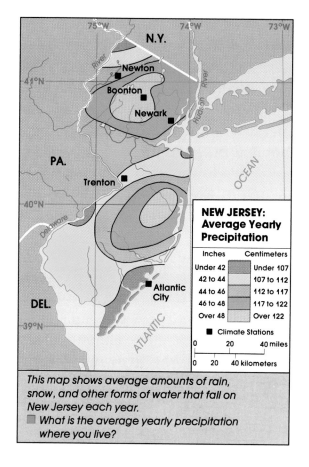

NEW JERSEY: Average Yearly Precipitation

Inches	Centimeters
Under 42	Under 107
42 to 44	107 to 112
44 to 46	112 to 117
46 to 48	117 to 122
Over 48	Over 122

■ Climate Stations

This map shows average amounts of rain, snow, and other forms of water that fall on New Jersey each year.

■ What is the average yearly precipitation where you live?

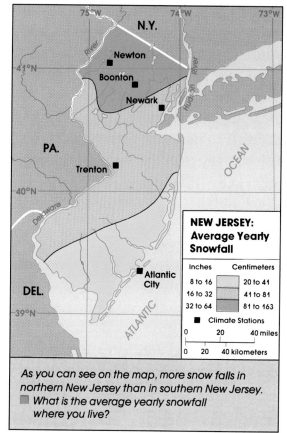

NEW JERSEY: Average Yearly Snowfall

Inches	Centimeters
8 to 16	20 to 41
16 to 32	41 to 81
32 to 64	81 to 163

■ Climate Stations

As you can see on the map, more snow falls in northern New Jersey than in southern New Jersey.

■ What is the average yearly snowfall where you live?

know about the weather in order to plan what they are going to do.

The kind of weather a place has over a long period of time is called **climate.** The maps on pages 63–64 and the graphs on pages 278–279 tell about our state's climate.

Precipitation One way to describe the climate of a place is to talk about how much **precipitation** (pri sip ə ta′ shən) it gets. Precipitation is any form of water that falls to earth. Rain and snow are the most common forms of precipitation.

Most places in New Jersey have a little more precipitation in the summer than in the winter. Look at the graphs on page 278. The letters along the bottom stand for the months of the year. Which are the three driest months for Newark? For Atlantic City? Which are the three wettest months for these two cities?

Now look at the precipitation map at the top of this page. As you can see, different parts of the state receive different amounts of precipitation during the year. On the average, how much precipitation falls in Trenton each year?

In the winter some of the precipitation that falls in New Jersey is snow. Look at the snowfall map above. How much snow does Newton receive on the average?

Temperature Precipitation is only part of the picture of a place's climate. To understand the entire picture, we must learn about **temperature.** Temperature tells us how hot or cold something is. A thermometer is used to measure temperature.

In the Northern Hemisphere it generally gets cooler as you go farther north. It is also cooler in the mountains. At the seashore it is usually a little cooler on summer days than it is inland. That's one reason why people visit the shore in the summer. In the winter the seashore does not get quite as cold as places inland. Is the northwestern part of New Jersey colder in January than the southern tip of our state? The map called Average January Temperatures will give the answer. Now look at the map titled Average July Temperatures. Is it cooler in the summer in Trenton or Atlantic City? How hot is it in Newton?

Turn to the graphs on page 279. Which of the five places shown has the coldest January? Which has the hottest July? In which place would you like to live in January?

The Many Effects of Climate Climate can affect the way people make a living. For example, climate affects the length of the **growing season.** This is the period when crops can

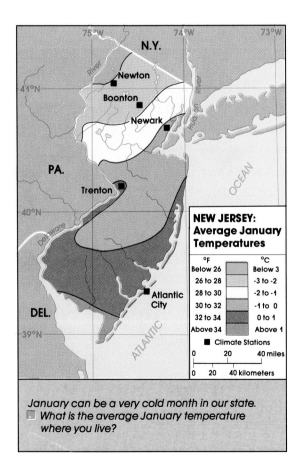

January can be a very cold month in our state.
☐ *What is the average January temperature where you live?*

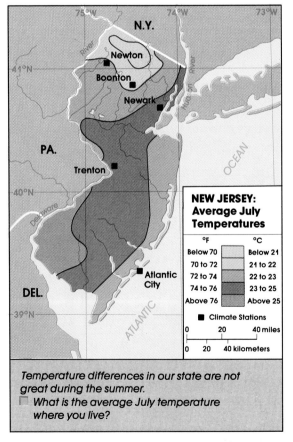

Temperature differences in our state are not great during the summer.
☐ *What is the average July temperature where you live?*

Although temperatures are generally lower in the winter, many people like to be outdoors. One way to be active in the winter is to play a winter sport.
■ What sport are this boy and girl playing?

grow. It is the number of days from the last spring frost to the first fall frost. Plants freeze and die when there is a frost. The growing season is about 200 days long near southern New Jersey's bay and seashore. It is only 140 days in the mountains in the northwestern part of the state. Where would farming be best?

Climate also affects outdoor recreation. Outdoor fun in New Jersey in the summer means swimming, boating, fishing, and hiking. In the winter in our state, people enjoy skiing, snowmobiling, and ice skating. New Jersey's climate affects all these activities.

CHECKUP
1. What is weather?
2. What is climate?
3. Name two kinds of precipitation.

4. **Thinking Critically** How does climate affect the way *you* live?

Using a Dictionary

WHAT IS A DICTIONARY?

A dictionary is a book that contains the words of a language. A dictionary tells several things about these words. The pronunciation and meaning of each word is given. The respelling shows you how to pronounce, or say, a word. It divides the word into parts and identifies the sounds of the letters.

The words are listed in alphabetical order. This helps you find the words easily. It also makes it possible for you to check the spelling of a word easily.

When you see a word that you do not know, you can find the meaning of the word in a dictionary. If you do not know how to use a word, a dictionary can help.

Look up the word *geography* in a dictionary. Why is it easy to find? (Words are in alphabetical order.) Notice that the word is divided into parts. Look at the pronunciation. Say the word, using the respelling. How many definitions are given for the word *geography*?

SKILLS PRACTICE

Find the following words in a dictionary. On a separate sheet of paper, write a sentence using each word.

1. population
2. county
3. patent
4. township
5. weather
6. nursery
7. agriculture
8. climate
9. mineral
10. ore

Some students say, "If I can't spell a word, how can I look it up in a dictionary?" Usually you can spell a word closely enough to search and find it in a dictionary. Use a dictionary to correct the misspelled words below. The misspelled parts of the words are underlined. Write the correct spellings on a separate sheet of paper.

1. den<u>c</u>ity
2. gra<u>fh</u>
3. grav<u>ol</u>
4. greenho<u>ws</u>e
5. shel<u>f</u>ish
6. pre<u>s</u>ipitation
7. tab<u>ul</u>
8. se<u>e</u>son
9. pi<u>k</u>tograph
10. tempera<u>chu</u>re

CHAPTER 3 REVIEW

MAIN IDEAS

1. Maps and other tools that help us learn about New Jersey include population density and counties maps; tables of cities, townships, and counties; and four kinds of graphs — pictographs, pie graphs, bar graphs, and line graphs.
2. New Jersey is the most densely populated state in our country.
3. There are 21 counties in New Jersey.
4. Minerals, forests, soil, and water are four important natural resources in New Jersey.
5. New Jersey's climate is mild.

VOCABULARY REVIEW

Beside the number of each sentence, write the word or words that best complete the sentence. Use a separate sheet of paper.

1. You can tell how crowded a place is by finding its _____.
2. A kind of drawing that uses pictures, circles, bars, or lines to compare things is a _____.
3. A _____ is something provided by nature that is useful to people.
4. Plants are grown for sale in a _____.
5. A _____ is something that can be burned to produce heat or power.
6. A place where water can be collected and stored for use is a _____.
7. The kind of weather a place has over a long period of time is its _____.
8. _____ is the way the air is at a certain time.
9. Something found in the earth that is neither plant nor animal is a _____.
10. _____ tells us how hot or cold something is.

CHAPTER CHECKUP

1. What two numbers must you have to find population density?
2. How does a pictograph show information about something?
3. Explain why New Jersey is called the Garden State.
4. **Thinking Critically** Why are people interested in the oil and natural gas found off the coast of New Jersey?
5. **Thinking Critically** What is the difference between weather and climate?

APPLYING KNOWLEDGE

1. List at least five things in your home or in school that come from natural resources. Next to each item write at least one natural resource used to make it (for example, paper — tree).
2. Keep a record of the weather in your area for 2 weeks. Record the temperature at the same time each morning and afternoon. Note whether it is rainy, cloudy, partly cloudy, or sunny.

4 The Regions of New Jersey

How the Regions Were Formed

How has nature formed the land of New Jersey?

VOCABULARY

region
elevation
contour line
glacier
moraine

Four Regions Now you are going to learn about the different land areas of New Jersey. These land areas are called physical **regions.** A region is an area that has something special about it that makes it different from other areas.

We can think of New Jersey as a giant jigsaw puzzle. The map on the left shows the pieces of the puzzle. Each piece is a region of the state. The four physical regions of New Jersey are the Atlantic Coastal Plain, the Piedmont (pēd′ mänt), the Highlands, and the Ridge and Valley Region. The land in each of the four regions is different.

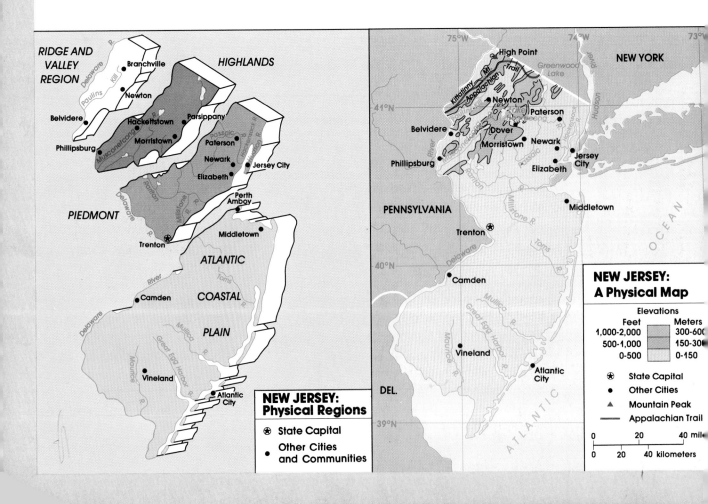

RIDGE AND VALLEY REGION — Branchville, Newton, Belvidere, Hackettstown, Phillipsburg, Morristown, Parsippany, Paterson, Newark, Elizabeth, Jersey City, Perth Amboy, Trenton, Middletown

HIGHLANDS

PIEDMONT

ATLANTIC COASTAL PLAIN — Camden, Vineland, Atlantic City

NEW JERSEY: Physical Regions
✳ State Capital
• Other Cities and Communities

NEW YORK

High Point, Greenwood Lake, Newton, Paterson, Belvidere, Dover, Morristown, Newark, Phillipsburg, Elizabeth, Jersey City, Middletown, Trenton, Camden, Vineland, Atlantic City

PENNSYLVANIA

DEL.

NEW JERSEY: A Physical Map

Elevations		
Feet		Meters
1,000–2,000		300–600
500–1,000		150–300
0–500		0–150

✳ State Capital
• Other Cities
▲ Mountain Peak
— Appalachian Trail

0   20   40 miles
0   20   40 kilometers

An Elevation Map New Jersey is a small state, but its land shows a great deal of variety. The map on the right on page 68 shows how the land in our state varies. It shows **elevations** in New Jersey. Elevation is distance above sea level. A map like this one is called a relief, or physical, map. Most relief maps use **contour lines.** Contour lines are the lines on a map that separate the colors used to show elevation of the land. All places along one contour line are the same distance above sea level.

Find Paterson on the map. What color is used to show the elevation of the land around it? Find this color in the map key. You will see that this color stands for 0 to 500 feet (0 to 150 m). What is the elevation of the land around Newton? What is the elevation where you live?

Nature Shapes the Land The differences in the look of the land from region to region are the result of many changes over many thousands of years. Some of these changes happened quickly. Others were slower. Great rivers of very hot melted rock flowed across the land. With earthquakes, huge cracks in the land appeared. Mountains were pushed up out of the earth. Valleys were formed. These things happened millions of years ago.

At 1,803 feet (550 m), High Point is the highest point in our state. Find High Point on the physical map.
■ In which region is it located?

About 1 million years ago, the earth was cooler than it is now. The summers were short and cool. The winters were long. Much snow fell. The snow did not melt in the summer. For many thousands of years, the snow got deeper and became very tightly packed. It formed thick sheets of ice and snow called **glaciers** (glā′ sherz). The glaciers formed in the area of the North Pole and pushed south. The glaciers were thousands of feet thick. They pushed huge amounts of earth around like bulldozers. They could carry everything from earth, sand, and pebbles to huge rocks the size of small cars. The glaciers were so heavy they could flatten hills and fill valleys with rocks and soil. This time in the earth's history is called the Ice Age. It ended about 10,000 years ago, when the earth got warmer and the glaciers melted.

Some glaciers left piles of rocks, sand, and soil in ridges, or raised strips of land. These ridges are called **moraines** (mə rānz′). In New Jersey a moraine runs east from the Delaware River valley near Belvidere. Near Morristown it dips to the south, ending near Perth Amboy. This moraine lies across both ridges and valleys in northern New Jersey. For a while it stopped the flow of the Hackensack and Passaic rivers. Two large lakes were formed. Today, swamps and marshes have taken their place. The Hackensack Meadows and the Great

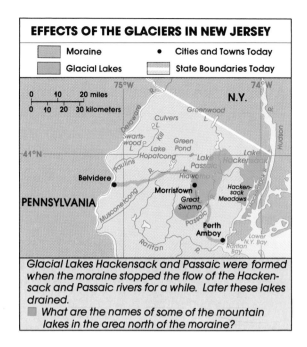

EFFECTS OF THE GLACIERS IN NEW JERSEY

Moraine · Cities and Towns Today
Glacial Lakes — State Boundaries Today

Glacial Lakes Hackensack and Passaic were formed when the moraine stopped the flow of the Hackensack and Passaic rivers. Later these lakes drained.
What are the names of some of the mountain lakes in the area north of the moraine?

Swamp stand where the lakes once were. North of the moraine are many mountain lakes that were formed by the glaciers. The largest of these is Lake Hopatcong.

Slow changes in the land continue to happen. Many are the work of moving water. Many, many years ago, New Jersey looked a little different than it does now. Many years from now, moving water will have shaped a New Jersey that is a little different from the one today.

CHECKUP

1. What is elevation?
2. How did glaciers shape the land of New Jersey?
3. What is changing the land of New Jersey today?

4. **Thinking Critically** How does the climate of New Jersey during the Ice Age compare to the state's climate today?

The Atlantic Coastal Plain

What do people do for a living and for fun on the Atlantic Coastal Plain?

VOCABULARY

plain	food processing
Pine Barrens	open space
conservation	resort

A Great Coastal Plain Along the coast of many countries, there is a broad strip of low, flat land called a **plain.** A coastal plain usually stretches from the ocean to higher land farther inland. Along the eastern coast of the United States, a plain runs from Georgia to New Jersey. It is called the Atlantic Coastal Plain.

The Atlantic Coastal Plain makes up more than half of our state. It is not perfectly flat. It has some low, rolling hills. But nearly half the coastal plain in New Jersey is less than 100 feet (31 m) above sea level.

The Inner Coastal Plain New Jersey's coastal plain can be divided into two parts. The map on this page shows these parts. The inner plain is the part toward the inside, toward other land. It is the smaller part. The outer coastal plain lies toward the outside, along the Atlantic Ocean and Delaware Bay.

Although the inner plain is three times smaller than the outer plain, it has many more people. Camden is the most populated city on the inner coastal plain. It is located on the Delaware River, across from Philadelphia. Perth Amboy, an important port and industrial center, is also on the inner plain.

Inner plain soils are a lot better for farming than those of the outer plain. From the 1600s, farmers have been able to farm most of the inner coastal plain. Many of the Garden State's fruits and vegetables are still grown here.

The Outer Coastal Plain Early New Jerseyans found that outer

NEW JERSEY:
The Atlantic Coastal Plain

Pinelands
• Cities and Other Communities
0   25   50 miles
0   25   50 kilometers

As you can see, the Atlantic Coastal Plain makes up about three fifths of our state.
■ Are the seaside resorts on the inner or outer coastal plain?
■ What large city is on the Delaware River?

71

Tom Brown, Jr. (1950 –   )

The Indian moved silently through the woods. Following carefully were the Indian's grandson, Rick, and Rick's best friend, Tom. The two boys watched everything that Stalking Wolf was doing. Stalking Wolf was an expert tracker. He knew how to "read" the tracks made by wild animals. He could stalk, or closely follow, animals so quietly that he could touch a deer before the deer knew he was there. Rick and Tom were learning much more from Stalking Wolf than how to track wild animals. They were learning how to understand the environment. The environment is all the things around us, such as water, land, animals, plants, and air. Where were the woods in which Rick and Tom learned by watching Stalking Wolf? The woods were part of the Pine Barrens or Pinelands, the largest area of wild land in New Jersey.

As he was growing up in southern New Jersey, the Pinelands were Tom's "backyard." He learned how to track, hunt, fish, build, and live off the land. When he was older, Tom spent a year living alone in the woods of the Pinelands. Tom is a teacher now. He has taught rescue teams and police groups how to track people. He also runs a school on his farm near Asbury. Tom's students sleep in his barn, cook in a pit in the barnyard, and observe nature on Tom's land. The students take Indian names. They learn how to find water, food, and shelter in the wild. They also learn how to make a bow and arrow. But perhaps the most important thing that Tom's students learn is how people fit into the world of nature.

coastal plain soils were difficult to use for farming. Since then, farmers have discovered that blueberries and cranberries do well.

Early farmers called the outer coastal plain barren. *Barren* means "not able to produce things." Because many pine trees grow in a large part of the outer plain, that area was called the **Pine Barrens.** Many people today call it the Pinelands. The **conservation** of the Pinelands is important to our state. Conservation is the careful use and protection of something, especially natural resources. The Pinelands cover over one quarter of our state. The area is rich in animal and plant life.

Vineland, a farming center and New Jersey's largest city in area, is on the outer coastal plain. Also on the outer plain are Millville and Bridgeton. Millville is known for its glass industry. **Food processing** is important in Bridgeton. Food processing is preparing, freezing, or canning food to be sold.

The Seashore The seashore is where the outer coastal plain meets the Atlantic Ocean. The shore is about 127 miles (204 km) long—from Sandy Hook in the north to Cape May in the south. About 7 miles (11 km) is **open space,** or unsettled or undeveloped land. The rest is lined with vacation homes, motels, and hotels. The towns along the shore are **resorts.** A resort is a place that peo-

Point Pleasant is a popular resort.
■ What fun do people have here?

ple visit for fun. Long Branch and Cape May are among the oldest seashore resorts in the country. Atlantic City is the biggest resort on the New Jersey shore.

Many people who live near the ocean make their living from the sea, in one way or another. Some fish in the ocean or nearby bays. Others make a living by selling or renting things to visitors.

CHECKUP
1. Which part of the Atlantic Coastal Plain is smaller in area, but has more people?
2. Explain why some early New Jerseyans called the Pinelands the Pine Barrens.
3. What is a resort?
4. **Thinking Critically** Why, do you think, do people like to live by the shore?

The Piedmont

Why do most people in New Jersey live in the Piedmont?

VOCABULARY

Piedmont	capital
mountain chain	suburb
Fall Line	oil refinery

The Fall Line The **Piedmont** in New Jersey lies between the low land of the Atlantic Coastal Plain and the higher land of the Highlands. *Piedmont* is an Italian word meaning "the land at the foot of the mountains," or "foothills." The region is an area of flat land and hills. The hills are part of the Appalachian (ap ə lā′ chən) **mountain chain.** A mountain chain is a long, unbroken line of mountains. The Appalachian Mountains run from Alabama to Canada. The Pied-

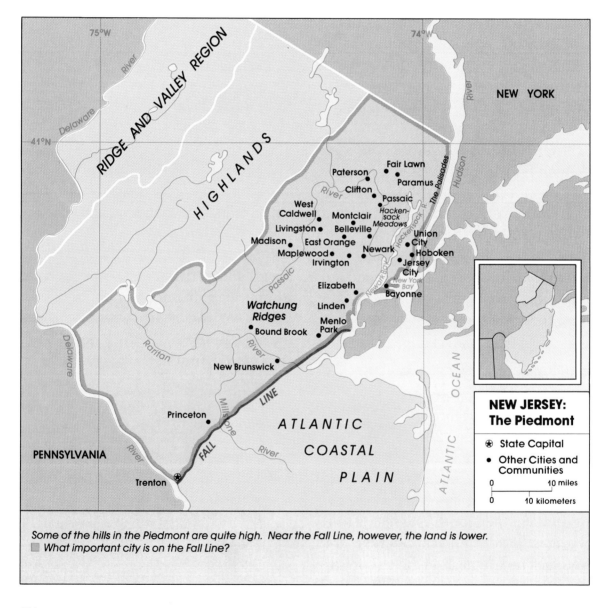

Some of the hills in the Piedmont are quite high. Near the Fall Line, however, the land is lower.
■ *What important city is on the Fall Line?*

mont in New Jersey is part of a larger region that stretches from Alabama to New York.

The place where the Piedmont meets the Atlantic Coastal Plain is called the **Fall Line.** The Fall Line is a line of small waterfalls and rapids. Rapids are places in rivers where the water flows quickly over rocks that are close to the surface. The Fall Line is formed by streams flowing from the older, harder rocks of the Piedmont onto the younger, softer rocks of the coastal plain. The flowing rivers and streams erode, or wash away, the softer rocks of the coastal plain. This causes the rivers and streams to fall, or drop, 40 to 70 feet (12 to 21 m) at the Fall Line.

A line of towns and cities lies along the Fall Line all the way from Georgia to New Jersey. Trenton, our state **capital,** is the northernmost Fall Line city. A capital is a city that is the seat of government of a country or state. Cities and towns grew up along the Fall Line because it was the farthest that ships could sail. Goods were traded here, and the rushing water provided power for water-wheels at mills.

Hills and Good Farmland Unlike the coastal plain, the Piedmont has some steep hills and valleys. The Palisades and the Watchung Ridges are in the Piedmont. The Palisades rise to over 500 feet (152 m) at the New Jersey-New York border. The Watchung

A palisade is a fence of pointed poles.
■ Why were these steep cliffs given the name Palisades?

Ridges reach elevations of over 800 feet (244 m). Tough rock lies under both the Palisades and the Watchung Ridges. A great deal of this rock has been used to build highways and sea-walls along the coast. Today, however, parts of the Palisades, at least, have been set aside as parkland. The Palisades look out over the Hudson River. Palisades Interstate Park, in both New Jersey and New York, gives visitors a beautiful view of the river and New York City.

Piedmont soils are among the best in New Jersey. Most of these soils were farmed until houses, factories, and shopping centers sprang up in place of strawberries and corn.

Big Cities and Industry The Piedmont in New Jersey is also called the Newark Basin. Newark is the largest city in the region and in our state. The Piedmont contains more than half of New Jersey's people, even though it is only about one fifth of the state's area.

Most of New Jersey's big cities are in the Piedmont. In addition to Newark, Piedmont cities include Elizabeth, Jersey City, Hoboken, East Orange, Clifton, Passaic, Union City, and Paterson. Many **suburbs** are also found in this region. A suburb is a smaller town or community near a large city. Some of the suburbs are Fair Lawn, Montclair, West Caldwell, Livingston, Madison, Maplewood, and Bound Brook.

The Piedmont also has much of our state's industry. Some of the largest **oil refineries** in the world are located in the cities of Elizabeth and Linden. An oil refinery is a plant where gasoline and other products are made from oil. Many electric products, such as radios, televisions, stoves, lamps, and motors, are made in Hudson, Union, and Essex counties. Drugs, paints, plastics, and other chemical products are also made in the Piedmont.

The pharmaceutical (fär mə süt′ i kəl), or drug, industry is one of the Piedmont's largest industries.
■ Why do you think this man wears a hat and gloves?

CHECKUP

1. What is the Fall Line?
2. What is another name for New Jersey's Piedmont?
3. What kinds of products are made in the Piedmont?
4. **Thinking Critically** What connection is there between the large number of people living in the Piedmont and the large amount of industry there?

The Highlands

What brings people to the Highlands?

VOCABULARY

dam   headquarters

A Land of Iron The Highlands are higher than both the Piedmont and the Atlantic Coastal Plain. The high land in this region is lower than that of the Ridge and Valley Region, but the Highlands are high hills. They, too, belong to the Appalachian mountain chain. Many of New Jersey's mineral resources are found in the Highlands. Iron ore has been the most important mineral resource for 200 years.

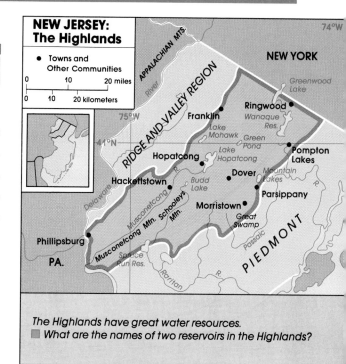

The Highlands have great water resources.
■ What are the names of two reservoirs in the Highlands?

A Land of Lakes The Highlands are rich in something besides minerals. Most of New Jersey's lakes are found here. The northern part of the Highlands was once covered by glaciers. The slowly moving ice scraped and dug many large holes that later filled with water and became lakes. Later, people helped make more lakes and made old lakes deeper and larger by building **dams.** Dams are like walls that keep water behind them. Two of the larger natural lakes in the Highlands are Green Pond and Lake Hopatcong. Lakes built by people include Mountain Lakes and Lake Mohawk. Many reservoirs are also found in the Highlands. Newark, Jersey City, and other cities use water from Highlands reservoirs.

Lake Hopatcong is lined with summer cottages and year-round homes.
■ Why do people like to live here?

77

Several divisions of Nabisco Brands' headquarters are located in Parsippany in the Highlands. These include divisions that have to do with the making and selling of Nabisco's products. Food processing is Nabisco's business.
■ **What steps in food processing are shown in these photographs?**

A Land of Growing Suburbs Many towns along the eastern edge of the Highlands are growing quickly. Morristown, Parsippany, Dover, and Pompton Lakes are the homes of more people each year. There are many jobs in the Highlands. Many big companies have their **headquarters** here. A headquarters is the business center of a company. It is where the head or heads of the company work. Companies with headquarters in the Highlands include AT&T (American Telephone & Telegraph) and Warner-Lambert Company.

The Highlands is also a beautiful area in which to live. Phillipsburg, an old metalworking center, and Hackettstown, a business center, are two attractive towns in the western part of the Highlands.

CHECKUP
1. What is the most important mineral resource of the Highlands?
2. Name two natural lakes located in the Highlands.
3. What is a headquarters?
4. **Thinking Critically** Compare the land of the Highlands with that of the Piedmont.

78

The Ridge and Valley Region

What has nature given to the Ridge and Valley Region?

VOCABULARY

Delaware Water Gap   dairy farm

The Look of the Land It would be easy to see from an airplane why this region has the name that it does. The mountains are in the form of long, narrow, steep-sided ridges. These ridges run in a northeast to southwest line. In between the ridges, long, narrow valleys follow the same direction. It is as though a giant garden rake had been dragged across the land. Like the hills of the Highlands and the Piedmont, the mountains of the Ridge and Valley Region are part of the Appalachian mountain chain. Almost all of the region was once covered by glaciers.

The Ridge and Valley Region has the highest point in New Jersey — High Point, which is 1,803 feet (550 m) above sea level. High Point is on Kittatinny Mountain. The mountain is about 36 miles (58 km) long. The Appalachian Trail runs the entire length of Kittatinny Mountain. Find the trail on the physical map on page 68. The Delaware River cuts more than 1,000 feet (305 m) through Kittatinny Mountain at the beautiful **Delaware Water Gap.** This water gap, or opening cut through a mountain by a river, is one of the most famous in the eastern United States.

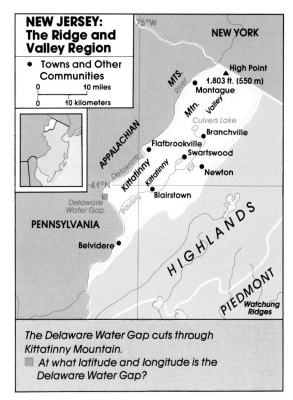

The Delaware Water Gap cuts through Kittatinny Mountain.
■ At what latitude and longitude is the Delaware Water Gap?

From the time of the Indians, paths, roads, and highways have passed through the great gap to avoid climbing the mountain. Today, Interstate Route 80 runs through the gap.

The Use of the Land Many of the people who live in the Ridge and Valley Region all year are farmers. Many summer visitors join them to enjoy the mountain scenery. People visit High Point State Park, Stokes State Forest, and Worthington State Forest. Visitors also enjoy the Delaware Water Gap National Recreation Area, which lies in both New Jersey and Pennsylvania.

The farmers in the Ridge and Valley Region find good soils in the

There are many dairy farms in the Ridge and Valley Region. Warren and Sussex counties lead the counties in milk production.
■ What buildings are shown on this dairy farm?

valleys. Most farms in this region are **dairy farms.** Farmers may have chosen to raise cows because they knew the land was too rocky and the climate too cool for many crops. Cows like cool summers and do not mind walking up and down hills.

Of course, not everyone in the Ridge and Valley Region is a farmer. Just as in the Highlands, the pretty and peaceful scenery is attracting people from more crowded parts of New Jersey. Belvidere, Blairstown, Swartswood, Flatbrookville, and Montague are some of the beautiful small towns of this region.

Regions and People   Now you have looked at all the pieces of the New Jersey puzzle. When you put all the pieces together, you have a picture that says, "This is New Jersey!" Nature has formed the land of New Jersey. It is up to the people of our state to use the land in the best way that they can.

CHECKUP

1. What mountain chain are the mountains of the Ridge and Valley Region a part of?
2. Why have travelers from the Indians to interstate truckers used the Delaware Water Gap?
3. What is a dairy farm?

4. **Thinking Critically** How do the mountains and valleys affect how people make a living in the Ridge and Valley Region?

Reading a Map: Contour Lines

CONTOUR LINES

Maps can do many things. One of the things maps can do is to show how high places are. The height of a place is its distance above sea level. As you know, this is called elevation. Maps show elevation by contour lines. The best way to understand contour lines is to draw some yourself. You can use the drawing below to do this.

The drawing is the beginning of an elevation map of a large island. It is an imaginary island. The drawing shows the shoreline of the island—where the land meets the sea. The elevation of the shoreline is 0 feet, or sea level.

On this island the elevation of the land has been measured at 23 points. Those points are shown by dots. At 10 points the elevation is 100 feet. At 8 points the elevation is 200 feet. At 5 points the elevation is 300 feet.

SKILLS PRACTICE

Trace the island and key below on a sheet of paper. Draw a curved line connecting all the 100-foot elevation points. Since all the points on this line are 100 feet above sea level, it is called a 100-foot contour line. Now do the same thing with the 200-foot and 300-foot contour lines.

Next add color to your map. Use green to color the space between the shoreline and the 100-foot contour line. Use yellow for the space between the 100-foot and 200-foot contour lines. Use brown between the 200-foot and 300-foot lines and red inside the 300-foot line. Then color your key.

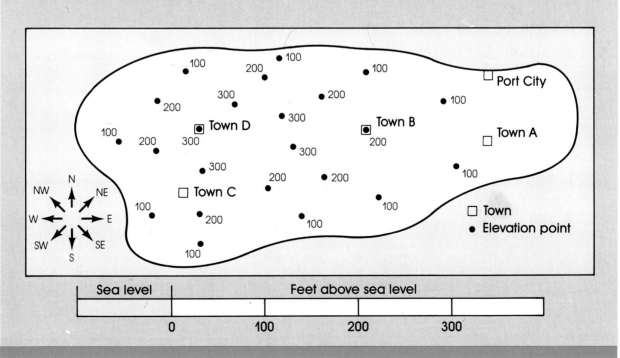

CHAPTER 4 REVIEW

MAIN IDEAS

1. Glaciers and other forms of moving water have helped to shape the land of New Jersey.
2. People work in industry and on farms on the Atlantic Coastal Plain. They also fish for a living and work in seashore resorts. People enjoy the Pinelands and the seashore of the Atlantic Coastal Plain.
3. Most people in New Jersey live in the Piedmont because there are big cities and important industry in the region.
4. People come to the Highlands to enjoy the beautiful lakes and attractive towns and countryside. Many also come to work in the big companies that have their headquarters there.
5. Nature has given the Ridge and Valley Region mountains, the Delaware Water Gap, good soils, peaceful scenery, and a cool climate.

VOCABULARY REVIEW

Write the numbers 1 through 10 on a separate sheet of paper. Match these words with the definitions.

   a. oil refinery
   b. glacier
   c. resort
   d. suburb
   e. plain
   f. Delaware Water Gap
   g. moraine
   h. contour line
   i. open space
   j. mountain chain

   1. A thick sheet of ice and snow
   2. A line on a map that separates the colors used to show the elevation of the land
   3. A broad strip of low, flat land
   4. Unsettled or undeveloped land
   5. A place that people visit for fun
   6. A plant where gasoline and other products are made from oil
   7. A smaller town or community near a large city
   8. Opening cut through Kittatinny Mountain by the Delaware River
   9. A raised strip of land formed by rocks, sand, and soil left by a glacier
   10. A long, unbroken line of mountains

CHAPTER CHECKUP

1. In what other ways besides glaciers and other forms of moving water can nature shape the land?
2. Why is Pinelands a better name than Pine Barrens for the forest area of the coastal plain?
3. Why are dams built?
4. **Thinking Critically** What problems might be caused by the great amount of industry in the Piedmont?
5. **Thinking Critically** In which region of New Jersey would you like to live, and why?
6. **Thinking Critically** Describe each of the regions of New Jersey as it would appear from the air.

APPLYING KNOWLEDGE

On an outline map of New Jersey, divide the state into the four regions you have learned about in this chapter. Find pictures in old magazines or draw pictures that show things that are important to each region. Paste these pictures in the regions on the map. Compare your map with those of your classmates. How do your maps differ? In what ways are your maps the same?

SUMMARIZING UNIT 1

REVIEWING VOCABULARY

1. Globe   A globe shows the shapes of land and water on the surface of the earth. How much of the earth is water? How much is land?

2. Compass Rose   Sometimes a compass rose shows more than just the four main directions. Name the other four directions a compass rose might show. What are these directions called?

3. Population Density   There are more people per square mile in New Jersey than in any other state. What is the population density of our state? What parts of New Jersey are the least crowded? The most crowded?

4. Glacier   Glaciers moved huge amounts of earth and carried rocks and sand from one place to another. Compare the land in northern New Jersey with that in southern New Jersey. What did glaciers have to do with the differences between the land in northern New Jersey and that in southern New Jersey?

5. Region   There are four physical regions in New Jersey. Name the regions. Explain how people make a living in each region. Which region has the most industry?

EXPRESSING YOURSELF

1. What If?   If you were going to make a map that would show four good places to spend a vacation in New Jersey, what places would you choose and why? What symbols would you use to show these places on the map?

2. Thinking Like a Geographer   A geographer is a person who studies the earth and how people use it. Write a paragraph explaining what you think is the most important use of the land in New Jersey.

3. Who Would You Rather Be?   If you were given the choice of being a cranberry farmer in the Pinelands, a member of an iron ore mining company in Morris County, or the owner of an oil refinery in Linden, which would you choose? Explain your choice.

4. In What Ways?   Imagine that you live in the mountains in the northwestern part of New Jersey. You enjoy the scenery and you like living in one of the least densely populated areas of the state. You have just learned that a ski area will be built within a few miles of your home. In what ways will the ski area change your life?

5. What Would You Do?   You have decided to open a store in one of the resorts on the New Jersey shore. In addition to refreshments for visitors, you would like to sell items that people use at the beach. What ten items would you choose to sell?

The Early History of New Jersey

New Jersey's history began thousands of years ago, when the first people came to the land that is now our state. In this unit you will learn about the first people of New Jersey — the Indians. You will also learn about other people who came here and about the beginnings of our state and our country, the United States of America.

This time line shows some of the main events that you will study in this unit.
■ What important event ended in 1781?

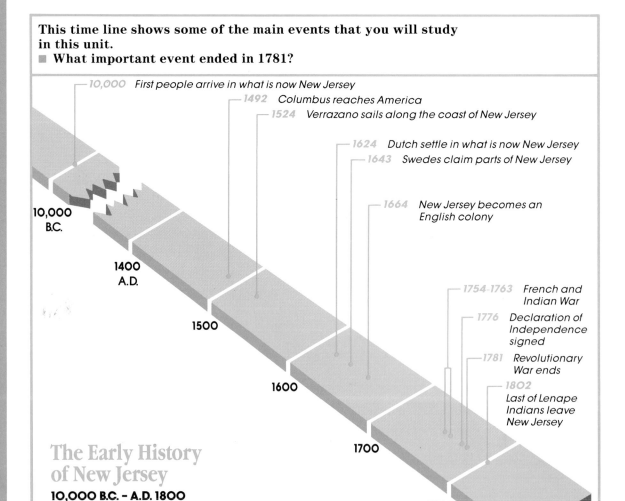

10,000 First people arrive in what is now New Jersey
1492 Columbus reaches America
1524 Verrazano sails along the coast of New Jersey
1624 Dutch settle in what is now New Jersey
1643 Swedes claim parts of New Jersey
1664 New Jersey becomes an English colony
1754-1763 French and Indian War
1776 Declaration of Independence signed
1781 Revolutionary War ends
1802 Last of Lenape Indians leave New Jersey

10,000 B.C.
1400 A.D.
1500
1600
1700
1800

The Early History of New Jersey
10,000 B.C. - A.D. 1800

The Indians above see the ship of the European explorer Henry
Hudson. The Europeans were interested in the furs in America.
■ What goods did the Europeans trade the Indians for furs?

There was no place called New Jersey when the Indians arrived. The Indians did not set boundaries to separate the land that is now New Jersey from other land. It was not really until the English took over the land that is now our state that boundaries were set and the land was finally called New Jersey.

The Indians and settlers had different ways of life. The settlers used the land in some different ways. But the Indians did teach some of the settlers about farming in America.

The settlers put their goods and services up for sale.
■ What is this craftworker doing?

The Indians farmed with simple handmade tools. Corn was an especially important food for them.
■ What other Indian food is shown here?

The Indians were the first farmers on the land that is now New Jersey. They raised a large number of crops that are still grown in our state.

A farm in early New Jersey met most of a family's needs. In addition to corn and other vegetables, the settlers grew wheat, which was ground into flour to make bread. The settlers also kept animals, such as cows, horses, chickens, and pigs. At the end of the 1700s, most people in New Jersey were farmers.

Carpenters, shoemakers, blacksmiths, glassmakers, leatherworkers, weavers, silversmiths, ropemakers, brickmakers, and other craftworkers had skills that were needed by others. These craftworkers usually worked in small shops. There were no real factories at the time. But there were forges, or places where iron was made. There were gristmills, where grain was ground into flour. There were also sawmills, where logs were cut into boards.

The Indians and other people in early New Jersey had much hard work to do just to stay alive. But they found fun in many everyday activities.

The Indians enjoyed singing, dancing, and storytelling. Contests involving work of all kinds were popular among the settlers. Log-rolling and log-burning contests helped to clear the land. People also enjoyed helping each other build homes.

A quilting bee was both work and fun. With many hands, much sewing could be done in a short time.
■ What do you think made a gathering such as this quilting bee so much fun?

Newark, our state's largest city today, was founded in 1666 by a group of settlers from Connecticut. The settlers were Puritans. They were looking for a place where the leaders of their church could also lead the government of the village.

The Puritans traded goods with the Indians for land by the Passaic River for their village. The settlers named the village Newark for the English home of one of their leaders.

By 1708, Newark had many buildings and a main street 132 feet (40 m) wide.
■ What kinds of transportation can you find?

CHAPTER 5 The Lenape Indians of New Jersey

The First People in New Jersey

Who were the first people to live in New Jersey?

VOCABULARY

Native American   dialect

The Lenape Indians   The first people to live in what is now New Jersey were the Indians. Another name for Indians is **Native Americans.** The Native Americans who settled in New Jersey were called the Lenni Lenape (len ē lə näp′ ē) or just Lenape Indians. In their language the name *Lenape* meant "common" or "ordinary people." Sometimes the Lenape Indians are also called the Delaware Indians. They were part of a group of Indians who lived on or near the Delaware River.

The Lenape Indians were made up of two groups. These two groups each spoke a different **dialect** of the Delaware language. A dialect is a variety, or form, of a language. One

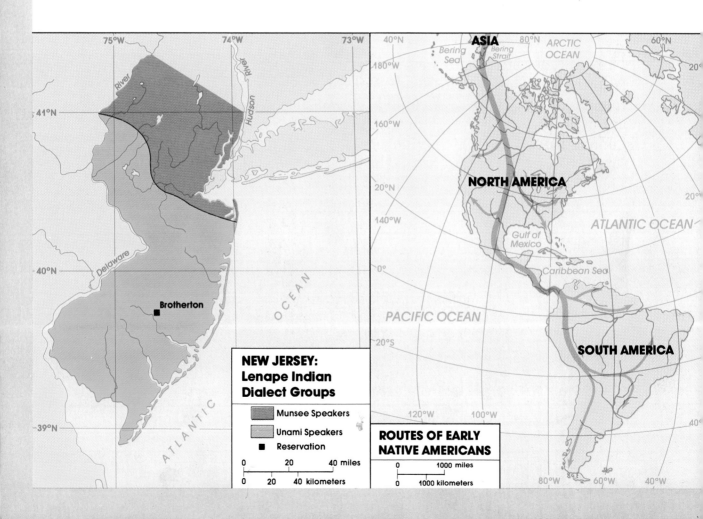

NEW JERSEY: Lenape Indian Dialect Groups

- Munsee Speakers
- Unami Speakers
- ■ Reservation

Brotherton

0   20   40 miles
0   20   40 kilometers

ROUTES OF EARLY NATIVE AMERICANS

0   1000 miles
0   1000 kilometers

ASIA · Bering Sea · Bering Strait · ARCTIC OCEAN · NORTH AMERICA · ATLANTIC OCEAN · Gulf of Mexico · Caribbean Sea · PACIFIC OCEAN · SOUTH AMERICA

group spoke the Munsee (mən′ sē) dialect. The other group spoke the Unami (ü nä′ mē) dialect. The map on the left on page 88 shows where these two groups lived. Which group lived in northern New Jersey? Which group lived in the south?

From Asia to North America   Ancestors of New Jersey's Indians once lived on the continent of Asia. A very long time ago, a strip of land connected Asia and North America. People from Asia probably walked across the strip of land to North America. That was many, many thousands of years ago. No one knows why these people left Asia.

Many historians believe that the people were following animals they were hunting.

The people who traveled from Asia to North America did not stay in one place. They moved around to hunt. The children of these people and their children after them moved around, too. After many thousands of years, people had settled in almost all parts of North and South America. The first people to come to what is now New Jersey arrived here about 12,000 years ago. These people were the first Indians in New Jersey.

From Tents and Caves to Villages
The first Indians in New Jersey lived

The Native Americans came across a strip of land from Asia.
■ Can you find where the strip of land between Asia and North America once was, on the map on the right on page 88?

89

Rock shelters offered protection from the rain and snow. They were used by Indians on the move and by hunters.
■ **What is each person in the picture doing?**

in tents made of animal skins or brush. In the mountain areas they lived in caves and under rock ledges.

After many thousands of years, the Indians began to live in simple villages. Indian villages were often near rivers and streams. Living near water was important to the Indians. Water was needed for fishing, washing, drinking, and cooking. The Indians traveled by water in canoes. Some Indian villages were also near forests or wooded areas. The Indians used saplings, or young trees, to build their houses.

After the Indians had lived in a place for a while, there were fewer

animals to hunt and fish to catch. So the Indians would move and set up a new village. The land of New Jersey was full of forests and rivers where the Indians could make their homes.

CHECKUP

1. What dialects of the Delaware language did the Lenape Indians in New Jersey speak?
2. Where did the first Native Americans come from?
3. Why did the Indians make their homes near water and forests?

4. **Thinking Critically** Compare the lives of the people who came from Asia and the Indians who settled in New Jersey.

90

Life in the Villages

How did the Lenape Indians meet their needs for housing and food?

VOCABULARY

longhouse	maize
celt	weir
slash and burn	

The Longhouse   The Lenape built their houses out of thin tree trunks and bark. These houses were called **longhouses.** A longhouse was just what it sounds like—a long house. Some Lenape longhouses were up to 20 feet wide (6 m), 60 feet long (18 m), and 5 to 6 feet (about 2 m) tall. Others were smaller. Up to 12 families could live together in a large longhouse.

The men of the village built the longhouses. They used **celts** (selts) to cut down saplings. A celt was a large, sharpened stone with a wooden handle. After the saplings were cut down, each was sharpened to a point and forced into the earth. The saplings were placed 12 to 20 inches (31 to 51 cm) apart. Then more saplings were tied across the others with strips of bark. The roof and walls of the longhouse were then covered with sheets of elm or chestnut bark for protection. After this was done, another set of saplings was tied to the outside of the bark to make the longhouse strong.

A single doorway was left open on one of the long sides of the house. Openings were also left in the roof to let out the smoke from indoor fires. Fires were used for cooking and for heat. Thin walls were built inside to give privacy to each family.

There were usually only a few houses in each Lenape village.
■ In which longhouse could several families live comfortably?

BUILDING A LONGHOUSE

1. Forcing Saplings into the Earth

2. Tying Saplings Crosswise with Strips of Bark

3. Covering the Framework with Sheets of Bark

4. Tying Saplings to the Outside of the Bark Covering

Farming the Land   The Native Americans divided the work of getting food. Women and girls planted gardens, and men and boys hunted and fished. Women and children also gathered berries, roots, and nuts.

The job of planting a garden was not an easy one. First the land had to be cleared of all trees. The men cut the trees down, using their celts. After days of hard work cutting the trees, the Indians built a fire to burn the logs, branches, and twigs, and the tree stumps left in the ground. This kind of work for preparing a garden is called **slash and burn.** The trees are first slashed, or cut, and then burned. The ashes from the fire helped to fertilize the soil, or make it better for growing crops. After the fire cooled, the men chopped at the soil to loosen it for planting. Large roots were pulled out. Then the women and girls took over and planted the garden.

Maize (māz), or corn, seeds were planted first. Later in the season, beans and squash seeds were planted. The Indians called these crops the "three sisters." They were the main crops planted, but other plants, like tobacco, were also grown.

Hunting and Fishing   Although the women and children gathered most of the food for the village, the animal meat and fish brought in by the men and boys were also impor-

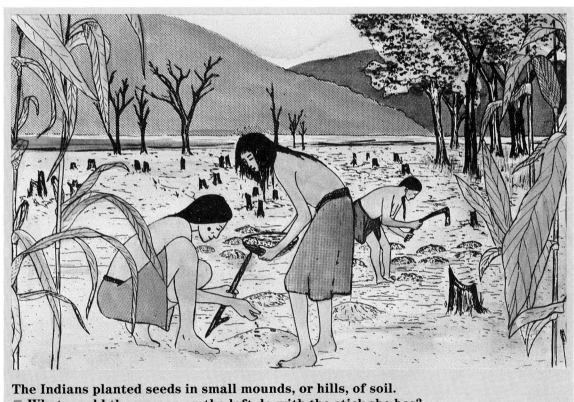

The Indians planted seeds in small mounds, or hills, of soil.
■ **What would the woman on the left do with the stick she has?**

The Lenape children worked hard, but they also had time to play.
■ What are the two children at the front of the picture doing?

tant foods. Skins from most animals were used for furs and leather goods. The Lenape hunted geese, turkey, deer, elk, black bear, squirrel, beaver, and raccoon. They used bows and arrows, spears, and traps. The Indians made their own hunting tools. Arrowheads were made from stone. Bows were made from wood.

Clams, mussels, and oysters were collected from the waters near the Lenape villages. The Lenape caught and ate trout, bass, shad, and other fish. The men and boys caught these fish with nets, spears, and fishhooks. They also used **weirs** (warz). A weir is a dam of sticks or fences. The dam trapped the fish as they swam. The Lenape also sometimes used canoes to go fishing.

The Children of the Village By now you have learned that Lenape children had very busy lives. Even though Indian children did not go to school, they learned by listening, watching, and helping adults. Children were very important members of the village. They helped the adults do many things. Later they would also carry on the Lenape way of life. Every family wanted many children.

CHECKUP
1. How large were some longhouses?
2. How did the Lenape divide the work of getting food?
3. How did the Lenape Indian children learn?

4. **Thinking Critically** How is farming easier today than it was when the Lenape lived in New Jersey?

94

The People and Their Ways and Beliefs

What is known about the ways and beliefs of the Lenape?

What They Looked Like Now that you know how the Lenape lived, you may wonder what they looked like. We can learn about how the Lenape Indians looked from documents written by the European **explorers** who sailed in New Jersey waters hundreds of years ago. An explorer is someone who searches for new places and things.

The European explorers described the Lenape as tall people with broad shoulders. Their skin was a dark golden color, but many were nearly white and others were of olive color. The Indians had black hair and dark eyes.

Indian Dress The Lenape Indians made all their clothing from the skins of animals. The skins of deer, elk, wolf, and other animals were often scraped and allowed to dry out. Then they were made into leather for moccasins, belts, pouches, and clothing. Only one side of some skins was scraped, and the fur was left on the outside. These skins were used for clothing and blankets in the winter. In the cold weather it was also important for the Lenape to wear moccasins. Moccasins are shoes made from one piece of deerskin. In the summer, the Indians wore little clothing. Most went barefoot in the villages.

The clothing of the Lenape was very plain. But the Indians were proud of their appearance. They liked to decorate their bodies in other ways. Indian men and women painted their bodies with natural dyes. Many men tattooed their bodies. Both men and women wore beads, bracelets, necklaces, and other jewelry. Jewelry was often made of bone or shell.

This pouch was made by a Native American whose ancestors belonged to a group of Indians who lived in the Monmouth County area.
■ What is the pouch made of?

95

Phratries   The Lenape Indians of New Jersey were made up of many family groups, or **phratries** (frā′ trēz). A phratry is a group of two or more smaller family groups known as clans. The families in a clan trace their background to a common ancestor. The Lenape had at least three phratries. Each phratry had an animal as its symbol. One phratry had the wolf as its symbol. Another had the turtle. A third phratry had the turkey as its symbol.

In the Lenape way of life, each child was a member of the mother's phratry. For example, a child born to a mother of the wolf phratry would also belong to the wolf phratry, even though the child's father was a member of the turkey or the turtle phratry. A person could not marry someone from the same phratry. That meant that a person from the turtle phratry had to marry someone from either the wolf phratry or the turkey phratry.

Each phratry had a male leader or chief. This chief was called a **sachem** (sā′ chəm). The word *sachem* means "powerful one" or "one above all others." The sachem represented all the members of his phratry. A new sachem was usually chosen by the old sachem before his death.

Religion   The Lenape Indians were a religious people. They believed that the world was controlled by a Great Spirit or Creator and by

The Big House Ceremony, held here by Delaware Indians in Oklahoma, may have been part of Lenape life.
■ What tells you this is a ceremony?

many lesser spirits. Some of these spirits were responsible for the corn harvest or the weather.

Throughout the year, the Lenape worshiped all the spirits with celebrations and ceremonies. The Harvest Ceremony, held in the autumn, allowed the Indians to give thanks to the spirits for what nature had given them that year.

CHECKUP
1. What did the Lenape use to make their clothing?
2. In what other ways did the Lenape decorate their bodies?
3. What were the symbols of the three Lenape phratries?
4. **Thinking Critically** What holiday that we celebrate does the Harvest Ceremony remind you of?

The Lenape Leave New Jersey

What happened to the Lenape Indians of New Jersey?

VOCABULARY

reservation   heritage

The Lenape and Their Neighbors   The Lenape Indians of New Jersey were only one group of Native Americans living in the eastern part of the United States. Many other Indian groups lived in what are now New York, Pennsylvania, Delaware, and other states. The Lenape were peaceful Indians. They respected their neighbors.

The Last of the Lenape   Before European settlers came in the 1600s, there were about 8,000 to 12,000 Lenape Indians living in the land of New Jersey. This was not a very large number of people. Because the land of New Jersey was not crowded with people, there were enough animals to hunt and fish to catch for everyone. The Indians could live the way they wanted to. When the European settlers arrived, the Lenape way of life changed. The settlers did not understand the Lenape way of life. The land became more crowded with people, and new illnesses brought by the Europeans caused many Indians to die.

The Lenape grew weaker, and their numbers grew smaller. By 1758 most Lenape Indians had moved west

The Europeans saw little or no value in the Indians' way of life.
■ **How must the Indians have felt about the arrival of settlers?**

Dr. Herbert C. Kraft (1927 –   )

Do you know what an archaeologist is? An archaeologist is a historian who learns about the past by studying objects made and used by people hundreds and thousands of years ago. Dr. Herbert Kraft is a New Jersey archaeologist. For many years, Dr. Kraft has been digging up objects used by the Lenape Indians. The objects that Dr. Kraft has found—such as arrowheads, tools, and pieces of pots—have helped him and others learn more about New Jersey's Indians.

Dr. Kraft also uses oral history to find out about how the Lenape

lived. He keeps in touch with people whose ancestors were Lenape Indians. He also visited one of the last full-blooded Lenape Indians in our country. Her name was Nora Thompson Dean, but her Lenape name was Touching Leaves. Dr. Kraft interviewed Touching Leaves just before her death and found out many things about the Lenape that he could not learn from objects.

To become an archaeologist, Dr. Kraft studied history at Seton Hall University in South Orange. He also studied anthropology at Hunter College and at the City University of New York in New York. Anthropology is the study of human beings. Dr. Kraft teaches anthropology at Seton Hall University. He is also the director of the Archaeological Research Center and Museum at Seton Hall. Dr. Kraft has written many articles and books about his discoveries and the life of the Indians of New Jersey. His most recent book, *The Lenape*, is a study of the artifacts, beliefs, and ways of the Indians who lived in what is now New Jersey for over 12,000 years.

and north. But some went to a **reservation** (rez ər vā′ shən) in the southern part of New Jersey, at Brotherton. A reservation is land that has been set aside, or reserved, for the Indians by the government. The Lenape who moved to the Brotherton reservation were unhappy with life there. These Lenape were later invited to join the Lenape Indians who had moved west. In 1802 the last Indians left the Brotherton reservation in New Jersey. The reservation at Brotherton was deserted. It was later renamed Indian Mills, even though no Indians were living there.

The Lenape traveled to the western part of the United States to find new homes. Some traveled as far as Oklahoma. Others went to Wisconsin and Ontario, Canada. Today there are only a few Lenape Indians living in our country.

The Indian Heritage   Even though the Lenape Indians left New Jersey long ago, there are many reminders of their **heritage** (her′ ət ij) in our state. Heritage is ways and beliefs handed down from one generation to the next. Some roads in our state follow old Indian trails. Many places in our state have Indian names. Some of these are Hackensack, Succasunna, Raritan, Hopatcong, Ramapo, Kittatinny, Musconetcong, and Oratam. With these everyday reminders of the Indians, the Lenape are still part of New Jersey today.

This Oklahoma woman's ancestors were Lenape Indians.
■ What are her shoes called?

CHECKUP
1. How many Lenape lived in what is now New Jersey before the Europeans arrived?
2. What is a reservation?
3. Where did the Lenape go when they left New Jersey?
4. **Thinking Critically** How would life on a reservation have differed from the life the Lenape Indians led before?

Making a Retrieval Chart

WHAT IS A RETRIEVAL CHART?

In this chapter you have read about New Jersey's first people—the Lenape Indians. You learned about how the Lenape set up villages and built longhouses. You also read about the ways in which the Lenape farmed the land and hunted for animals. It may be hard for you to remember all these facts, but there are two things you can do to remember.

1. You can organize the facts.
2. You can compare the facts.

A retrieval chart is a good way to organize facts. The chart helps you retrieve, or recall, important information.

SKILLS PRACTICE

Copy one of these charts on a separate piece of paper. Fill in the boxes on the chart with facts. You may wish to add facts from other books, too.

THE LENAPE WAY OF LIFE			
	Farming	*Food*	*Clothing*
Men			
Women			
Children			

Now compare the facts on your chart by answering these questions:

1. How did the jobs of Lenape men and women differ in farming the land?
2. Who brought in what food?
3. How did men and women both help to make clothing?
4. What jobs did children do?

HOW HAS LIFE CHANGED?		
	Life During Lenape Times	*Life Today*
Food		
Clothing		
Housing		
Transporta-tion		
Fun		

Answer these questions by comparing the facts on your chart:

1. How was life during Lenape times different from life today?
2. How was life during Lenape times like life today?
3. What are some of the greatest changes that have taken place since Lenape times?
4. How would *your* life have been different during Lenape times?

MORE PRACTICE

Now you are ready to make your own chart. You may wish to make a retrieval chart after you have read the next chapter. The headings in the chapter will help you make your chart. Write questions and answers for your chart.

CHAPTER 5 REVIEW

MAIN IDEAS

1. The first people to live in what is now New Jersey were the Indians, or Native Americans. The Indians who settled in New Jersey were the Lenape.
2. The Lenape lived in longhouses, which were built by the men of the village out of young tree trunks and bark. The Indians divided the work of getting food — the women and girls planted and harvested such crops as corn, beans, and squash; the men and boys hunted and fished.
3. It is known that the Lenape were proud of their appearance. It is also known that the Lenape were divided into family groups called phratries and that they were a religious people who worshiped many spirits.
4. The Lenape moved from New Jersey to the north and the west.
5. Today there are very few Lenape Indians left in the United States.

VOCABULARY REVIEW

Write the numbers 1 to 10 on a sheet of paper. Match the words with the definitions. Write the matching word by the number of the definition. One word does not have a definition. Find the word and write your own definition by No. 10.

a.	celt	**f.**	heritage
b.	sachem	**g.**	weir
c.	longhouse	**h.**	reservation
d.	dialect	**i.**	phratry
e.	maize	**j.**	explorer

1. A Lenape house
2. A large, sharpened stone with a wooden handle
3. Another word for corn
4. Leader of a phratry
5. A variety, or form, of a language
6. A dam used to trap fish
7. A person who searches for new places and things
8. A group of two or more clans
9. Ways and beliefs handed down from one generation to the next
10.

CHAPTER CHECKUP

1. Where did the two dialect groups of Lenape Indians live?
2. How was a longhouse built?
3. How did the arrival of European settlers change the life of the Lenape Indians?
4. **Thinking Critically** What work would you have liked to do as an Indian, and why?
5. **Thinking Critically** What does a child's membership in the mother's phratry say about the importance of women among the Lenape Indians?

APPLYING KNOWLEDGE

1. Today some people go camping in the woods for vacation. How is this similar to living like the Lenape Indians? How does camping in the woods differ from living like the Indians?
2. Lenape children did have some time to play with toys, even though there was much work to do. What are some of the toys Indian children might have played with? Remember, everything the Indians used came from natural resources. This will help you think of some toys. (An example of an Indian toy is a simple doll made out of corn husks, or the dry outer covering on corn.) Make an Indian toy.

6 Europeans Come to New Jersey

Early Explorers

How did Europeans discover America?

VOCABULARY

New World   colony

A Route to the Indies Five hundred years ago, the Indians were living in North and South America. At the same time, people were living very differently in Europe. During the 1400s the people of Europe did not know that two large continents lay across the Atlantic Ocean from Europe. But they did know about a far-away place called the Indies. The Indies was another name for China, Japan, and India. Find these countries on the map on pages 260–261. Europeans were interested in trading goods with the people living in the Indies. They were especially interested in the jewels, spices, and other riches found there.

The land route from Europe to the Indies was long and hard. Robbers sometimes attacked travelers. Europeans wanted to find another

After a long sea voyage, Columbus and his crew of 90 men were glad to see land.
■ What do these two pictures tell you about what their voyage must have been like?

way to get to the Indies. They hoped to find a water route. A water route could be dangerous, too. The ships at that time were very small. They were only about 50 feet (15 m) long and half as wide. They were built of wood and had no engines. Instead the ships had sails and oars. The ships needed wind and manpower to sail. Sometimes very strong winds could turn a ship over. Giant ocean waves could wash sailors overboard.

Discovering the New World Finding a water route to the Indies would not be easy. But many European sailors decided to try. Some sailors believed that the best way to reach the Indies was by sailing east. China,

Japan, and India are east of Europe. But one Italian ship captain had a different plan. His name was Christopher Columbus. Columbus believed that if he sailed far enough west, he could find a direct ocean route to the Indies. Since most Europeans by this time believed that the earth was round, no one doubted that this route to the Indies was possible. But many people thought that the distance was too great and the voyage would take too long.

Christopher Columbus did not give up easily. In 1492 he set sail for the Indies under the Spanish flag. He had three ships, the *Nina*, the *Pinta*, and the *Santa Maria*. Columbus and his crew sailed for many days. When

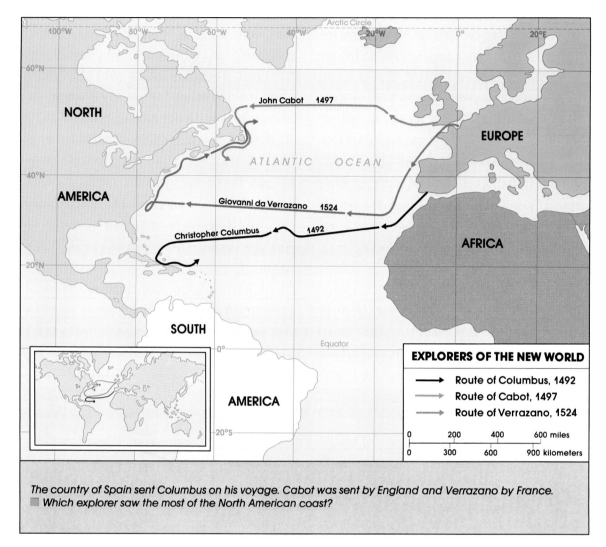

EXPLORERS OF THE NEW WORLD

→ Route of Columbus, 1492
→ Route of Cabot, 1497
→ Route of Verrazano, 1524

| 0 | 200 | 400 | 600 miles |
| 0 | 300 | 600 | 900 kilometers |

The country of Spain sent Columbus on his voyage. Cabot was sent by England and Verrazano by France.
■ *Which explorer saw the most of the North American coast?*

Columbus finally saw land on October 12, 1492, he thought he had reached the Indies. Columbus called the people he found Indians.

But Columbus had not reached the Indies at all. The land he had reached was an island between the coasts of North and South America. He had discovered a whole new land by accident! The Europeans called this new land the **New World.** Of course it was not a new world to the Indians. They had lived in the Americas for thousands of years.

John Cabot After Christopher Columbus brought back the exciting news of the New World, many other Europeans wished to explore it. Different countries in Europe sent explorers to the New World. In 1497 the country of England sent ship captain John Cabot to explore the New World and try to find a route to the Indies. Cabot sailed with a crew of only 18 men. After sailing for over a month, Cabot and his men landed on the North American coast. They probably arrived in what is now eastern

Canada. Cabot and his men picked up Indian fishnets and brought them back to England as souvenirs.

Because of John Cabot's voyage in 1497, the country of England claimed that it owned North America. At that time the rulers of England and other countries believed that they owned any land that had been explored for them. These countries also set up **colonies** in the New World. A colony is a place that is settled at a distance from the country that rules it.

Giovanni da Verrazano The explorers sent by Spain and England had found a new world. But they had not yet found what everyone was looking for — a water route to the Indies. In 1524 the country of France

Verrazano was an Italian ship captain.
■ **Trace his route on the map on page 104.**

decided it would try to find this route. It sent an Italian ship captain named Giovanni da Verrazano (jō-vän′ nē dä vär rä tsä′ nō) to find the way to the Indies.

In April 1524, Verrazano came to the coast of North America. He explored more of the coastline from eastern Canada to Florida than any other explorer before him. Verrazano was probably the first European to see the land that would later be called New Jersey. As he sailed along the coast of what is now New Jersey, Verrazano wrote that it was "green with forests."

Verrazano discovered a large inlet, or bay, along the seacoast between New Jersey and New York. Today this is called New York Bay. Verrazano did not stay long in this bay. He did not think that it would lead him to the Indies, and he was right. So he sailed back out into the ocean. Today, the Verrazano Narrows Bridge, which connects Staten Island to Long Island, is named after this explorer.

CHECKUP
1. Why did Europeans want to find a water route to the Indies?
2. Which explorer gave the country of England the right to claim land in the New World?
3. Who was probably the first European to see the land that is now New Jersey?
4. **Thinking Critically** How would Verrazano describe the coast of New Jersey today?

The Colony of New Netherland

How was the land of New Jersey claimed and settled by the Dutch?

VOCABULARY

trading post	patroonship
patroon system	thatched roof
patroon	

Henry Hudson For more than 100 years after Columbus discovered the New World, no one closely explored the waters around New Jersey. Even after Verrazano's voyage, the coastline of New Jersey remained a mystery to the Europeans.

In 1609 an explorer named Henry Hudson left for the New World on a small ship called the *Half Moon.* Hudson was an English ship captain, but he was sailing for the country of Holland, or the Netherlands. The people of Holland are called the Dutch. Like other explorers, Hudson hoped to find a way to the Indies through the American continent. Hudson arrived along the southern coast of New Jersey in late August 1609. He passed Cape May and the waters around Barnegat and continued north. On September 4, Hudson anchored his ship inside New Jersey waters, around present-day Sandy Hook Bay. Here he hoped to find fresh water for drinking and to give his sailors some rest. While at Sandy Hook, Hudson and his crew met some Lenape Indians. The Indians were invited on the ship. They brought knives and beads for the sailors.

Henry Hudson met Indians at several places along his route.
■ How did the Indians greet Hudson?

Henry Hudson left Sandy Hook and continued north. Along the northern coast of New Jersey, Hudson found the bay that Verrazano had discovered. Hudson sailed into this bay farther than Verrazano. Hudson found that the bay turned into a large inland river. Hudson thought that this river might lead him to the Indies. He sailed up the river about 150 miles (241 km). Today this river is called the Hudson River.

After sailing up the river for many days, Hudson reached shallow water. He knew then that the river would not lead him to the Indies. Hudson turned the *Half Moon* around and headed south again. Then he sailed out into the Atlantic Ocean and returned to Holland.

The Dutch Settle New Netherland

Holland used Henry Hudson's voyage to claim land in America. They called that land the colony of New Netherland. New Netherland included parts of what are now New Jersey and New York. The Dutch were excited about what Hudson had found in America. Many Dutch people believed that they could become wealthy by trading with the Indians. Soon after Henry Hudson's visit, the Dutch set up **trading posts** in New Netherland. A trading post is a place where things can be bought, sold, or traded. The Dutch traded goods with the Indians living along the Hudson River for furs.

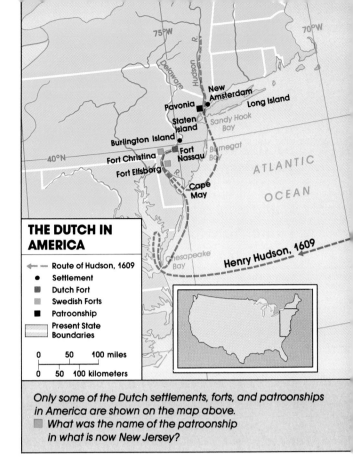

THE DUTCH IN AMERICA

← — Route of Hudson, 1609
● Settlement
■ Dutch Fort
■ Swedish Forts
■ Patroonship
　 Present State Boundaries

0　50　100 miles
0　50　100 kilometers

Only some of the Dutch settlements, forts, and patroonships in America are shown on the map above.
■ *What was the name of the patroonship in what is now New Jersey?*

In 1624 the first Dutch settlement was started on New Jersey soil in the colony. A man named Cornelius Mey brought families to live on what is now Burlington Island. Two years later, the Dutch also set up a trading post on New Jersey soil. They called this trading post Fort Nassau. By 1626, other settlements had been started across the Hudson River on Manhattan Island in what is now New York. The trading post on Manhattan Island was called New Amsterdam. The Dutch purchased the land of Manhattan Island from the Indians living there. The Lenape Indians were part of this Indian group. The Dutch traded beads and other goods for the land.

Patroons and Pavonia The colony of New Netherland grew slowly. It was not easy to attract people to live in the new colony, because living conditions were so hard. In 1629 the Dutch came up with a plan to get more people to move to New Netherland. This plan was called the **patroon** (pə trün´) **system.** Under this plan a person called a **patroon** was given a large piece of land in New Netherland. The land he was given was called a **patroonship.** In exchange for this land the patroon promised to bring 50 settlers to New Netherland to work on the land.

One patroon, named Michael Pauw, was given land on New Jersey soil. This land was near present-day Jersey City. Michael Pauw called his land Pavonia. New Jersey's first permanent settlers lived in Pavonia. But Michael Pauw never found as many as 50 people to settle in Pavonia. He had to give his land back to the Dutch West India Company in 1634. This company was in charge of running the colony of New Netherland. Some settlers decided to stay in Pavonia. Two houses were built there. They were the first houses to be built on New Jersey soil. These early New Jersey houses were made of wood and built into the side of a hill for protection. They had stone chimneys and **thatched roofs.** A thatched roof is made of straw or other plant matter.

Paulus Hook was a Dutch settlement on the site of present-day Jersey City. The windmill was a common Dutch building.
■ Why, do you think, was the windmill so close to the water?

Today the waterfront area of Jersey City has a different look.
■ **What kinds of buildings stand along the waterfront today?**

Facing the Indians In the beginning the Dutch and the Lenape Indians lived together in peace. The Indians helped the settlers in many ways. Many Dutch traded with the Lenape Indians.

As time went by, there were more Dutch settlements in New Jersey. This meant that more and more of the Indians' land was being used by the Europeans. In time, relations between the Dutch and the Indians grew less friendly. Finally, in 1643, a war broke out between the Indians and the Dutch. The war started when some Dutch killed 80 Indians. In return the Indians destroyed Dutch farms and burned many houses. Many of the New Jersey Dutch farmers fled to New Amsterdam for protection. This war lasted nearly 2 years. In 1645, peace was declared. The Dutch returned to rebuild their homes, and the Lenape went back to their villages.

CHECKUP

1. What did Henry Hudson explore in North America?
2. What was the name of the Dutch colony that included parts of what are New Jersey and New York?
3. Where was the first Dutch settlement on New Jersey soil?
4. How was the settlement of Pavonia started?

5. **Thinking Critically** What made life in the colony of New Netherland harder than life in Holland?

109

The Dutch and the Swedes

How did the colony of New Netherland grow and finally come to an end?

VOCABULARY

fort   surrender
govern

The Colony of New Sweden The country of Sweden also decided to send settlers to America. Sweden set up its own colony, called New Sweden, along the Delaware River. The Swedes built a **fort** called Fort Christina near what is now Wilmington, Delaware. A fort is a place built to protect people.

The Dutch were not happy about New Sweden. The Swedes needed a strong leader. In 1643, Johan Printz was sent by Sweden to **govern,** or rule, New Sweden. He had a fort built on the New Jersey side of the Delaware River. The name of the fort was Fort Elfsborg. From this fort, the Swedes could control all the Dutch ships using the river. Fort Elfsborg was built at Finn's Point. Finn's Point was named for people from the country of Finland who had come with the Swedes to America.

The colony of New Sweden had a short life. A man more powerful than Johan Printz was made governor of New Netherland. His name was Peter Stuyvesant (stī′ ve sənt). Peter Stuy-

Johan Printz was a tough governor.
■ How did this help New Sweden?

The Swedes came to America on this ship.
■ What is behind the ship?

Bergen was the first organized village on New Jersey soil. It was surrounded by a palisade, or wall made of pointed logs.
■ **What buildings stand inside the palisade?**

vesant was determined to get rid of the Swedish colony on the Delaware River.

The End of New Sweden In 1651, Governor Stuyvesant of New Netherland challenged Governor Printz of New Sweden for control of the Delaware River. Governor Stuyvesant led a small army to New Sweden and forced the Swedes to **surrender,** or give up. Peter Stuyvesant gave the settlers of New Sweden a choice. They could return to Sweden or stay and be loyal to the Dutch. Many of the Swedes decided to stay. Some of the Finns who had come with them stayed, too.

Life in Villages Fighting began again between the Dutch and the Indians. Peter Stuyvesant ordered the settlers to band together and live in villages for protection. The first planned New Jersey village was surrounded by a high wooden wall for protection. This village was called Bergen. It was built in 1660 near what is now Jersey City.

Life in a village began when the sun came up. Work began then. The women milked the cows and lit a fire in the fireplace for cooking the day's meals. The men fed the animals. The children helped by doing chores such as bringing in firewood. All this was done before breakfast.

During the day, the women might mend clothing, make candles, prepare the meals, clean the house, and take care of the children. The men would farm the land, build fences and barns, or make furniture. The children helped with some of the work. Girls helped prepare food, weave cloth, and make soap. Boys split wood for the fire, cleaned stables, and plowed the fields.

The children also went to school. Lessons were usually taught in a church or a meetinghouse. Not all boys and girls went to school, because often they were needed at home. Children also had some time for fun. They could skate and fish or play with simple homemade games.

The End of New Netherland As you remember, the country of England claimed it owned the land in North America. The English were angry that the Dutch had started a colony on what they considered to be their land. Finally England decided to take over New Netherland.

The king of England gave the colony of New Netherland to his brother. The king's brother was called the Duke of York. In 1664 the Duke of York sent a man named Richard Nicolls to take control of the colony for the English. Nicolls and an army of soldiers demanded that the Dutch give up New Netherland. On August 27, 1664, the Dutch surrendered to the English. There had been

The Dutch surrendered New Netherland to the English in 1664.
■ How can you tell this was a coastal settlement?

Tall tree trunks split in half were used to build this cabin.
■ What does the inset photograph on the right show?

no fighting. Governor Stuyvesant left the colony with his soldiers.

The Dutch colony of New Netherland became an English colony with a new government. But life did not change much for the settlers in the colony. If they promised to be loyal to England, they could stay on their land. Most of the Dutch and Swedes stayed. No matter who ruled the colony, it was their home.

The Past Lives On In New Jersey today there are many reminders of the Dutch, Swedes, and Finns who first settled here. In some places in northern New Jersey, there are old Dutch homes and churches made of stone. In the southern part of our state, some of America's first log cabins are still standing. They were built by the Swedes and Finns who lived there. The Swedes and Finns brought the idea of the log cabin from their homelands to New Jersey.

CHECKUP

1. Where was the colony of New Sweden started?
2. What did Governor Stuyvesant do that changed life for the settlers in New Netherland?
3. How did New Netherland become an English colony?
4. **Thinking Critically** How would you have felt if you had been a Dutch, Swedish, or Finnish settler in New Netherland when it was taken over by England?

Using a Time Line

WHAT IS A TIME LINE?

Time is difficult to understand. Knowing the order of events in the past helps us to understand the idea of time. A time line is used to show the order of events. A time line, like a map, is drawn to scale. A certain length on the time line represents a certain period of time. One inch, for instance, could stand for 1 year, 10 years, or 100 years.

READING A TIME LINE

Look at the time line below. It begins in 1950 and ends in 1990. Each ⅞-inch section stands for 10 years. The time line shows when each of the following became governor of New Jersey:

Robert B. Meyner	1954
Richard J. Hughes	1962
William T. Cahill	1970
Brendon T. Byrne	1974
Thomas H. Kean	1982

SKILLS PRACTICE

Now you can make your own time line. You might want to make a time line of important events in your family. Remember events in your own life. Then talk with family members. Try to get a date for each event. One date should be easy—the year you were born. Put all your information down on paper. Next, try to put the events in order.

To get started, you might ask some of these questions:

1. What events should be included?
2. In what years did they happen?
3. In what year will the time line begin? When will it end?
4. How many years will an inch stand for on the time line?

Now draw your own time line. Use a dot to place each event, and then label each dot. You have now created your very own time line.

The time line below shows the governors of our state from 1950 to the present.
■ Who was governor from 1970 to 1974?

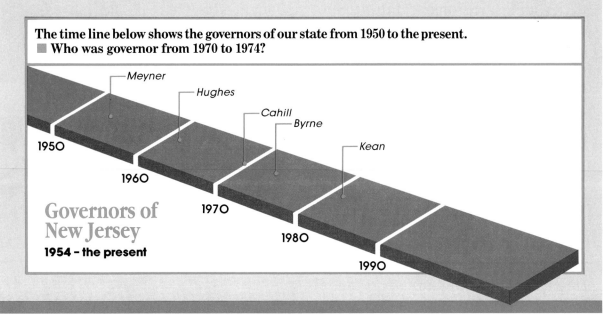

Meyner — Hughes — Cahill — Byrne — Kean

1950   1960   1970   1980   1990

Governors of
New Jersey
1954 – the present

CHAPTER 6 REVIEW

MAIN IDEAS

1. European explorers looking for a water route to the Indies discovered the New World.
2. Giovanni da Verrazano was probably the first European to see the land that would later be called New Jersey.
3. Holland used Henry Hudson's voyage in the waters off the coast of New Jersey and up the Hudson River to claim the land in America that is now New Jersey. Cornelius Mey led Dutch settlers to Burlington Island. A trading post called Fort Nassau was set up by the Dutch, and Pavonia was started in what is now New Jersey under the patroon system.
4. Swedes and Finns started a colony called New Sweden along the Delaware River.
5. The governor of New Netherland, Peter Stuyvesant, forced the governor of New Sweden, Johan Printz, to surrender the colony to the Dutch. New Netherland was finally taken over by the English, who claimed the land as theirs.

VOCABULARY REVIEW

On a separate sheet of paper, write the word or words that best complete each sentence.

1. A _____ is a place that is settled at a distance from the country that rules it.
2. To _____ means "to give up."
3. The land that a patroon is given is called a _____.
4. A _____ is a place that is built to protect people.
5. To _____ means "to rule."

CHAPTER CHECKUP

1. Why did Europeans want to travel to the Indies?
2. Do you think that it was fair for a country to claim as its own any land that it explored?
3. Why is Hudson's trip to the New World important in the history of the state of New Jersey?
4. How did the Dutch West India Company get more people to settle in the colony of New Netherland?
5. **Thinking Critically** Imagine that you are a patroon; how would you persuade people to settle in New Netherland?
6. **Thinking Critically** Why was it necessary for the Dutch to live in villages?
7. **Thinking Critically** Why were log cabins good homes for the Swedish and Finnish settlers in what is now New Jersey?

APPLYING KNOWLEDGE

1. Make a list of all the explorers mentioned in this chapter. Include the country they explored for, the dates of their explorations, and what they discovered. Organize this information in a chart. Give a report to your class, using the chart. Compare and contrast the explorers for your classmates. Which of the explorers, do you think, did the most to increase people's knowledge of the New World?
2. You know what the log cabins built by the Swedes and Finns looked like on the outside. Each had only one room and a dirt floor inside. Draw a picture of the inside of a cabin.

CHAPTER 7

The English Colony of New Jersey

A New Colony

What problems did the English colony of New Jersey face?

VOCABULARY

proprietor	assembly
religious freedom	tax

Governor Nicolls and Albania
After the English took over the Dutch colony of New Netherland in 1664, Richard Nicolls became the governor of the new colony. He gave the part of the colony that was west of the Hudson River the name Albania. The land that would later be called New Jersey was now called Albania. Richard Nicolls chose the name Albania to honor the Duke of York. The Duke of York was also the Duke of Albany in England.

Governor Nicolls knew that Albania needed more settlers in addition to the Dutch, Swedes, and Finns who already lived there. He invited people living in other colonies in America to come and live in Albania. The land in Albania could be bought

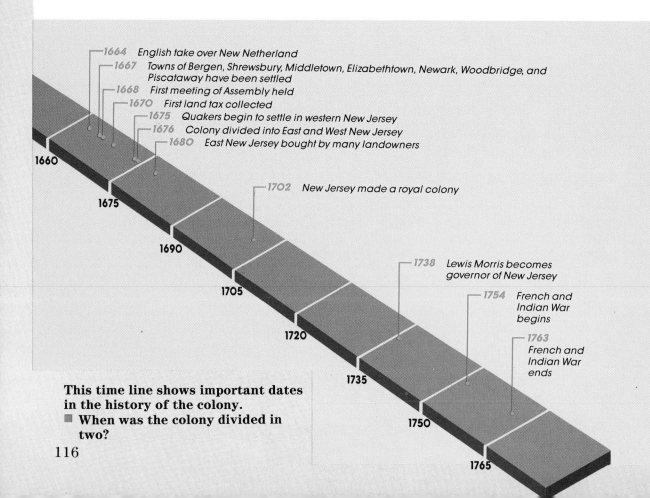

1664 English take over New Netherland
1667 Towns of Bergen, Shrewsbury, Middletown, Elizabethtown, Newark, Woodbridge, and Piscataway have been settled
1668 First meeting of Assembly held
1670 First land tax collected
1675 Quakers begin to settle in western New Jersey
1676 Colony divided into East and West New Jersey
1680 East New Jersey bought by many landowners

1660
1675
1690

1702 New Jersey made a royal colony

1705

1738 Lewis Morris becomes governor of New Jersey

1720

1754 French and Indian War begins

1735

1763 French and Indian War ends

1750

1765

This time line shows important dates in the history of the colony.
■ When was the colony divided in two?

116

from the Indians for a small price. Governor Nicolls promised the new settlers that they would have great freedom in Albania. He told them that they would have the right to make their own laws.

Albania had good farmland, clean rivers, many forests, and a good climate. Soon, new settlers began to move to Albania. Settlers from Long Island bought a very large piece of land in Albania from the Indians. This land was located in what is now Union County. Another group of settlers from Long Island bought land near Raritan Bay, in what is now Monmouth County.

The Indians were given guns, cloth, kettles, and other goods as payment. Although the Indians were given something in return for the land, they did not know they were giving up their claim to the land. The Indians believed that the land should be shared by all people.

Once the settlers moved to their land in Albania, they began to plan new towns. More settlers arrived, and Albania began to grow.

Lord Berkeley and Sir George Carteret The Duke of York had sent Richard Nicolls to govern the new English colony. But only 1 month after Richard Nicolls had left England for America, the Duke of York gave land in the new colony to two other people. These two people were

The Duke of York's land included the Arthur Kill area in Union County.
■ What is found in the area today?

Lord Berkeley and Sir George Carteret. On June 23, 1664, the Duke of York gave these two men all the land in America between the Hudson and Delaware rivers. He named this land New Jersey, after the island of Jersey in England.

Governor Philip Carteret After Lord Berkeley and Sir George Carteret were given the land of New Jersey, they became the **proprietors** of the colony. A proprietor is an owner. These two men chose Philip Carteret to be the governor of their colony. Philip Carteret was a relative of George Carteret.

In 1665, Philip Carteret arrived in America. He told Richard Nicolls that he was the governor of New Jersey. This news took Richard Nicolls completely by surprise. No one had written to tell him about Berkeley and Carteret. Besides that, he had already named the land to the west of the Hudson River Albania. Richard Nicolls wrote an angry letter to the Duke of York, but the duke would not listen. The land west of the Hudson was New Jersey, and the new governor was Philip Carteret.

Governor Philip Carteret had much to tell the colonists of New Jersey. He said that all the colonists

The English island of Jersey lies between England and France.
■ **Where might you find a scene like this in New Jersey?**

Philip Carteret did not receive a warm welcome in New Jersey. The man to his left in the picture is reading a message to the colonists.
■ What do you think Carteret's message to the colonists was?

would have **religious freedom.** In other words, they would be free to follow their own religion. He also told them that they would be allowed to have their own **assembly.** An assembly is a lawmaking group made up of elected people.

Philip Carteret also brought some unpopular news. He said that the colonists would have to pay a **tax** on the land they owned. A tax is money paid to a government or to the people who rule the land. The land tax would be collected every year, starting in 1670. The tax would go to the New Jersey proprietors.

The New Jersey colonists were unhappy about the land tax. Many believed that they, and not the proprietors, owned the land. After all,

the colonists had paid the Indians for their land. But the year was 1665, and the land tax would not be collected until 1670. Five years was a long time.

CHECKUP

1. Why did Richard Nicolls call the land west of the Hudson River by the name Albania?
2. How did Governor Nicolls attract new settlers to Albania?
3. What two men were given the land west of the Hudson River by the Duke of York?
4. What news did Governor Carteret bring to the settlers in the colony of New Jersey?
5. **Thinking Critically** Who had a stronger claim to the land in New Jersey, the Indians, the proprietors, or the colonists?

119

A Colony Divided

How did the colony of New Jersey change between 1667 and 1738?

VOCABULARY

merchant	royal colony

New Towns, New Colonists By 1667 the colony of New Jersey had seven important towns. The town of Bergen had been settled by the Dutch. English settlers from Long Island started the towns of Shrewsbury, Middletown, and Elizabethtown. Governor Carteret had invited English settlers from Connecticut to live in New Jersey. These Connecticut settlers had begun the town of Newark in 1666. People from the colonies of Massachusetts and New Hampshire started the towns of Woodbridge and Piscataway.

Each New Jersey town had a church or meetinghouse, markets, and houses. Many people in the towns were farmers. Some were **merchants.** A merchant is a person who buys and sells goods to make money. Other people in the towns were craftworkers.

Merchants were important members of communities in the colony.
■ What kinds of goods did the merchant in this picture sell?

Traces of early German settlers are still to be found in Hope.
■ **What did the settlers use for building materials?**

Many of the new colonists who settled in New Jersey towns were English people. People from other countries also came to New Jersey. Settlers from France and Germany came to America. They left their homelands because they could not follow their religion there. Some of the French and German settlers came to New Jersey because of its good farmland. The Moravians were among the Germans who came to America seeking religious freedom. Moravians founded the town of Hope in New Jersey. Today a number of Moravian buildings still stand there.

The Assembly Meets At first, the colonists did not have much say in how the colony was governed. The governor ran the colony for the proprietors and later for the English government. But the New Jersey colonists had been promised that they could help make laws for the colony. Finally, in 1668, the first meeting of the Assembly was held in Elizabethtown. Two men came from each New Jersey town to discuss laws for New Jersey. They also argued about taxes. New Jersey colonists did not want to pay any taxes. The Assembly told the governor that the New Jersey people would not pay the land tax. This led to many fights between the governor and the colonists. By the third meeting of the Assembly, in 1675, it was finally agreed that the colonists could pay the land tax with corn and grain instead of money.

Lord Berkeley and the Quakers As you know, Lord Berkeley and Sir George Carteret were the proprietors of New Jersey. Lord Berkeley owned the land in the western part of New Jersey, and Sir George Carteret owned the land in the east. Lord Berkeley decided to sell his land. The people who wanted to buy the land from him were called Quakers. The Quakers were a group of English people who had their own kind of religion. They were not well liked in England. This was because they had beliefs that were different from those of most of the people in England. They wanted to come to New Jersey to practice their religion freely.

When Lord Berkeley sold his land to a group of Quakers, they became the proprietors of western New Jersey. The new Quaker owners began to settle their land in 1675. Later, many more Quakers moved to New Jersey. They started the towns of Greenwich and Salem.

The Quaker settlers in New Jersey wrote a document that told how they would govern themselves. This document was called the Concessions and Agreements. It gave the Quakers religious freedom and many other rights. This document is a very special part of history. It tells us how people in our state believed in freedom and fairness over 300 years ago.

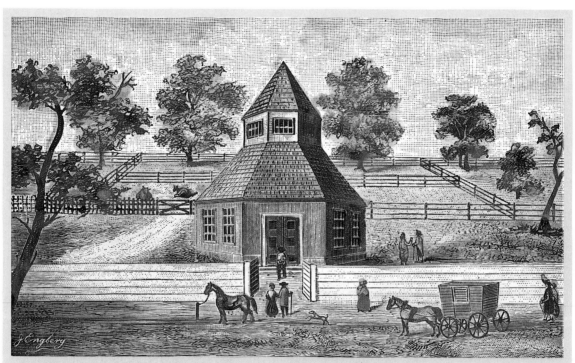

The Quakers did not worship in churches or have ministers. They gathered in silence in meetinghouses such as this one in southern New Jersey. Anyone who had a special message or concern could speak to the group during the Quaker meeting for worship.
■ Name three ways that people traveled to the meetinghouse.

New Jersey Splits in Two In 1676 the colony of New Jersey was owned by the Quakers and Sir George Carteret. They decided to divide the colony in half and make it into two separate colonies. These two colonies were called East New Jersey and West New Jersey. The Quakers in West New Jersey had their own government and their own capital. Burlington was made the capital of West New Jersey.

In 1680, Sir George Carteret died. His land in East New Jersey was bought by many landowners. They became the new proprietors of East New Jersey. These proprietors decided to make Perth Amboy the capital of East New Jersey. New Jersey was now two colonies with two governments and two capitals.

The Two Jerseys Joined Again At Last The two New Jersey colonies did not last for long. In 1702, Queen Anne of England brought the two colonies together. New Jersey was made a **royal colony.** This meant that it would be governed by England. The proprietors still had rights to the land, but they could no longer rule it. The colony of New Jersey had to share a governor with the colony of New York. This made New Jersey colonists unhappy. They believed that the governor did not understand their problems. He seemed to be more interested in New York.

In 1738, New Jersey was given its own governor. His name was Lewis Morris. Morris had been born in New Jersey. He had been a member of the Assembly. The colonists felt that he would understand their problems.

The colony of New Jersey was divided into two colonies from 1676 to 1702.
What was the capital of East New Jersey?
What was the capital of West New Jersey?

CHECKUP
1. Name the seven important towns in New Jersey in 1667.
2. Where did the Quakers settle in New Jersey?
3. What was the Concessions and Agreements?
4. How did New Jersey become a royal colony?
5. **Thinking Critically** Imagine that you are a new settler in New Jersey; explain why you came to live in the colony.

Life in the Colony

What was life like for the colonists in New Jersey?

VOCABULARY

indentured servant   apprentice
slave

Farming the Land Most of the people in the colony of New Jersey were farmers. Farming was very hard work. Trees had to be cut down or burned to make space for crops. Then the farmers had to dig out the stumps. When the land had been cleared, plows pulled by oxen were used to dig up the soil. Then different crops, such as wheat and corn and other vegetables, were planted.

The lumber from the trees that were cut down was used for firewood and for building houses, barns, and fences. Some farmers also sold some of the lumber.

Trade and Travel The farmers could not produce all the goods their families needed. Some goods, such as sugar, tea, paint, and nails, had to be purchased from merchants in the towns. The farmers sold their crops or lumber for money to buy goods.

Many farms were located near rivers and streams. The rivers and streams helped farmers to get their products to town markets. The easiest way to travel was by boat. Many farm products were shipped to big towns like Perth Amboy, Burlington, and Newark.

Apples grown on New Jersey farms could be made into cider.
■ **Where do you suppose the wagon full of kegs of cider is going?**

Miller-Cory Museum

Would you like to learn more about colonial life? The people at the Miller-Cory Museum in Westfield would be happy to show you what life was like in early New Jersey. On the grounds of the museum are the Miller-Cory House, a farmhouse built in 1740; the Frazee Building and woodshed; a necessary house or outhouse; several gardens; and an orchard. You can tour the Miller-Cory House. A guide in colonial costume will take you through the house, which holds the furniture and belongings of a colonial farm family. You can also watch people in colonial dress doing crafts and chores that would have been done daily and during the season in which you visit. In the Frazee Building there is an open-hearth fireplace and a beehive oven. There you can watch eighteenth-century cooking and fireside tasks.

If your class cannot visit the Miller-Cory Museum, the people from the museum can bring the museum to your classroom. In a special museum-without-walls program, costumed workers will come to your school to demonstrate colonial crafts. These crafts include butter and cheese making, candle making, stencil painting, basket weaving, spinning, corn crafts, and paper crafts. You can even make something to take home with you. Your teacher can also invite Sabra Miller to your class. Sabra and Samuel Miller built the farmhouse in the 1700s. Sabra, really a woman in costume, will bring a trunk full of things with her. She will explain how she uses each item.

Colonial history will come alive for you. The Miller-Cory Museum is a true living museum, where you can learn firsthand about the life of a colonial farm family in New Jersey.

Indentured Servants Many people wanted to come to America. But some were too poor to pay the fare on a ship. These people came to America as **indentured servants.** An indentured servant had his or her travel paid for by a person living in America. In return the indentured servant agreed to work for that person without pay for about 5 to 7 years. When the time of service was over, the servant was free. The life of an indentured servant was not easy. Most servants did not have a great deal of freedom. But they worked hard and learned important skills that helped the colony grow.

Slaves Some people came to America because they were forced to, not because they wanted to. These people were brought here as **slaves.** A slave is a person who is owned by another person. Many black people were brought from Africa to be slaves in America.

Most of the slaves that came to New Jersey lived around the large towns. Some slaves worked on farms. Slaves did not receive any pay. They could not live the way they wanted. Most were slaves until they died.

Not all the people in New Jersey believed in slavery. Most Quakers did not feel that slavery was right.

At least half of the white people coming to America came as indentured servants. Here new servants are met by their masters.
■ **How must these servants have felt upon their arrival?**

Travelers stayed overnight at inns on their way across New Jersey.
■ How does this inn compare to a present-day motel?

Apprentices Some young people in the colony became **apprentices.** An apprentice learns a trade from a master craftworker. The craftworker might be a shoemaker, a blacksmith, a baker, a tailor, or a carpenter. The apprentice agreed to work for a certain amount of time while he learned a trade. The craftworker taught the apprentice and provided food, clothing, and a place to live. Sometimes an apprentice worked from the age of 7 until the age of 21.

New Jersey Grows As more and more people came to live in New Jersey, the towns grew. New Jersey soon welcomed people from Ireland and Scotland. By 1745, New Jersey had over 61,000 people.

Transportation became important in the colony. People wanted to travel from one town to another. Soon roads and paths crisscrossed the colony. Horse-drawn wagons, coaches, carts, and sleighs carried people from town to town. They also brought travelers through New Jersey on their way to New York and Philadelphia. The towns and roads of the colony were busy.

CHECKUP
1. What made farming hard work in the colony of New Jersey?
2. How are slaves different from indentured servants?
3. What was the population of New Jersey around 1745?
4. **Thinking Critically** Why was the apprentice system a good system?

The French and Indian War

What part did New Jersey play in the French and Indian War?

VOCABULARY

barrack

Disagreements About Land Starting in 1689, the countries of France and England fought many wars against each other. The French and English fought mostly over land rights. The wars were fought mainly in Europe.

Both France and England claimed land in North America. The French claimed land in Canada and were beginning to move south into the Ohio River valley. The English believed that the Ohio River valley was theirs. It was not long before the wars between France and England turned to North America.

War in North America In 1754 the British had begun to fight the French in North America. (By this time, England was called Great Britain. The people who live in Great Britain are known as the British.) This war in North America is known as the French and Indian War. On one side were Great Britain and its 13 American colonies. On the other side were France and most of the Indian groups.

At first the colony of New Jersey did not want to send soldiers to help the British fight the French. But as

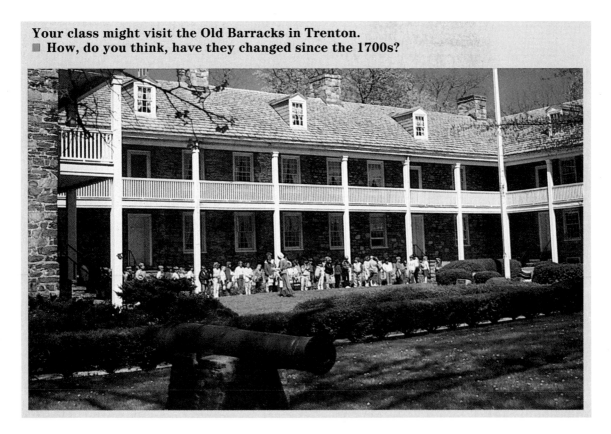

Your class might visit the Old Barracks in Trenton.
■ **How, do you think, have they changed since the 1700s?**

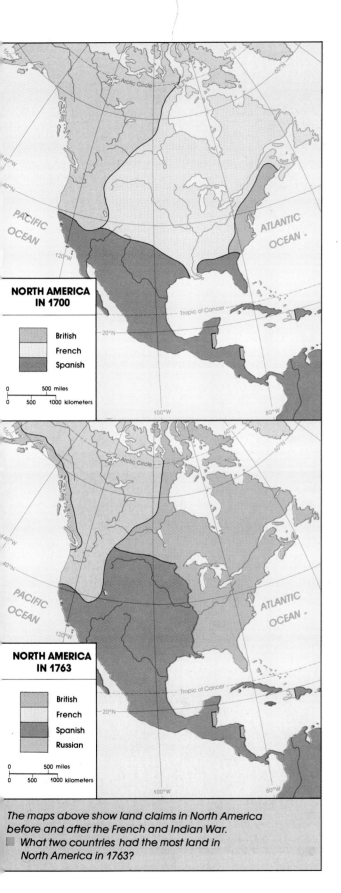

British
French
Spanish

0   500 miles
0 500 1000 kilometers

**NORTH AMERICA
IN 1763**

British
French
Spanish
Russian

0   500 miles
0 500 1000 kilometers

The maps above show land claims in North America before and after the French and Indian War.
■ *What two countries had the most land in North America in 1763?*

the war came closer and closer to New Jersey, the New Jersey Assembly finally voted to send men to fight.

During the war, many **barracks** were built for British soldiers in New Jersey. A barrack is a large building or group of buildings in which soldiers live. Barracks for British soldiers were built in five New Jersey towns. They were built in Trenton, Perth Amboy, Elizabethtown, Burlington, and New Brunswick. The barracks at Trenton still stand today.

In the first few years of the war, the French won most of the battles. But then in 1759, the British began to win more battles. When the war ended in 1763, France gave up all its land in Canada and all the land east of the Mississippi River.

The French and Indian War made Great Britain the strongest country in the world. The colonists living in the British colonies were glad to have a strong country ruling them. In a few years, however, these same colonists would be fighting to break away from Great Britain.

CHECKUP
1. How did New Jersey help the British in the French and Indian War?
2. Where were barracks built in the colony of New Jersey?
3. What happened to France's land in North America after the French and Indian War?

4. **Thinking Critically** Why, do you suppose, did the Indians fight on the side of the French during the French and Indian War?

Reading for Understanding

JOHN WOOLMAN, NEW JERSEY QUAKER

John Woolman was a Quaker who lived in Burlington County during the early years of the colony. Like most Quakers, he was against slavery. Many people in New Jersey and the other colonies—including some Quakers—held slaves. In 1746, John Woolman visited the southern colonies of Virginia, Maryland, and North Carolina. He saw many slaves on his trip. Woolman wrote about his feelings about slavery. Read the following piece from his writings.

A TRIP TO THE SOUTH

"Two things were remarkable to me in this journey: first, in regard to my entertainment. When I ate, drank, and lodged free-cost with people who lived in ease on the hard labor of their slaves I felt uneasy; and as my mind was inward to the Lord, I found this uneasiness return upon me, at times, through the whole visit. Where the masters bore a good share of the burden, and lived frugally, so that their servants were well provided for, and their labor moderate, I felt more easy; but where they lived in a costly way, and laid heavy burdens on their slaves, my exercise was often great, and I frequently had conversation with them in private concerning it. Secondly, this trade of importing slaves from their native country being much encouraged amongst them, and the white people and their children so generally living without much labor, was frequently the subject of my serious thoughts. I saw in these southern provinces so many vices and corruptions, increased by this trade and this way of life, that it appeared to me as a dark gloominess hanging over the land . . ."

From *The Journal of John Woolman and a Plea for the Poor.* Used by permission of Citadel Press, Inc., a subsidiary of Lyle Stuart, Inc.

SKILLS PRACTICE

On a separate sheet of paper, answer these questions about what you read.

1. What made John Woolman feel uneasy, or uncomfortable, on his visit?
2. Were all the slaves that he saw treated in the same way by their masters?
3. Did Woolman share his feelings about slavery with the owners of the slaves?
4. How did Woolman feel about the bringing of blacks from Africa to America to be slaves?
5. What, do you think, did Woolman mean when he wrote that some masters "lived frugally"?

CHAPTER 7 REVIEW

MAIN IDEAS

1. The colony of New Jersey faced several problems: 1) The Duke of York had made two men, Richard Nicolls and Philip Carteret, governors of the colony, 2) There was to be a tax on land to be paid to the proprietors, and 3) People who had bought land questioned whether the proprietors really owned all the land in the colony.
2. Between 1667 and 1738, Lord Berkeley sold the western part of the colony to a group of Quakers. Then the colony was divided into East New Jersey and West New Jersey. The two colonies were finally brought together again as a royal colony.
3. Although most of the people in early New Jersey were farmers, the merchants and businesses in the towns were also important to the colony. Indentured servants, slaves, craftworkers, and apprentices worked in New Jersey's early communities.
4. The French and Indian War was a war fought between France and Great Britain over land in North America. At the end of the war, France turned over its land in Canada and east of the Mississippi River to Great Britain.
5. New Jersey sent soldiers to help the British fight the French and Indians, and barracks for the British soldiers were built on New Jersey soil.

VOCABULARY REVIEW

On a separate sheet of paper, match these words with the definitions.

a. proprietor
b. assembly
c. apprentice
d. slave
e. religious freedom

1. A lawmaking group made up of elected people
2. A person who learns a trade from a master craftworker
3. An owner
4. Freedom to follow one's own religion
5. A person who is owned by another

CHAPTER CHECKUP

1. Why was the land of New Jersey first called Albania?
2. What did Richard Nicolls do when he heard that Philip Carteret was governor of New Jersey?
3. Who settled the seven important towns in New Jersey in 1667?
4. When was New Jersey split into two separate colonies?
5. **Thinking Critically** Compare the indentured servant system and the apprentice system.
6. **Thinking Critically** How did the people of New Jersey feel about slavery?
7. **Thinking Critically** Which country had a greater right to land in North America in 1754, France or Great Britain?

APPLYING KNOWLEDGE

By 1667, New Jersey had seven important towns. Using an outline map, locate and label these towns. Next to the name of each town, write down the people who settled there. (For example, English people from Long Island settled the town of Shrewsbury.) Find out whether the seven towns are towns or cities today. Choose one of the towns that still exists and explain why it grew. Would you like to live there now? Why or why not?

8 New Jersey During the American Revolution

The Road to Revolution

Why did the American colonists rebel against British tax laws?

VOCABULARY

Parliament	Patriot
Sons of Liberty	revolution
delegate	Loyalist
First Continental Congress	

Reasons for Rebellion Great Britain had spent a lot of money to win the French and Indian War. The British king, George III, wanted the colonists in America to help pay for the war. So the British government decided to make American colonists pay more money in taxes. Many new taxes were placed on goods sold in the colonies.

The colonists were very angry about these new taxes. They thought

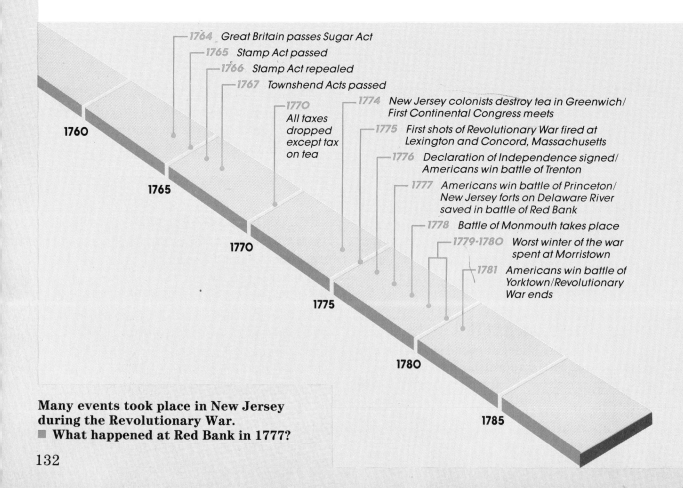

1764 Great Britain passes Sugar Act
1765 Stamp Act passed
1766 Stamp Act repealed
1767 Townshend Acts passed
1770 All taxes dropped except tax on tea
1774 New Jersey colonists destroy tea in Greenwich/ First Continental Congress meets
1775 First shots of Revolutionary War fired at Lexington and Concord, Massachusetts
1776 Declaration of Independence signed/ Americans win battle of Trenton
1777 Americans win battle of Princeton/ New Jersey forts on Delaware River saved in battle of Red Bank
1778 Battle of Monmouth takes place
1779-1780 Worst winter of the war spent at Morristown
1781 Americans win battle of Yorktown/Revolutionary War ends

1760 1765 1770 1775 1780 1785

Many events took place in New Jersey during the Revolutionary War.
■ What happened at Red Bank in 1777?

that it was unfair of the British to tax them. The taxes had been passed by **Parliament,** which is the part of the British government that makes laws. The colonies were not allowed to elect anyone to speak for them in Parliament. The colonists believed that only people elected by them had the right to make laws for them. The American colonists did not want to obey the tax laws because they had not voted for them. "Taxation without representation" was the cry heard in the 13 colonies.

Standing Up to Taxes   Three British laws, or acts, said that taxes had to be paid on different goods sold in the American colonies. One of the first laws was the Sugar Act of 1764. This law said that a tax had to be paid on all sugar and molasses sold in the colonies. The next year a tax law called the Stamp Act said that tax stamps had to be placed on newspapers, legal papers, some books, and even playing cards!

The Americans rebelled against these taxes. In many colonies, people formed groups called the **Sons of Liberty** to fight against the Stamp Act. In the colony of New Jersey, there was little violence. But the New Jersey colonists made it clear that they would not stand for the Stamp Act tax. In fact, New Jersey's stamp tax

New Jersey colonists raise a liberty pole to protest Great Britain's unfair treatment of the colonies.
■ **What does the sign above say about the colonists' feelings?**

collector, William Coxe, gave up his position without collecting anything!

Because of the actions of the colonists, the Stamp Act was repealed, or taken back, in 1766. But the next year, Parliament passed the Townshend Acts. These laws placed taxes on other goods, such as glass, paint, paper, and tea. Again the colonists rebelled against the taxes. In 1770 all of the taxes were dropped except the tax on tea.

A Tea Party   The British lowered the price of tea, but many colonists refused to buy the tea as long as it was taxed. This was a hardship for many colonists because tea was the most popular drink in the colonies at the time.

One of the most famous ways that Americans showed their anger over the unfair tea tax was to destroy the tea that was shipped into the colonies. In 1774 a group of colonists in New Jersey destroyed some British tea. This event was called the Greenwich Tea Party. On a cold December day the British ship *Greyhound* arrived at the small port of Greenwich. The ship was loaded with tea. The captain of the *Greyhound* did not want to take any chances. The chests of tea were taken off the ship and stored in the cellar of a Greenwich house for safety. But the tea was not safe for long. During the night a small group of colonists dressed as Indians en-

This monument was set up in remembrance of the Greenwich Tea Party.
■ **What part did the people listed play in the tea party?**

tered Greenwich. They broke open the cellar of the house where the tea was stored. They dragged the tea out into the street and burned it.

The First Continental Congress The colonies decided to hold a meeting about the problems they were having with Great Britain. All the colonies except Georgia sent **delegates** to this meeting. A delegate is a person who acts or speaks for other people. This meeting of delegates from the colonies was called the **First Continental Congress.**

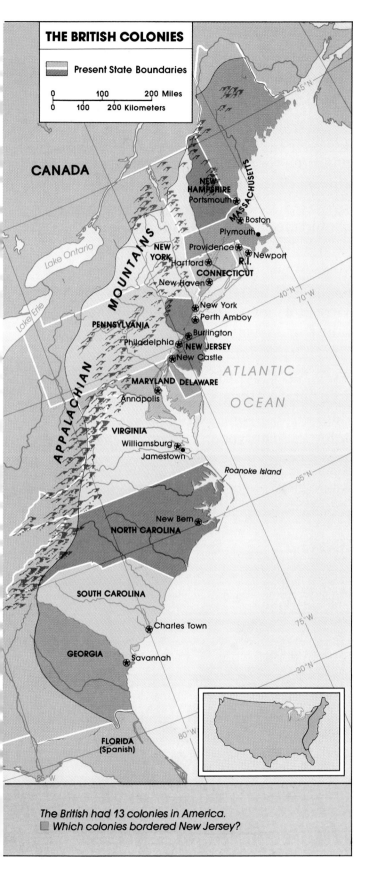

THE BRITISH COLONIES

Present State Boundaries

0   100   200 Miles

0   100   200 Kilometers

CANADA

NEW HAMPSHIRE
Portsmouth

MASSACHUSETTS
Boston
Plymouth

NEW YORK
Providence
Hartford   Newport
R.I.
CONNECTICUT
New Haven

MOUNTAINS

Lake Ontario

Lake Erie

PENNSYLVANIA

Philadelphia

New York
Perth Amboy
Burlington
NEW JERSEY
New Castle

ATLANTIC

OCEAN

APPALACHIAN

MARYLAND   DELAWARE
Annapolis

VIRGINIA
Williamsburg
Jamestown

Roanoke Island

New Bern
NORTH CAROLINA

SOUTH CAROLINA

Charles Town

GEORGIA   Savannah

FLORIDA
(Spanish)

The British had 13 colonies in America.
Which colonies bordered New Jersey?

'The First Continental Congress met on September 5, 1774, in Philadelphia, Pennsylvania. New Jersey sent five delegates. They were Stephen Crane, James Kinsey, John De-Hart, William Livingston, and Richard Smith.'

Patriots and Loyalists   By 1774 many people in the 13 colonies were against the unfair treatment of the colonies by the British. These people were called **Patriots.** They wanted to put an end to British rule in the colonies and form their own government. The Patriots felt that a **revolution** was needed to break away from the British. A revolution is a complete and often violent change of government. Some colonists did not wish to go against Britain. They remained loyal to the British king and government. These people were called **Loyalists.** There were both Patriots and Loyalists in New Jersey.

CHECKUP

1. Name three tax laws that Parliament passed in the 1760s and the goods that were taxed by each.
2. Why did the colonists rebel against the taxes passed by the British Parliament?
3. Who were New Jersey's delegates to the First Continental Congress?
4. Why did the Patriots believe that a revolution was needed?
5. **Thinking Critically** What did an act such as the Greenwich Tea Party tell the British?

135

The Colonies Face War

How did most New Jersey colonists feel about breaking away from Great Britain?

VOCABULARY

Continental army	**Declaration of Independence**
independence	

War Begins at Lexington and Concord   The American Revolution, or Revolutionary War, began on April 19, 1775. On that day, fighting broke out between Massachusetts colonists and British soldiers. Two battles were fought. One took place at Lexington, Massachusetts; the other at Concord. These battles were the beginning of a war that would change the way Americans lived.

Raising an Army   The Continental Congress met a second time soon after the fighting at Lexington and Concord. At this meeting the Second Continental Congress voted to raise an army to fight the British. It asked for soldiers from all of the colonies. These troops would be called the **Continental army.** George Washington was made commander in chief of the army. He was in charge of all the American soldiers.

In October 1775 the men of New Jersey were asked to serve in the Continental army. They had to supply their own weapons and uniforms. New Jersey decided to send soldiers to fight in the Revolutionary War.

Between 1775 and 1778, New Jersey sent 9,000 men to fight in the war.

Votes for Independence   The year 1776 was important for New Jersey and the other American colonies. On July 2, 1776, the Second Continental Congress voted that all 13 colonies should declare their **independence,** or freedom, from Great Britain. The vote for a declaration of independence was 12 to 0. The colony of New York did not vote. New Jersey had sent five delegates to vote at the Second Continental Congress. They were Abraham Clark from Rahway, John Hart from Hopewell, Francis Hopkinson from Bordentown, and John Witherspoon and Richard

New Jersey's Loyalist governor, William Franklin, was thrown out of office in 1776 by the Patriots.
■ How does Franklin react here?

The Declaration of Independence was approved on July 4, 1776. Here, Thomas Jefferson and others who helped to write the declaration present the document to the Second Continental Congress.
■ **Why do we celebrate Independence Day on July 4?**

Stockton from Princeton. The New Jersey delegates all voted for independence at the meeting.

The Second Continental Congress asked Thomas Jefferson to write about its decision to break away from Great Britain. He did this in the **Declaration of Independence.** It said that the colonies were "free and independent states." On July 4, 1776, the Second Continental Congress approved what Jefferson had written. Later all the delegates from the 13 colonies signed the Declaration of Independence. The 13 colonies were now 13 states. A new country was born—the United States of America. But this new country still had a long and hard road ahead. Great Britain would not give up the colonies without a fight. The United States would have to win its independence from Britain through war. New Jersey and the other new states could not turn back now.

CHECKUP

1. Where were the first two battles of the Revolutionary War fought?
2. What did the Declaration of Independence say?
3. **Thinking Critically** If you were a Patriot, how would you explain to a Loyalist the importance of independence from Great Britain?

137

The Continental Army in New Jersey

Why was New Jersey important in the American Revolution?

VOCABULARY

| redcoat | Hessian |

Crossroads of the Revolution New Jersey's location was very important during the Revolutionary War. New Jersey lay between the big cities of New York and Philadelphia. Both the Americans and the British wanted to control these two cities. New Jersey was like a highway or crossroads between them. Soon after 1776, New Jersey found itself in the middle of the fighting. General George Washington moved the Continental army back and forth across New Jersey four times during the Revolutionary War. Before the war was over, almost 100 battles were fought on New Jersey land. For these reasons, New Jersey is sometimes called the Crossroads of the Revolution.

New Jersey had large iron mills in Hanover, Ringwood, Dover, Morristown, and other places. The iron was used to make guns, cannonballs, and musket balls. New Jersey also had good farmland that could supply food for the soldiers.

The Battle of Trenton On December 26, 1776, a battle was fought

Washington and his troops won a great victory at Trenton in 1776.
■ How does the Continental army appear in his picture?

in Trenton. The fighting lasted only 1 hour, but it was an important battle for the Continental army.

Until the battle of Trenton, the Americans were being badly beaten by the British. The Continental army was much smaller than the British army. The American soldiers wore old and ragged uniforms. They sometimes did not have enough to eat. Many of the soldiers were far from home and no longer wanted to fight. The British soldiers, on the other hand, were used to fighting. They had good weapons and wore bright red uniforms. Because of their red uniforms, the British were called **redcoats** by the Americans. The redcoats had plenty to eat and received regular pay for fighting.

General Washington knew that his American soldiers needed to win a battle to give them hope. He thought of a clever plan to beat the British at Trenton. During the cold Christmas of 1776, a group of **Hessians** (hesh′ənz) was resting in Trenton. The Hessians were German soldiers who were paid by the British to fight the Americans. The Hessians at Trenton did not expect the Americans to attack on Christmas.

General Washington and his troops were waiting in nearby Pennsylvania. On Christmas night, Washington ordered his men to cross the icy Delaware River in boats to New Jersey. The next morning the American soldiers marched to Trenton.

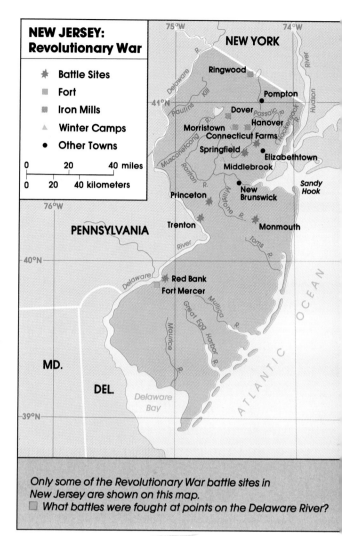

NEW JERSEY: Revolutionary War

* Battle Sites
■ Fort
▦ Iron Mills
▲ Winter Camps
● Other Towns

Only some of the Revolutionary War battle sites in New Jersey are shown on this map.
□ *What battles were fought at points on the Delaware River?*

They took the Hessians completely by surprise and won the battle. The victory at Trenton gave the Continental army new hope.

The Battle of Princeton   When British General William Howe learned of Washington's victory at Trenton, he sent troops to attack the Continental army in New Jersey. British soldiers arrived in Princeton on January 2, 1777. At the time, General Washington and his troops were still nearby, in Trenton.

139

Washington decided to send General Hugh Mercer and 350 soldiers ahead of the main army. These troops fought with some British soldiers on their way to Princeton. With the help of the main army, they drove the British back to New Brunswick. The British in town also left Princeton. The Americans had been successful once again in New Jersey. After the battle of Princeton, Washington and his army rested in Morristown for what remained of the winter.

The Battle of Red Bank   In the fall of 1777, another important battle was fought in New Jersey. This was the battle of Red Bank. In this battle, American soldiers stopped the British and the Hessians from capturing some New Jersey forts along the Delaware River. Then General Washington and his troops moved on to Valley Forge, Pennsylvania, where they spent the freezing winter of 1777–1778.

Molly Pitcher and the Battle of Monmouth   In June 1778 the British left Pennsylvania for New York. Washington and his troops left Valley Forge and followed the British across New Jersey. The British were planning to cross from Sandy Hook to New York, but the Americans met them at Monmouth. The battle of Monmouth took place on June 28, 1778. The day was hot and steamy. The temperature was over 90°F (32°C), and the soldiers were tired and thirsty. On the battlefield that

Hugh Mercer (front center) lies wounded at Princeton.
■ **What kinds of weapons were used in the battle?**

Mary Ludwig Hays, better known as Molly Pitcher, was at her husband's side during the battle of Monmouth. When William Hays was wounded, Mary took his place at the cannon.
■ **What was the bucket at her feet used for during the battle?**

day was a woman named Mary or Molly Hays. She had left her home to join her husband during the fighting of the war.

Mary was at her husband's side during the battle at Monmouth. She brought him water when he was thirsty. Mary also brought pitchers of water to the other Continental soldiers. They would call out to her, "Molly, bring the pitcher!" or simply, "Molly! Pitcher!" Because of this, Mary got the nickname Molly Pitcher. When Mary's husband was wounded during the fighting, she took his place firing the cannon. She was a brave woman.

The battle of Monmouth lasted 1 day. Many men were killed. After all the fighting, neither side really won the battle. Although the Continental army had fought well, the British were able to move on to New York.

CHECKUP

1. Why is New Jersey called the Crossroads of the Revolution?
2. What was George Washington's clever plan for the first battle fought in New Jersey?
3. Why was Mary Hays important during the battle of Monmouth?

4. **Thinking Critically** Describe what it must have been like to be a soldier in the Continental army.

The War Ends

What happened during the last years of the war?

VOCABULARY

ally   **militia**

Hard Times at Home   After the battle of Monmouth, the fighting turned away from New Jersey for a while. But times were still hard for the New Jersey colonists left at home. The war tore New Jersey families apart. Farms had to be taken care of and work had to be done. Women and children kept things going. Everywhere in New Jersey, farms were burned by Hessian and British soldiers. The New Jersey colonists hoped the war would end soon.

The Worst Winter of All   Three times during the Revolutionary War, New Jersey was the winter home of the Continental army. Twice the soldiers camped at Morristown, in 1777–1778 and in 1779–1780. They made winter camp at Middlebrook in 1778–1779. During the winter months, fighting stopped because of the cold weather. Both armies rested and made plans for the spring.

Washington made the Ford Mansion in Morristown his headquarters during the terrible winter of 1779–1780. Mrs. Jacob Ford and her four children lived in two rooms that winter. Washington and his staff took over the rest of the house.
■ **What use did Washington make of the room shown below?**

Until huts were ready, the soldiers at Morristown lived in tents.
■ **What must it have been like to build huts during the winter?**

There was no rest for the American soldiers during the winter of 1779–1780. It was the coldest and worst winter of the war. Snow was piled high, and rivers were frozen over. George Washington and almost 13,000 American soldiers spent this worst winter of all in Morristown. Before the winter was over, many soldiers died from the cold, disease, and hunger.

France Helps the Americans General Washington knew that help was needed to fight the rest of the war. He asked the French people to help the Americans in the war against the British. By the end of the winter at Morristown, there was good news. France agreed to be an **ally** of the Americans. An ally is a friend or helper. The government of France promised to send ships and soldiers to help the Americans.

The British Gain Strength Soon after the good news of help from France arrived, the British were in New York and stronger than ever. British General Howe had been replaced by a new general. His name was Henry Clinton.

General Washington feared that Clinton's army would try to attack his weakened troops in New Jersey. He was right. In June 1780, Hessian

143

and British soldiers marched toward Morristown. But they were stopped by New Jersey **militia** at Connecticut Farms, which is Union today. A militia is an army of local citizens. Its members are part-time soldiers. The New Jersey militia tried to push back the Hessian and British soldiers. During the battle the Hessians burned many houses and farms.

In the confusion of the battle, the enemy shot the wife of the local minister by mistake. Her name was Hannah Caldwell. The New Jersey militia was so angered by the killing of innocent Mrs. Caldwell that they fought as hard as they could. The British army was finally forced back to Elizabethtown.

The Battle of Springfield The British were not stopped by the battle of Connecticut Farms. On June 23, 1780, about 6,000 British and Hessian soldiers marched toward Morristown again. They were stopped again by hundreds of American soldiers and New Jersey militiamen at Springfield. The Americans forced the British to turn back.

Peace At Last In August 1781, General Washington and his army marched across New Jersey for the last time. They were on their way to Yorktown, Virginia. In October a great battle was fought at Yorktown. At the end of the battle, the Americans and French had badly beaten

Parson James Caldwell helped the New Jersey militiamen at the battle of Springfield.
■ Find Springfield on the map on page 139.

the British. With the victory at Yorktown, the Americans had won the Revolutionary War.

When the war ended, Washington met with the Second Continental Congress at Nassau Hall in Princeton. The Congress thanked Washington for all he had done for the new nation. Everyone was happy that the fighting was over.

CHECKUP

1. Who took care of life at home during the war?
2. Where did Washington camp during the winter of 1779–1780?
3. How did the French promise to help the Americans?
4. **Thinking Critically** Describe how George Washington helped the United States of America during the war.

144

Understanding Cause and Effect

WHAT IS CAUSE AND EFFECT?

One thing sometimes causes something else to happen. For example, when there is a heavy rainstorm, the soil is washed away. We call this cause and effect. The *cause* of what happened was the heavy rain. The *effect* was the soil washing away.

It is important to learn how one event causes another. Picking out cause and effect is a part of the important skill of thinking clearly.

MATCH THE PICTURES

Look at the pictures below. Match each cause with an effect.

Now let us see how well you matched the causes and effects.

1 matches B.
The effect of the tornado was the collapsed house.
2 matches A.
The effect of the heavy snowstorm was that the school had to be closed.

3 matches C.
The effect of the child's playing with matches was that the grass and trees caught fire.

SKILLS PRACTICE

Write the numbers 1 to 5 on a separate sheet of paper. Match each cause below with the correct effect.

CAUSES

1. The British Parliament needed money to pay for the French and Indian War.
2. Americans were angry about the tax on tea.
3. The 13 American colonies decided to break away from Great Britain.
4. New Jersey is located between the cities of New York and Philadelphia.
5. The United States needed help to win the Revolutionary War.

EFFECTS

a. British tea was not bought and was often destroyed by the colonists.
b. New taxes were placed on certain goods used by those living in the 13 American colonies.
c. George Washington asked the country of France to help the Americans fight against the British.
d. About 100 battles of the American Revolution were fought on New Jersey soil.
e. The Revolutionary War began.

CHAPTER 8 REVIEW

MAIN IDEAS

1. The American colonists rebelled against British tax laws because the laws were passed by the British Parliament, in which the American colonists had no representation.
2. In New Jersey there were many Patriots, or people who wanted to end British rule in the colonies. New Jersey delegates to the Second Continental Congress voted for and signed the Declaration of Independence. New Jersey also sent soldiers to fight for independence from the British.
3. The American colonists declared their independence from Great Britain on July 4, 1776.
4. During the American Revolution, New Jersey was in the middle of the fighting and was the scene of about 100 battles. New Jersey's iron and farmland were also important.
5. The battle of Trenton was a major victory for the Americans during the Revolutionary War.
6. During 1780–1781 a weakened Continental army faced strong British troops. The Americans won the last battle of the war at Yorktown with the help of their French allies.

VOCABULARY REVIEW

On a separate sheet of paper, write the word or words that best complete each sentence.

1. A person who wanted independence for the American colonies was a **(a)** Loyalist, **(b)** Patriot, **(c)** soldier.
2. A person who acts or speaks for other people is a **(a)** delegate, **(b)** commander, **(c)** revolutionary.
3. The lawmaking body of Great Britain is the **(a)** Continental army, **(b)** royal government, **(c)** Parliament.
4. A complete and often violent change in government is called a **(a)** war, **(b)** revolution, **(c)** battle.
5. An ally is a **(a)** friend, **(b)** enemy, **(c)** Loyalist.

CHAPTER CHECKUP

1. Why was the Declaration of Independence written?
2. Where was the last battle of the Revolutionary War fought?
3. **Thinking Critically** Do you think that it was fair of Great Britain to make the American colonists pay more money in taxes after the French and Indian War?
4. **Thinking Critically** Why were so many battles fought in New Jersey?
5. **Thinking Critically** Name one reason why France was so willing to be an ally of the Americans.

APPLYING KNOWLEDGE

1. Imagine that you are a Patriot living in New Jersey at the beginning of the Revolutionary War. What are your reasons for opposing the government of Great Britain? Write a letter to William Franklin, the Loyalist governor of New Jersey, explaining why you have become a Patriot.
2. Newspapers were important in New Jersey during the Revolutionary War. If you had been a reporter for a New Jersey newspaper in 1778, what would you have written about the battle of Monmouth?

SUMMARIZING UNIT 2

REVIEWING VOCABULARY

1. Native American The Native Americans, or Indians, were the first people to live in what is now New Jersey. By what names were the Native Americans in New Jersey known?

2. Colony Several European countries started colonies in the New World. What countries had colonies in the area that is now New Jersey?

3. Tax Taxes were placed on many things in the colonies. How did the colonists feel about the taxes passed by the British government in the 1760s?

4. Patriot There were both Patriots and Loyalists in New Jersey. Compare the two. Name one Patriot and one Loyalist from New Jersey.

5. Militia The New Jersey militia played a part in the battles of Connecticut Farms and Springfield. Explain the difference between a militia and the Continental army. Who was the commander of the Continental army?

EXPRESSING YOURSELF

1. How Would You Feel? Imagine that you are a Lenape Indian living in New Jersey. How would you feel about the arrival of European settlers?

2. Thinking Like a Historian The Dutch and the English both claimed land in America that had been explored for them. Who, do you think, had a stronger claim to land in the New World? Explain your answer.

3. What Would You Do? If you had been Richard Nicolls, what would you have done when you heard that the Duke of York had given the land between the Hudson and Delaware rivers to Lord Berkeley and George Carteret?

4. In What Ways? The colonists protested the tax on tea by destroying the tea that was shipped into the colonies. In what other ways, do you think, could the colonists have shown their anger over unfair taxes?

5. Who Would You Rather Be? If you were given the choice of being a Continental soldier, a redcoat, or a Hessian, which would you rather be? What reasons can you give for your choice?

New Jersey Moves into the Nineteenth Century

In this unit you will read about New Jersey in the new nation and the war that tore our nation apart. You will also learn about the changes that took place in life in our state. In the nineteenth century, New Jersey was becoming the great state of industry, agriculture, cities, and resorts that it is today.

In Unit 3, you will learn about the many areas in which New Jersey made progress in the nineteenth century.
■ What important events for our state are shown below?

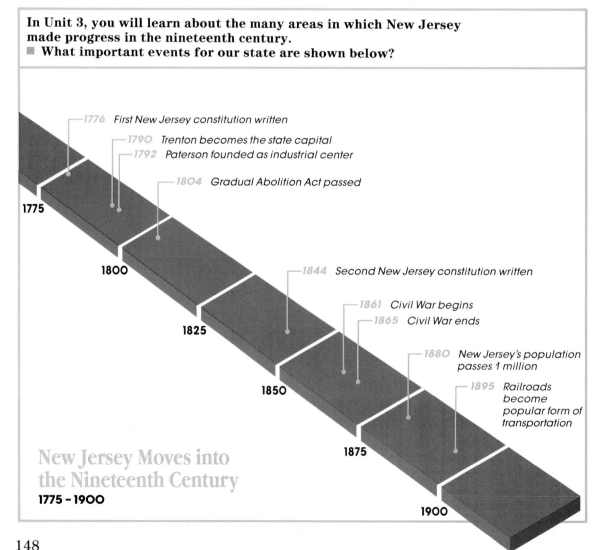

1776 First New Jersey constitution written
1790 Trenton becomes the state capital
1792 Paterson founded as industrial center
1804 Gradual Abolition Act passed
1775
1800
1844 Second New Jersey constitution written
1825
1861 Civil War begins
1865 Civil War ends
1850
1880 New Jersey's population passes 1 million
1895 Railroads become popular form of transportation
1875

New Jersey Moves into the Nineteenth Century
1775 – 1900
1900

Railroads were a great step forward in transportation. The picture
below shows New Brunswick in the nineteenth century.
■ What different forms of transportation were used there?

The 1800s were a time of great change for our country and state. After the Revolutionary War the states learned to work together as a nation. As part of a strong nation, New Jersey grew. Like the other states, it saw great changes.

The period of change beginning in the late 1700s and continuing into the 1800s is known as the Industrial Revolution. This revolution marked a sharp change from the use of muscle power to the use of machine power in industry. Machines were powered by different forms of energy instead of by humans or animals. Paper, wire, iron, pottery, glass, cloth, and rubber were some of the products made in factories in our state.

The men here are using a harvesting machine.
■ How would a farmer harvest wheat without this machine?

People worked with machines in factories.
■ **What is being made here?**

Agriculture remained strong in New Jersey. Most farms in the state were small family farms. Farm work became a little easier than it had been in the past. There were new kinds of plows, mowers, and power tools. These machines worked faster and better than the tools the farmers had been using.

Like the other large cities of New Jersey, Camden grew rapidly during the 1800s. In the early part of the century, Camden was a quiet town on the Delaware River, across from Philadelphia. With railroads and steam power, important industry came to Camden. Camden was close to good farmland. In 1869, New Jersey tomatoes began to be canned in large quantities in Camden. The Joseph Campbell Preserve Company, which did the canning, came out with soups in 1897. This was the beginning of the Campbell Soup Company, which is still in Camden today.

People enjoy the seashore at South Amboy.
■ How is this seashore scene unusual?

Tomato Soup

From sun-ripened Jersey tomatoes

12 cents a can

CAN'T YOU JUST TASTE IT!

This is a 1924 advertisement for Campbell's tomato soup.
■ How much did the soup cost in 1924?

As work could be done faster both in factories and on farms, there was more time for pleasure. Many people enjoyed walking, visiting, and other simple forms of entertainment. The sports of hunting and fishing remained popular. There were also new sports—baseball and football. The first organized games of each were played in New Jersey. Resorts sprang up in the mountains and on the coast of our state. The lakes of northern New Jersey also began to welcome their first visitors. The natural setting and amusement parks drew large numbers of people to the resorts.

9 The New State in the New Nation

The New Nation

What important part did New Jersey play in making a plan for the government of the new nation?

VOCABULARY

currency	compromise
federal	ratify
New Jersey Plan	

New Problems   The Revolutionary War was over. A great victory had been won, and a new nation had been born. But the new and independent United States of America faced a number of problems.

Trade was one problem. American ships and American goods were not welcome now in the British colonies in the Caribbean Sea. That trade had been important to America. In addition, many British goods were being shipped into America. Americans bought these goods because they were cheaper than the same goods made in the United States. This did not help industry in the new nation. New Jersey industry had an

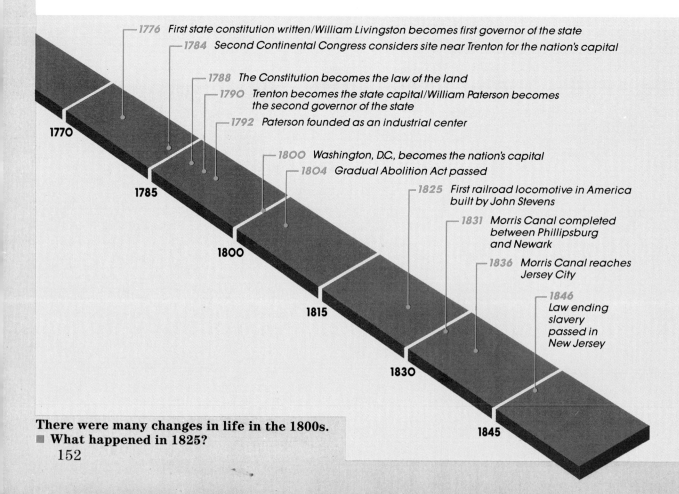

1776 First state constitution written/William Livingston becomes first governor of the state

1784 Second Continental Congress considers site near Trenton for the nation's capital

1788 The Constitution becomes the law of the land

1790 Trenton becomes the state capital/William Paterson becomes the second governor of the state

1792 Paterson founded as an industrial center

1800 Washington, D.C., becomes the nation's capital

1804 Gradual Abolition Act passed

1825 First railroad locomotive in America built by John Stevens

1831 Morris Canal completed between Phillipsburg and Newark

1836 Morris Canal reaches Jersey City

1846 Law ending slavery passed in New Jersey

1770
1785
1800
1815
1830
1845

There were many changes in life in the 1800s.
■ What happened in 1825?

especially hard time. British goods came into the state easily from the ports of New York and Philadelphia.

Money itself was a problem. The states could have their own **currencies,** or coins and paper money. But the states would not always accept each other's currencies. New York and Pennsylvania merchants would not take New Jersey bills or coins. The states could also tax goods from other states. New York and Pennsylvania wanted to tax New Jersey goods coming into their states. The states seemed more interested in themselves than in the nation. They had begun to treat each other like foreign countries.

The United States Constitution

The government of the new nation was not strong enough to hold the states together. In 1787 a meeting was held in Philadelphia to solve some of the problems with the government. Delegates from all the states except Rhode Island attended the meeting. The New Jersey delegates were William Livingston, David Brearley, William Churchill Houston, William Paterson, and Jonathan Dayton.

The different states had different ideas about the government of the country. Virginia, a state with many people, wanted a strong **federal,** or national, government. It

Above are some examples of the currencies of different states.
■ **Which are examples of New Jersey bills?**

wanted two houses, or groups of representatives, in the Congress. It said that states with the largest populations should have the largest number of representatives. The New Jersey delegates did not like this idea. William Paterson came up with a different idea, called the **New Jersey Plan.** It was fairer to states with fewer people. Under the plan there would be one house of Congress. All states would have the same number of representatives in the Congress.

Finally there was a **compromise.** A compromise is a decision that gives each side something. It was decided that there would be two houses of Congress. In one house, the Senate, the states would each have two representatives. This pleased the states with smaller populations. In the other house, the House of Representatives, the number of representatives each state had would be based on the state's population. This made states such as Virginia happy.

Finally a whole new plan for the United States government was agreed upon. It was called the United States Constitution. In addition to a Congress of two houses, there would be a President. The President would

William Paterson (top) presented a plan to the other delegates.
■ **Who is standing at the right with a paper in his hands?**

On his way to New York to become President, George Washington passed through Trenton.
■ What is the importance of the date on the arch?

Washington became President of the United States on April 30, 1789, in New York.

Choosing a Capital Between 1776 and 1800, the government of the United States made its home in many places — Philadelphia, New York, Annapolis, Trenton, and Princeton. In 1783, New Jersey had offered the Continental Congress 20 square miles (52 sq km) of land near the town of Trenton for the nation's capital. The land would belong to the nation. It would no longer be part of New Jersey. Other northern states liked the idea of building the capital of the country near Trenton. The capital would be close to them. In 1784 the Continental Congress considered the site near Trenton for a capital. But a location on the Potomac River near Virginia was finally chosen instead. That place, which was called the District of Columbia, was more in the center of the country. In 1800, Washington, D.C., named after George Washington, became the capital of the United States.

carry out the laws made by Congress. There would also be a Supreme Court to explain the laws.

Adopting the Constitution The Constitution was finished on September 17, 1787. Nine of the 13 states had to **ratify,** or approve, it before it could be put into use. In December 1787, New Jersey became the third state to approve the Constitution, after the states of Delaware and Pennsylvania.

The Constitution became the law of the land in 1788. George Washington was chosen as the first President.

CHECKUP
1. What problems did the United States face after the Revolutionary War?
2. What is a compromise?
3. When did New Jersey ratify the Constitution of the United States?

4. **Thinking Critically** Compare the New Jersey Plan with the plan suggested by Virginia.

The New State

What changes were made in the constitution of New Jersey between 1776 and 1844?

Choosing a State Capital Trenton had not been chosen as the site of the nation's capital, but it was made the capital of New Jersey. As you remember, New Jersey had two capitals — Perth Amboy and Burlington — when it was divided into the two colonies of East New Jersey and West New Jersey. When the two colonies were made a royal colony in 1702, both towns remained capitals. The government moved back and forth between them. During the Revolution the state government met at Princeton, Trenton, Burlington, and Haddonfield. It was not until 1790 that Trenton was made the state capital.

The State Constitution New Jersey had had a constitution since 1776, when the United States of America had declared its independence from Great Britain. It was the third state to adopt a state constitution. The constitution set up a government for New Jersey. It said that there would be a **legislature,** or lawmaking body, made up of two houses — the Council and the Assembly. There would also be a governor to carry out the laws. Any New Jer-seyan who owned property could vote, including women and blacks. The people of New Jersey elected the members of the Council and Assembly. The governor was elected by the state legislature.

The first state constitution had been written in a hurry. Many New Jerseyans were unhappy with it from the start. In 1807 it was decided by the legislature that women and blacks could not vote. In 1844 an entirely new constitution was written. All men who were white, United States citizens, and at least 21 years old could vote. Voters also had to have lived in New Jersey for 1 year

The leaders of the state government met in this building in Trenton.
■ What, do you suppose, were the posts in front used for?

Women who owned property had the right to vote in eighteenth-century New Jersey. This picture shows several women casting their votes.
■ In what ways is voting different today?

and in one county for 5 months. Voters no longer had to own property. Women and blacks still were not allowed to vote. A Bill of Rights, describing people's freedoms, was included. Women, blacks, and others, such as criminals and some poor people, were not given many of these rights. The new constitution set up courts to explain the laws. It also said that the governor was to be elected by the state's voters.

The First Governors New Jersey's first governor was William Livingston. He was chosen governor in 1776 and was elected every year after that until 1790. No other person has ever

served as long. New Jersey's second governor was William Paterson. William Paterson resigned from the United States Senate to become governor. He served as governor for 3 years before being named to the United States Supreme Court.

CHECKUP
1. When did Trenton become the state capital?
2. Who had the right to vote in New Jersey before 1807?
3. Who served the longest term as governor of New Jersey?

4. **Thinking Critically** Why, do you think, was the right to vote taken away from women and blacks in 1807?

New Jersey Moves Ahead

What changed life in New Jersey in the first half of the nineteenth century?

Paterson Leads the Way Paterson was planned as a great center of factories. The idea had started with Alexander Hamilton of New York. During the Revolutionary War, Hamilton and George Washington had visited the Great Falls of the Passaic River. The waterpower of the Falls gave Hamilton the idea that a great **manufacturing** center could be started at that point on the Passaic. Manufacturing is the making of goods by hand or machine, especially in large quantities. In 1791 the New Jersey legislature set up a group called the Society for Establishing Useful Manufactures (S.U.M.). The next year the group bought 700 acres (284 ha) of land by the Great Falls on which to build an industrial center. The new city was named after the governor of the state at the time, William Paterson. A cotton mill was opened. Industry got off to a slow start in the town of Paterson, but it was booming by the mid-1800s.

The Corridor State New Jersey is sometimes called the Corridor State. Like a great corridor, or passageway, the state is constantly being crossed

Water rushes over the Great Falls.
■ Why was this a good location for industry?

by people going somewhere. Even in the early 1800s, New Jersey could be called the Corridor State. There were many roads in the state by that time. Most of the roads were not good, but they were well traveled.

In 1801 a new and better kind of road opened in New Jersey. It was called a **turnpike.** At different places on the road, travelers had to pass through a turning pike, or gate. There they paid money called a **toll.** The toll helped pay for the building costs of the road and its care. The Morris Turnpike, which ran from Elizabeth to Milford, Pennsylvania, was the first of these toll roads.

Batsto Village

Batsto, located in the Pine Barrens, was one of the largest of many ironmaking towns in New Jersey. Cannons and cannonballs made at Batsto helped to win the Revolutionary War. Batsto iron was used in peacetime, too. Iron plates were made at Batsto for the backs of fireplaces. Many kitchen items of the day were made of iron. Batsto frying pans were used in many households. An iron fence made at Batsto once stood outside Independence Hall in Philadelphia, where the Constitution was written.

The Batsto iron furnace went out in 1848. Iron was being made more cheaply in the Midwest. Batsto then turned to glassmaking. Like the iron furnaces, the glass furnaces were fueled by wood from the pine and oak trees of the area. Sand from the area was also used to make glass. In the second half of the nineteenth century, the furnaces stopped producing glass. Batsto's industrial days were over. The town was nearly deserted.

A modern visitor to Batsto, though, will find a busy place. Today the state of New Jersey owns the land and buildings at Batsto Village. The village looks much as it did over a century and a half ago. The water-powered sawmill there puts out boards and shingles. These boards and shingles have been used to rebuild houses in the village. The gristmill grinds different kinds of grains. You can buy some cornmeal, if you wish. Batsto truly lives again as an early nineteenth-century manufacturing center. Places like Batsto helped our state become a mighty center of industry.

Canals Traveling by boat in the 1800s was easier than by wagon, stagecoach, or horseback. It was cheaper to move goods by water. Boats could carry many more goods than wagons.

People began to talk about joining the rivers in New Jersey. Deep, water-filled ditches called **canals** could be built between the rivers. Boats and barges would be moved along the canals by teams of horses or mules. A barge is a roomy, flat-bottomed boat. The animals would walk on a path beside the canal. They would pull the boats and barges through the canal by rope.

The Morris Canal, which was begun in 1825, ran across northern New Jersey from the Delaware River to the Hudson River. The canal connected Phillipsburg and Newark by 1831. It reached Jersey City in 1836. The canal was called "the impossible canal" because it started at sea level at Jersey City and rose to 914 feet (279 m) at Lake Hopatcong. The canal ran up, across, and down mountains. The canal was able to run up and down through the use of locks and inclined planes. Locks are like steps for boats. The inclined planes worked like hillside railways. The boats and barges were carried up the mountains on railroad cars. The Morris Canal's most important job was to bring Pennsylvania coal to manufacturing towns to the east.

Horses or mules pulled boats and barges by rope through the Morris Canal. Cars on inclined planes on the canal carried the boats and barges up the hills on the canal's route.
■ What is the boat in the center of the picture carrying?

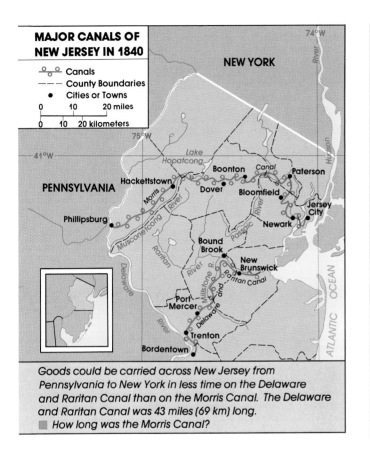

MAJOR CANALS OF NEW JERSEY IN 1840

Goods could be carried across New Jersey from Pennsylvania to New York in less time on the Delaware and Raritan Canal than on the Morris Canal. The Delaware and Raritan Canal was 43 miles (69 km) long.
■ How long was the Morris Canal?

John Fitch ran a steamboat between Pennsylvania and New Jersey.
■ How do the banks of the Delaware River look here?

In 1834 the Delaware and Raritan Canal was finished. The canal joined the Delaware River and the Raritan River. It was 43 miles (69 km) long and 70 feet (21 m) wide. Coal, clay, grain, and other farm products were carried on the Delaware and Raritan Canal. For about $4, 25 tons (23 t) could be carried 25 miles (40 km) in 1 day.

The Steamboat Another change came to the waterways of New Jersey around this time. Several people had already tried a new kind of boat, called a **steamboat,** on the rivers. The boat was not moved by oars or sails but by steam power. A steam engine on the boat burned coal or wood to heat water. The heated water made steam. The power from the steam made the engine work. The engine made the boat move. Steamboats could carry people and goods faster and more cheaply than other kinds of boats.

By 1788, John Fitch of Philadelphia was running a regular steamboat service across the Delaware River to New Jersey. Ten years later, John Stevens of Hoboken built his own steamboat. His 100-foot-long (31-meter-long) steamboat, called the *Phoenix,* was finished in 1808. It traveled out on the Atlantic Ocean and around New Jersey to reach Philadelphia. The *Phoenix* was the first steamboat to travel on the sea.

161

Railroads   John Stevens was even more interested in building a steam **locomotive.** A locomotive is an engine that moves on its own power. In 1825, Stevens built the first railroad locomotive in America. It was powered by steam. Stevens ran it on a track at Hoboken. It could travel 12 miles (19 km) per hour and could also go uphill.

Traffic on the canals was still heavy. It was some time before railroads took the place of canals. New Jersey's most successful railroad, the Camden and Amboy, helped connect Philadelphia and New York. Steam ferryboats were used on the Delaware and Hudson rivers to make the final connection. By the 1830s there were many railroads in New Jersey. Railroads linked most of the important towns of the state. In the mid-1800s, railroads were carrying farm products north from southern New Jersey. In 1854 the Camden and Atlantic Railroad carried the first passengers to a new resort on the Atlantic Ocean. The resort was called Atlantic City.

New Jersey Begins to Grow   After the Revolutionary War, New Jersey's population grew slowly. But industry, steam power, canals, and railroads changed this. From the 1830s on, New Jersey grew rapidly. Factories and industry brought workers from other states and the countries of Great Britain and Ire-

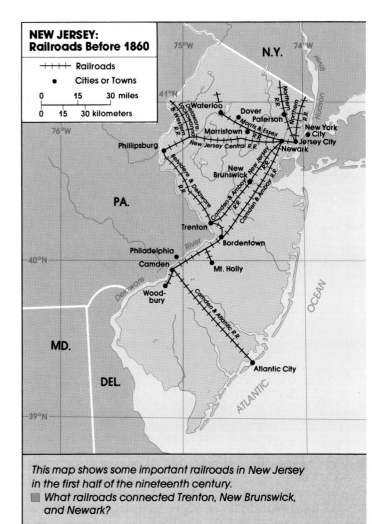

This map shows some important railroads in New Jersey in the first half of the nineteenth century.
■ What railroads connected Trenton, New Brunswick, and Newark?

land. Germans also came in large numbers. Towns became cities as more workers came to the factories. Between 1830 and 1860 the population of New Jersey doubled, rising from 320,000 to 674,000.

CHECKUP
1. How was Paterson started?
2. What is a turnpike?
3. What rivers were joined by the Morris Canal?

4. **Thinking Critically**   Discuss how turnpikes, canals, and railroads helped improve life in New Jersey.

162

Making Life Better

In what areas did people work to make life better in New Jersey?

VOCABULARY

asylum	Underground
abolitionist	Railroad

Education In the early 1800s there was a great need in New Jersey for schools that all children could attend. State law provided for some schooling for poor children, slaves, and apprentices. Children whose parents could afford it were also sent to school. But there were many children in between the rich and the poor. Their chance for an education was not good.

In 1836 the first free public schools were opened in the city of Newark. Taxes paid for the schools.

Very slowly other towns in New Jersey set up free schools. By 1871 there was a good system of free schools in the state.

Prisons, Poorhouses, and Asylums
Tax money was also used to fix up the jails, poorhouses, and mental **asylums,** or homes for the mentally ill. Dorothea Dix spoke out against the terrible living conditions in these places. Dix was from Massachusetts. In 1843 she toured prisons and homes for the poor and mentally ill in New Jersey. Dix wrote a report on her findings. Her report led to the building of a state mental hospital north of Trenton. When finished, the hospital was called the finest mental asylum in America.

A state mental hospital was built north of Trenton in the 1840s.
■ What did Dorothea Dix have to do with the hospital?

Quakers in Randolph helped slaves on the Underground Railroad.
■ **How, do you think, slaves felt during their trip to freedom?**

The Movement to End Slavery By the mid-1800s, New Jerseyans and other Americans faced an even more important problem — slavery. People who wanted to put an end to slavery were called **abolitionists** (ab ə lish′ ə nists). Peter Johnson and Henry Drayton of Newark were abolitionists. They helped start a group called the Antislavery Society to protest slavery. They and others tried to get New Jersey and other states to pass a law to end slavery.

As early as 1786 it was against New Jersey state law to bring slaves into the state. In 1804 the state legislature passed the Gradual Abolition Act. The act did not do away with slavery. But it did say that female slaves became free at age 21 and male slaves at age 25. In 1846, New Jersey passed a law that put an end to slavery. But the new law did not give all slaves in New Jersey freedom right away. Instead, before they were freed, slaves had to work for their masters as apprentices for a certain number of years. In 1860 there were still slaves in New Jersey.

The Underground Railroad Many other states still allowed slavery. Many slaves lived in the South. They were not free. Some escaped from their owners. In the 1830s, abolitionists in New Jersey and other states began to help Southern slaves escape to freedom in the North. The abolitionists worked together on the **Underground Railroad.** The Underground Railroad was a secret escape route for slaves. It was a system of paths that slaves could take to freedom. On the paths there were safe resting stops for the slaves in homes, churches, and other places.

The Underground Railroad went from the Southern states to the Northern states or Canada, where slaves could be free. Many of the paths passed through New Jersey. Slaves rode on wagons or walked along the New Jersey paths. Many Quakers living in southern New Jersey worked on the Underground Railroad. The most famous person who guided slaves to freedom on the Underground Railroad was Harriet Tubman. She had escaped to freedom from Maryland when she

Harriet Tubman was a runaway slave.
■ How did she help others to escape to freedom?

was about 28 years old. Tubman went back to the South many times to lead people to freedom.

By 1860 the Underground Railroad had helped over 50,000 slaves to escape. But the Underground Railroad was not a real answer to the problem of slavery. Differences between the North and the South were greater than ever before.

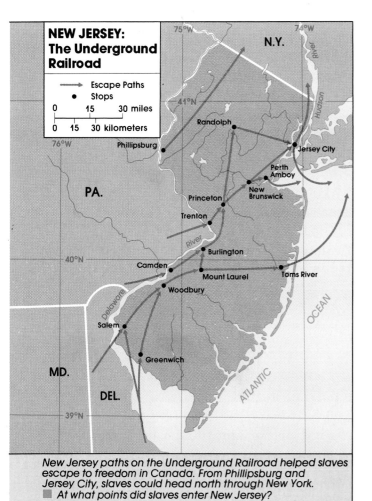

NEW JERSEY:
The Underground
Railroad

→ Escape Paths
• Stops

0   15   30 miles
0   15   30 kilometers

New Jersey paths on the Underground Railroad helped slaves escape to freedom in Canada. From Phillipsburg and Jersey City, slaves could head north through New York.
■ At what points did slaves enter New Jersey?

CHECKUP
1. Who could attend school in New Jersey in the early 1800s?
2. How did Dorothea Dix of Massachusetts help to make life better for some New Jerseyans?
3. Explain how the Underground Railroad worked.
4. **Thinking Critically** Why wasn't the Underground Railroad a real answer to the problem of slavery?

Finding Information in a Library

WHAT IS A CARD CATALOG?

A library is a source of much information. You know that a library has many books. Do you know how to find the book that has the information you need?

One way is by using the card catalog. A card catalog is a listing of all the books in the library. The books are listed on cards that are kept in drawers. Each book is listed alphabetically by the subject, the title, and the author's last name.

In this book you have already learned much about New Jersey. Now you might want to find a book that will tell you more about New Jersey. How can you use the card catalog to find a book about New Jersey?

USING A CARD CATALOG

First, you will look in the card catalog under *N* for the subject *New Jersey*. You will find many cards under this heading. These are subject cards. A subject as broad as New Jersey will be broken down further into smaller subjects. You will probably see subheadings for cities, climate, geography, government, and so on. These subheadings help to narrow the subject. One subheading, History, lists a book entitled *New Jersey* by Allan Carpenter. On the card is a group of numbers or letters that will help you find the book on the shelf in the library.

You may already know the title of the book you want. Perhaps someone told you that *Capsules of New Jersey History* is a good book. You will look under the letter *C* for the first word of the title, *Capsules*. The complete title of the book will be on the title card.

A friend of yours may say, "A cookbook by Ridgway has some interesting old recipes from New Jersey, but I've forgotten the title." Then you will look under the letter *R* to find Ridgway. There might be more than one book by authors named Ridgway. These cards are author cards. If you do not know the author's first name, you may have to look through the book titles until you find the title that seems to be right. If you find a book called *Chicken Foot Soup and Other Recipes from the Pine Barrens*, you have the right book.

SKILLS PRACTICE

Now see how well you can use the card catalog. Write down the type of card and the letter under which you will find the following books:

   a. A book about Atlantic City
   b. A book written by Henry Beck
   c. A book about William Paterson
   d. A book called *Iron in the Pines*

You can find information quickly when you know how to use the card catalog. Each time you use the catalog, it will be easier. If you have any questions about the use of the library, the librarian is there to help.

CHAPTER 9 REVIEW

MAIN IDEAS

1. At the Constitutional Convention, New Jersey delegate William Paterson put forth the New Jersey Plan. Under the plan there would be one house of Congress in which all states would have the same number of representatives. This plan was the idea behind the United States Senate.

2. The constitution of 1776 said that any New Jerseyan owning property could vote and the governor was elected by the legislature. In 1807, female and black property owners lost their right to vote. Under the constitution of 1844, voters did not have to own property and the governor was elected by the voters.

3. In the first half of the nineteenth century, people in New Jersey began to use machines to manufacture things in factories. There were many changes in transportation. Better roads, including turnpikes, were opened. Goods were carried on canals and railroads. Steam was used to power boats and railroad locomotives.

4. People worked to make education better and free for all. They made living conditions in poorhouses, prisons, and asylums better. They also worked to end slavery in New Jersey and other states.

VOCABULARY REVIEW

Write the word or words that best complete each sentence. Use a separate sheet of paper.

1. A _____ is a lawmaking body.
2. _____ means "to approve."
3. A decision that gives each side something is a _____.
4. A _____ is an engine that moves on its own power.
5. An _____ is a person who wants to put an end to slavery.

CHAPTER CHECKUP

1. What did the compromise about the two houses of Congress give states with small populations and states with large populations?

2. Which states would have preferred Washington, D. C., as a national capital to Trenton?

3. **Thinking Critically** Why was the 1807 decision of the state legislature about voting rights a step backward?

4. **Thinking Critically** Compare life in New Jersey before and after the invention of the steam engine.

5. **Thinking Critically** Describe the steps taken in the state of New Jersey to end slavery.

6. **Thinking Critically** Explain the name Underground Railroad.

APPLYING KNOWLEDGE

1. Pretend you are Alexander Hamilton. Explain why you believe the Great Falls of the Passaic River would be a good location for a factory town. Discuss the importance of manufacturing to the growth of the new nation.

2. Make a poster that advertises one of the improvements in transportation in the 1800s. The advertisement should explain how the new form of transportation is better than earlier forms. Illustrate your ad so that it will catch people's eye.

10 New Jersey from 1860 to 1900

New Jersey in the Civil War

What did New Jersey do to help during the Civil War?

VOCABULARY

states' rights	Civil War
secede	

A Nation in Trouble Many people in New Jersey and other Northern states wanted to put an end to slavery in the United States. They also did not want slavery to begin in the western part of the country, which was just being settled.

In the South, many people believed that they had a right to own slaves. The people of the South said they needed slaves to work on their farms and in the cities. Southerners also wanted to be able to take slaves into the new lands being settled in the western part of the country.

By 1860, people from the North and the South had still not agreed about whether to keep slavery or end it. The people of the South believed in **states' rights.** They believed that

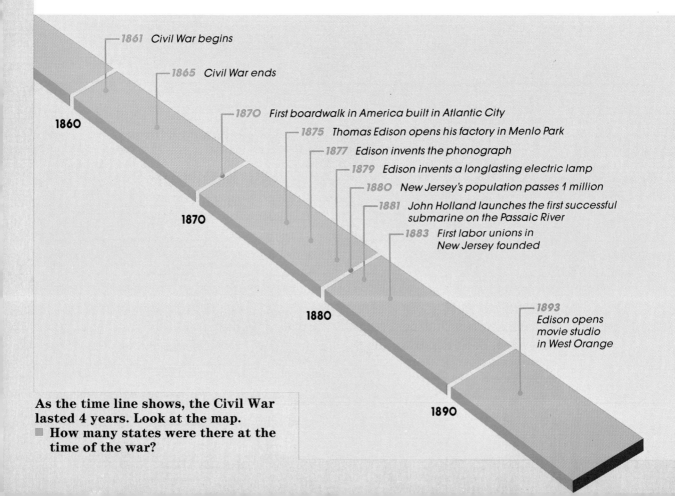

1861 Civil War begins

1865 Civil War ends

1860

1870 First boardwalk in America built in Atlantic City

1875 Thomas Edison opens his factory in Menlo Park

1877 Edison invents the phonograph

1879 Edison invents a longlasting electric lamp

1880 New Jersey's population passes 1 million

1881 John Holland launches the first successful submarine on the Passaic River

1883 First labor unions in New Jersey founded

1870

1893 Edison opens movie studio in West Orange

1880

1890

As the time line shows, the Civil War lasted 4 years. Look at the map.
■ How many states were there at the time of the war?

each state should decide what was best for that state. They did not want the federal government to have the power to tell the states what they could or could not do within their own boundaries. Some Southern states decided they did not want to be part of the United States any more. They wanted to form their own country. Then they could keep their slaves. These states **seceded,** or withdrew from, the United States.

Abraham Lincoln was President of the United States at this time. Lincoln and many people from the North felt that the Southern states should not be allowed to break away. President Lincoln believed that all the states should stay together. He de-cided to use the United States Army to stop the Southern states.

But the Southern states were de-termined to break away. This led to the start of the **Civil War.** A civil war is a war fought between people of the same country. The American Civil War was fought between the North and the South. It began in 1861 and ended in 1865.

New Jersey—a Northern State

New Jersey was the first state to send an organized group of soldiers to Washington, D. C., to fight on the side of the North. Between 1861 and 1865 over 80,000 New Jersey men left home to fight in the Civil War. Many were killed in battle.

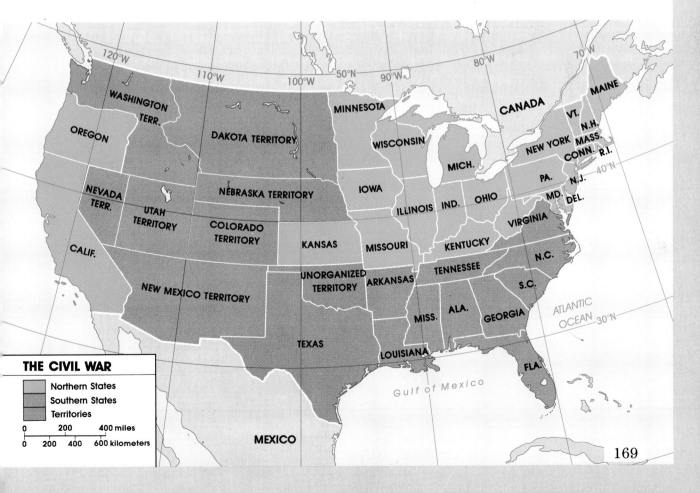

THE CIVIL WAR

- Northern States
- Southern States
- Territories

0   200   400 miles
0 200 400 600 kilometers

169

James Still (1812 – 1885)

James Still was born in Indian Mills, in the Pine Barrens, in 1812. He was one of 21 children. His parents had once been slaves. From his early years, James knew what it was like to work hard. His family had almost no money. James and the other children helped their parents earn enough money to pay for food, clothing, and shelter for the family. James worked at many jobs. There was not much time for James to play when he was a child. In fact, there was hardly time for him to go to school. James had only about 3 months of schooling. At the age of 21, James left home to find another job. After he had saved some money, he bought some land and married.

Still also began to heal sick people who lived in the Pine Barrens. He made medicines for the sick from herbs and other plants. The people of the Pine Barrens valued his skills. They paid him whatever they could afford. Even though Still was not a doctor who had gone to a school of medicine, people began to call him the Black Doctor of the Pines. People from Philadelphia and from other parts of New Jersey began to learn of Still's cures. Even real doctors began to ask his advice about cures.

In 1877, after many years of healing the sick, "Doctor" Still decided to write the story of his life. He also offered advice to black people about how they could improve their lives. Still believed that black people could have better lives if they moved out to the country. There they could buy land and teach their children the value of hard work. Still's beliefs were based on his own experience. Life in the country, hard work, and care for others were the secrets of his success.

Many generals of the Northern army were from New Jersey. One of the most famous Civil War generals from New Jersey was George McClellan from West Orange. General McClellan led the whole Northern army for part of the war. Later he became governor of New Jersey. Philip Kearny was another Civil War general from New Jersey.

Producing Supplies to Win the War
Many businesses in New Jersey produced goods for use in the war. New Jersey's clothing factories helped to supply uniforms for the soldiers. The city of Camden was an important center for building ships for the war. Trenton factories made iron goods, such as cannons and guns.

Railroads were also important during the war. Trains were needed to move soldiers and supplies. No state in the country made more train engines than New Jersey. Most of the engines that pulled the nation's trains were made in Paterson. The locomotive the *General* was built in 1856 by the Rogers Locomotive Company of Paterson. Northern soldiers stole the *General* from Southern soldiers in Georgia in 1862. The Southern soldiers chased them in the *Texas*, another New Jersey-made locomotive. For a picture of the *General*, see page 149.

The state of New Jersey helped in many ways to fight the Civil War. Finally, in 1865, the North won the

General Philip Kearny led the First New Jersey Brigade.
■ How, do you suppose, did he lose his left arm?

war. The end of the Civil War meant the end of slavery in the United States. It also meant that all the states were still part of the nation. New Jerseyans could be proud that they helped to win the war.

CHECKUP
1. Why did the Southern states want to break away from the nation?
2. When was the Civil War fought?
3. Name two Northern generals from New Jersey.
4. What did the end of the Civil War bring about?

5. **Thinking Critically** Compare the South's view of slavery with the North's view.

New Jersey's Economy Grows

How did New Jersey's economy change and grow in the second half of the nineteenth century?

Railroads Help the Economy After the Civil War, New Jersey's **economy** began to grow very quickly. The word *economy* means "the making and selling of goods and services."

Railroads played an important part in New Jersey's growth. Many new railroads were built after the Civil War. In fact, almost every community in the state was on or near a railroad line. By 1895, railroads were the most popular form of transportation in New Jersey. Railroads provided jobs for thousands of New Jerseyans. Workers were needed to build tracks, bridges, and tunnels for the railroads. Many other workers helped to repair or make railroad engines and cars.

The Growth of Industry As the railroads grew, so did New Jersey industry. Most New Jersey industries were in Newark, Paterson, Trenton, Elizabeth, and other large cities. But as railroad tracks began to be laid all over the state, industry also began to grow in smaller towns.

New Jersey industry grew for other reasons, too. New Jersey had many people to fill jobs in the factories. In addition, because the state's population was growing, more people needed to buy goods.

This locomotive can be seen today at Allaire State Park.
■ **What kind of power drives the locomotive?**

Strikes sometimes became violent. Here, striking coal handlers at the Weehawken docks drive new handlers from their work.
■ **Why, do you think, were the strikers angry at the new workers?**

All kinds of machine-made goods were produced in New Jersey. Factories in Newark produced hats, carriages, spools of thread, jewelry, and leather goods. Trenton was known for iron products, china, and pottery. Elizabeth was home to the large Singer Sewing Machine Company, which made thousands of sewing machines each year. Camden was a furniture-making center.

The Worker in the Factory Factory workers had long hours. Their pay was not good. Sometimes, people in a factory worked 12 or 14 hours a day. Many worked 6 days a week. Women and children worked in fac-

tories, too. They helped their families make enough money to live. The factories were sometimes dangerous. Fires could easily start, and machines broke down. Many factories were dirty and noisy.

In 1883 an important new law was passed in New Jersey. This law allowed factory workers to organize into groups to protest poor working conditions. These groups were called **labor unions.** A labor union tries to get employers to improve working conditions and pay. An employer is a person who hires other people to work for him or her. **Striking** was one way that labor unions tried to get the pay and changes they wanted.

173

When workers strike, they stop working until they get what they want. Some strikes lasted for several days or even weeks. Often the workers on strike did not get the changes they wanted. But other times a strike would be successful, and conditions were improved.

Another state law was passed, which said that a state inspector had to visit the factories. The job of the inspector was to check working conditions in the state's factories.

Railroads, Industry, and the Farmer

The railroads helped New Jersey farmers to send their goods to all parts of New Jersey and other states. But railroads also brought about competition between farmers. For example, farm goods from other states could be brought quickly and without spoiling to Philadelphia and New York by train. Many New Jersey farmers decided to sell their farms and move to the cities. Some farmers sold their land to industries that needed more space for building factories. By 1880 a farmer in New Jersey could sell an acre of land for $90. This was a very good price. Still, many farmers decided to stay on their farms.

New Jersey — the Little Giant

By 1880, New Jersey was the fourth smallest state in area in the country. But because of the growth in railroads and factories, New Jersey

Pick-your-own farms were popular even in the nineteenth century.
■ What is the woman doing at the stand at the left?

was the fifth most important industrial state. By the end of the nineteenth century, New Jersey had already earned the nickname the Little Giant because of the great industry within its boundaries.

CHECKUP

1. How did railroads help New Jersey grow between 1860 and 1900?
2. Why did workers form groups called labor unions?
3. Why did some New Jersey farmers sell their land at this time?
4. **Thinking Critically** Describe how industry was able to grow in New Jersey.

Inventing the Way to the Future

What are some New Jersey inventions?

VOCABULARY

phonograph

From Plastic to Submarines The years 1860–1900 were also a time of new ideas. New ideas led to inventions. Many important things were invented in New Jersey.

A man named John Hyatt invented the world's first kind of plastic. This plastic was used to make such things as piano keys, knife handles, and pool balls. These goods were made in Hyatt's factory in Newark. Plastic was also used to make film. The man who invented the first plastic film was the Reverend Hannibal Goodwin from Newark. Goodwin's invention led to the camera and movie film we use today.

America's first submarine was invented by a teacher in Paterson named John Holland. Holland built his first submarine in 1875. It was not a success. It went down into the Passaic River but did not come back up. In 1881, Holland tried again with a new and larger submarine. This time his invention worked. Later the United States Navy asked John Holland to build submarines for the navy to use.

Submarines sink when water is pumped into special tanks on board.
■ How do people get into the submarine shown here?

175

Thomas Edison One of the most famous inventors of all time was Thomas Alva Edison. Thomas Edison was born in Ohio in 1847. In 1871 he came to New Jersey. He spent the rest of his life here.

Edison had an unusual idea. He wanted to build a special kind of factory just to make inventions. In 1876, Edison built this factory at Menlo Park. Then he invited people with different ideas to help him invent things there. It was at Menlo Park

that the world's first **phonograph** was invented. A phonograph is a machine that produces sounds. Today we call this machine a record player.

Thomas Edison and his fellow inventors then started on another invention. Electricity had already been discovered, and the light bulb had already been invented. But no one had found a way to make electric lighting useful to all people. In 1879, Edison invented an electric lamp that could last for many hours. Edison also found a way to bring electricity to many lamps at the same time. By 1883, people were using Edison's invention to light up their homes, offices, and stores. Candles and gas lanterns became old-fashioned.

Edison also invented a new way to make motion pictures, or movies. In 1893 he opened a movie studio in West Orange. A movie called *The Great Train Robbery* was made at this studio. Later, many more movies were made and shown all over New Jersey. Edison's invention helped make New Jersey America's first movie capital.

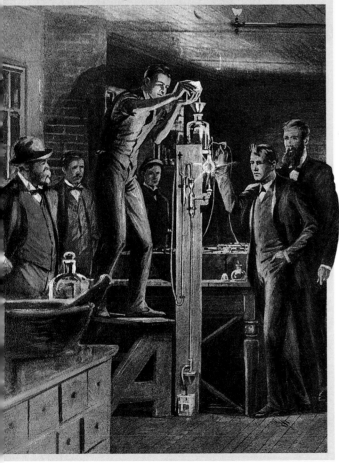

Thomas Edison did many kinds of experiments in his factory, or laboratory, in Menlo Park.
■ What invention are he and others working on in this picture?

CHECKUP

1. Name four things invented in the state of New Jersey.
2. Where did John Holland test his first submarine?
3. What unusual idea did Thomas Edison have for inventing things?
4. **Thinking Critically** Compare the inventions discussed in this lesson and their importance today.

A New Way of Life

What was life like in the cities, suburbs, and resorts of New Jersey in the late 1800s?

The cities were crowded, and living conditions were poor.
■ **What kind of shelter did this family find in the city?**

Life in the City   By 1880, New Jersey's population had grown to over 1 million. More than half of the people lived in cities. New Jersey was now called an **urban** state. *Urban* means "of or relating to a city."

Newark was New Jersey's most populated city. It had many jobs in all kinds of factories. Jersey City was another growing urban center. Here, people took jobs building and repairing railroad cars and working on the ship docks.

The cities became crowded. More houses were needed. Some houses were divided to provide homes for more families. Sometimes one or more families lived in only a few rooms. Many poor people lived in **tenements.** These were large, crowded apartment buildings. Often tenements did not have indoor plumbing or bathrooms. There was dirt and garbage in the streets around the tenements. This way of living was not healthy. It caused some people to become ill.

But life in the city was not all bad. Cities provided education in schools for young people. Young people needed to learn new skills to work in the factories. Many cities opened special schools to teach pupils these new skills.

The Beginning of Suburbs   Many wealthier New Jerseyans decided to move out to the new suburbs. The suburbs were located near the train routes so that people could commute to the cities. Some early suburbs included Morristown, the Oranges, Teaneck, and Montclair. Suburbs were slower to start in southern New Jersey. This was because the railroads did not grow in this part of the state until later on.

Life in the suburbs was much different from life in the cities. In the suburbs there was more space, fewer people, and peace and quiet.

177

Atlantic City was one of the most popular resorts on the Jersey shore. The country's first boardwalk was built there in 1870. Both New Jerseyans and people from out of state visited the resort.
■ What did Atlantic City have to offer visitors?

Shore Resorts Become Popular In the 1880s and 1890s, more people began to visit New Jersey's seashore. The seashore towns of Cape May and Long Branch had been popular among the wealthy in the 1860s. But now, more working people could easily travel by railroad to many places on the shore to relax on the beach.

People who worked in the cities went to the Jersey shore on Sundays for a day of rest and fun, just as they do today. A round-trip ticket to the Jersey shore from Newark, Jersey City, or Camden cost $1. This may seem like a small price to pay, but most people at the time only earned about $4 a week!

By the end of the 1800s, New Jersey had good railroads, a large population, and strong industry. If that was not enough, the state also had beautiful beaches and other vacation spots that attracted people from near and far.

CHECKUP
1. Why was New Jersey called an urban state?
2. How did people in the suburbs get to work in the cities?
3. Why did people visit the shore resorts in the late 1800s?
4. **Thinking Critically** Why, do you think, did many wealthier New Jerseyans move to the suburbs at this time?

178

Using Context Clues

MORE THAN ONE MEANING

You have learned how to use a dictionary to find the meaning of words. But sometimes a dictionary is not close at hand. Sometimes, too, a dictionary gives more than one meaning for a word. Take the word *leaf*, for example. It is used differently in each of the following sentences.

1. The last dead leaf on the tree fluttered in the winter wind.
2. Before our cousins came for dinner, we put another leaf in the old dining-room table.
3. Each leaf of the old book was brown and faded.

WHAT ARE CONTEXT CLUES?

In each sentence above, the word *leaf* has a different meaning. But you probably knew what the word meant each time it was used. You looked at the other words in the sentence to learn the meaning. The words that are around another word are called context. In each sentence above, these words helped you to know the meaning of the word *leaf*. A clue is something that helps you figure out the answer to a problem. Words that you know in a sentence and that help you understand the meaning of one or more words in a sentence are called context clues.

SKILLS PRACTICE

In the exercise below, look for context clues for the underlined word in each sentence. On a separate sheet of paper, write what you think is the meaning of each underlined word. Then look up the word in a dictionary. See if the meaning you wrote was correct in the context of the sentence.

1. Many people living in New Jersey in 1860 wished to <u>abolish</u> slavery.
2. In the late 1800s many New Jerseyans spent their <u>leisure</u> time at shore and other resorts.
3. During the Civil War the Northern states <u>opposed</u> the Southern states.
4. New Jersey <u>exported</u> many goods to other states by railroad.
5. Workers went on strike to <u>protest</u> poor working conditions.
6. Factory workers <u>labored</u> long and hard for their weekly paycheck.
7. Thomas Edison had one of the most <u>inventive</u> minds in the United States.
8. Railroads were a popular <u>mode</u> of transportation.

CHAPTER 10 REVIEW

MAIN IDEAS

1. New Jersey sent important generals and thousands of soldiers to help fight the Civil War. Uniforms, cannons, guns, ships, and train engines were made in New Jersey for use in the war.
2. After the Civil War, railroads became the most popular form of transportation in the state. Railroads also provided jobs for many New Jerseyans. Railroads helped New Jersey industry grow in both cities and small towns. The growth in industry meant that more workers were needed and more different kinds of goods were produced. Farms continued to be important, although some farmers sold their land to industry.
3. Inventions from New Jersey include plastic film, the submarine, the phonograph, a new kind of electric lamp, and a new way to make movies.
4. In the late 1800s, New Jersey cities were crowded, and living conditions were poor for many people. In the suburbs there was more space and less noise. Fewer people lived in the suburbs than in the cities. The seashore resorts became popular vacation spots among New Jerseyans and people from out of state.

VOCABULARY REVIEW

Match the terms with their definitions.
- **a.** urban
- **b.** Civil War
- **c.** labor union
- **d.** tenement
- **e.** economy

1. The war between North and South in the United States of America
2. Of or relating to a city
3. An organized group of workers that tries to get higher pay and better working conditions
4. The making and selling of goods and services
5. A large, crowded apartment building

CHAPTER CHECKUP

1. How were railroads important to New Jersey before and after 1860?
2. What did Thomas Edison invent?
3. What was New Jersey's population around 1880?
4. **Thinking Critically** What effect, do you think, did the end of slavery have on the economy of the South?
5. **Thinking Critically** In your own words, explain New Jersey's nickname the Little Giant.
6. **Thinking Critically** Why were some people willing to put up with overcrowding and poor living conditions in the cities of New Jersey?

APPLYING KNOWLEDGE

1. Make a list of the industries and other businesses in your area. Tell what each industry produces or what each business does. Have industry and business helped your area to grow?
2. Make a poster comparing life in a New Jersey city in the late 1800s with life in a suburb. Use categories such as housing, transportation, jobs, and recreation to organize your poster. Draw pictures to illustrate the differences between city and suburb.

SUMMARIZING UNIT 3

REVIEWING VOCABULARY

1. New Jersey Plan Under the New Jersey Plan for the government of the nation, there would be one house of Congress with the same number of representatives from all the states. Who thought of the New Jersey Plan? Why did states with smaller populations like this plan?

2. Manufacturing Manufacturing is the making of goods by hand or machine, especially in large quantities. Paterson was planned as a center of manufacturing. What important source of power for machines was found at the location of Paterson?

3. Abolitionist Abolitionists were people who wanted to put an end to slavery. In what ways did abolitionists work to end slavery in our country? Who were two well-known abolitionists from New Jersey?

4. Civil War The American Civil War was fought between the North and the South. On which side did New Jersey fight? Discuss how New Jersey helped the war effort.

5. Economy The economy of New Jersey, or the making and selling of goods and services in the state, grew rapidly after the Civil War. Give three reasons for the growth of New Jersey's economy after the war.

EXPRESSING YOURSELF

1. What Would You Do? Pretend that you are a delegate to the meeting about a national constitution in Philadelphia. You have heard the plans for the national government suggested by New Jersey and Virginia. What would you suggest doing to reach an agreement about one plan for the government of the United States?

2. How Would You Feel? In 1807 the state legislature voted not to give women and blacks the right to vote. How would you feel if you were a woman or a black living in New Jersey?

3. In What Ways? Imagine that you have run a manufacturing business in Camden since the beginning of the nineteenth century. The Camden and Amboy Railroad has just been completed. In what ways will the railroad help your business? In what ways will it hurt your business?

4. What If? In 1860 the Southern states began to break away from the United States to form their own country. President Lincoln used the army to stop this, but he was not successful. What if the army had been able to stop the South from breaking away at this time and the Civil War had not broken out? How would history have been different?

5. Thinking Like an Inventor Pretend that you are one of the inventors at Edison's factory in Menlo Park. Describe how you and the other inventors think of inventions. Explain why you like inventing things.

New Jersey in the Twentieth Century

New Jersey has kept on moving forward. In the late 1800s and early 1900s, more new people came to our state to live. These people were of many backgrounds. They brought different ways of life to New Jersey. This made life more interesting for all New Jerseyans. The people of our state experienced good times and bad times in the first half of the twentieth century. Progress was made in many areas. There were also two world wars.

Two world wars were fought during the first half of the twentieth century.

■ **How long did each war last?**

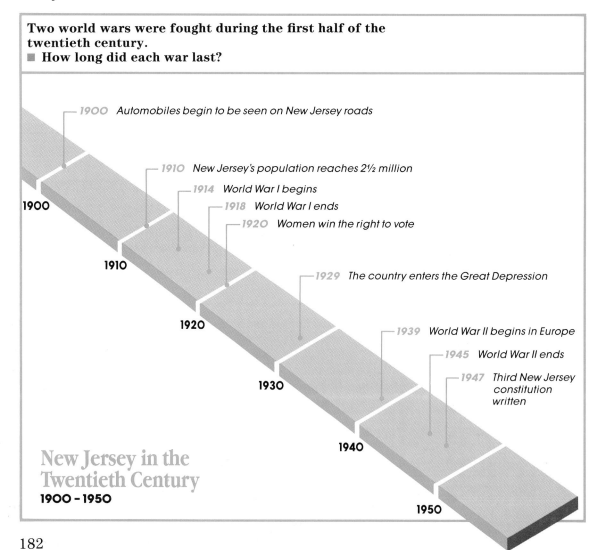

1900   Automobiles begin to be seen on New Jersey roads

1900

1910   New Jersey's population reaches 2½ million

1914   World War I begins

1918   World War I ends

1920   Women win the right to vote

1910

1929   The country enters the Great Depression

1920

1939   World War II begins in Europe

1945   World War II ends

1947   Third New Jersey constitution written

1930

1940

New Jersey in the Twentieth Century
1900 - 1950

1950

The automobile changed life.
■ How did the automobile make the scene below possible?

In this unit you will learn about how the good times, bad times, and wars affected New Jerseyans. You will also learn about how life has become not only easier but better in this century.

In the twentieth century, new sports became popular. One of these was cycling. Both women and men enjoyed bicycling, sometimes together on a "bicycle built for two."

Vaudeville also was popular. Vaudeville shows were variety shows that included magic shows, comedy, animal acts, and song-and-dance acts. Movies drew people to theaters, too. Before long there was radio. By the 1950s, millions of Americans had television in their own homes.

The radio was the center of home entertainment in the 1920s, 1930s, and 1940s.
■ What did this family do while listening?

New Jersey cities like Jersey City reached their peak in the twentieth century. Jersey City, already a leading transportation center, was connected to New York City early in the century by the Hudson Tubes, a railroad tunnel, and the Holland Tunnel, a passage for cars, trucks, and buses. Both ran under the Hudson River. These links were important to Jersey City's continuing role as a transportation center. At its height in 1950, Jersey City's population neared 300,000. Today the city is still a busy place. The Holland Tunnel is now used by over 20 million motor vehicles each year.

Early cars use the Holland Tunnel.
■ What was used to cover the inside walls of the tunnel?

Although change came to the cities, life on many farms in New Jersey was backward even as late as the 1920s and 1930s. Some farmers still used horses to pull machines. Many of the hard chores on the farm were still done by hand.

Many New Jersey farms disappeared in the first half of the twentieth century. The hard times of the 1930s hit farmers as hard as others. Many farms did not pull through. Some farmers left their farms to look for work in the cities.

When more land was needed for industry later in the century, some farmers sold their land for a good price. The suburbs also began to spread into farmland. Farmers were able to get even more money for their land. Nevertheless, many farmers stayed on their farms, and agriculture continued to keep New Jersey green.

Suburbs spread into farmland in the twentieth century.
■ How would you describe this suburb?

In the first half of the century, there was great growth in the variety of industry in New Jersey. Some industries, such as silk, died out. New industries, such as chemicals, were born. Industry boomed at different times. The war years (1914–1918 and 1939–1945) were a busy time for industry in the state. During the years between the wars, however, many businesses closed. Research became an important industry in the state. Ideas born in New Jersey research centers brought the United States into the space age.

Lightwaves are used here to send information.
■ Why is research like this important today?

11 New Jersey at the Beginning of a New Century

The Immigrants

Why did immigrants come to the state of New Jersey?

VOCABULARY

immigrant   custom
steerage ticket

New People Arrive   Between 1840 and 1920, thousands of **immigrants** (im′ ə grənts) came to New Jersey from all over Europe. An immigrant is a person who comes to a country to make a home. The immigrants who came to New Jersey were from Ireland, Italy, Greece, Russia, and many other countries.

These people decided to move to the United States for many reasons. The biggest reason of all was to find a new and better life. There were better jobs in America. The factories in the cities needed workers. Many of the immigrants had heard that any-

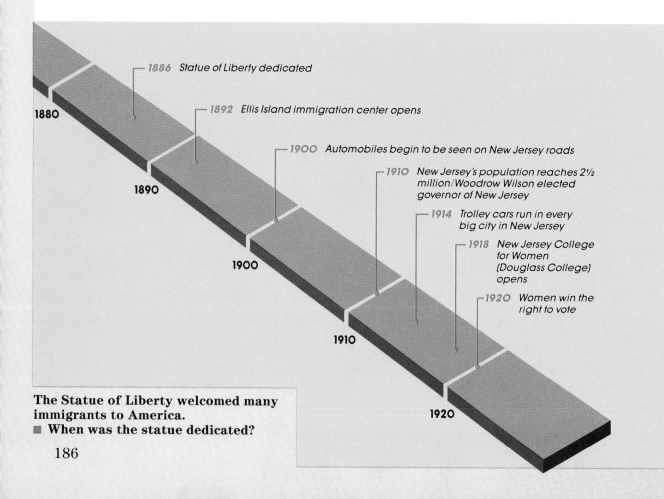

1886 Statue of Liberty dedicated

1880

1892 Ellis Island immigration center opens

1900 Automobiles begin to be seen on New Jersey roads

1890

1910 New Jersey's population reaches 2½ million/Woodrow Wilson elected governor of New Jersey

1914 Trolley cars run in every big city in New Jersey

1900

1918 New Jersey College for Women (Douglass College) opens

1920 Women win the right to vote

1910

1920

The Statue of Liberty welcomed many immigrants to America.
■ **When was the statue dedicated?**

one who worked hard in America could get ahead.

Another reason people came to the United States was that they were poor and hungry. Many of the immigrants were farmers who had been able to own little or no land in their homelands. They had heard that there was a lot of good farmland to be found in this country.

Some young men left so that they would not have to serve in the army. Other people left their homelands because they did not have religious freedom there. Religious freedom was one of many rights all Americans had. Many immigrants wanted to live in America so that they could follow their own religion.

The Hard Voyage to a New Home

The immigrants came to America by ship. An immigrant could buy either a first-class, second-class, or **steerage ticket** on the ship. A steerage ticket was the lowest-priced ticket. Those who bought first- or second-class tickets stayed on the upper levels of the ship during the trip. People who bought steerage tickets had to stay on the bottom level of the ship. Most immigrants could only afford a steerage ticket.

The ships that brought immigrants to the United States were crowded. The food was poor, and living conditions in the steerage section were bad. The bottom level of the ship did not let in sunshine or fresh

The voyage to America was not comfortable for most immigrants.
■ What were conditions like for the immigrants on this ship?

air. The voyage from Europe to the United States usually took a few weeks or even a month! Some people became ill during the voyage.

After traveling for many days, the ships would finally reach the coast of the United States. One of the first sights the immigrants saw was the Statue of Liberty.

Miss Liberty   The Statue of Liberty arrived in America in 1885 as a gift from the people of France. The statue came to America by ship. The different parts of the statue were made in France. But because the statue was so huge, it could not be sent to America in one piece. Over 214 boxes were sent from France to America. The boxes held the different parts of the statue. Some boxes held pieces of the statue's hair and ears. Other boxes held the statue's eyebrows and feet.

On June 17, 1885, the boxes arrived at Bedloe's Island, now called Liberty Island, in New Jersey waters. The island was to be the Statue of Liberty's new home. American workers put the statue together. When they were finished, she stood 305 feet (93 m) tall on a beautiful rock pedestal. In October 1886, thousands of people gathered at Bedloe's Island for a special ceremony. Grover Cleveland, the President of the United States at the time and a New Jerseyan, officially accepted the statue on that day as a gift from the French.

Miss Liberty (top) stands tall against the New Jersey skyline.
■ What does the picture below show?

The Statue of Liberty is a symbol of friendship between two countries, France and the United States. She has welcomed many immigrants to the United States. To the immigrants she has been a symbol of freedom, hope, and opportunity in the United States of America.

Entering the United States After ships passed the Statue of Liberty, they left the immigrants at Castle Garden. At Castle Garden there was a large brick building where the immigrants were checked in to the United States. The immigrants were asked questions by the officers at Castle Garden. Criminals or very sick people were not allowed to come into this country. They were sent back to their homelands. Passing through Castle Garden was sometimes very easy. But for some immigrants, getting through the long waiting lines at Castle Garden took many hours and was a difficult experience.

In 1892 the immigration center at Castle Garden was replaced by Ellis Island. Ellis Island was a bigger and better center for immigrants. But so many thousands of immigrants came to the United States each year, the waiting lines at Ellis Island were just as long as those at Castle Garden. There were still questions to answer and tests to pass.

There were long lines and hours of waiting at the immigration centers at Castle Garden and Ellis Island. Immigrants were asked a variety of questions and given different tests. For many, arrival in America was a frightening and tiring experience.
■ What kind of test is this young German girl taking?

189

Starting a New Life Many immigrants decided to live in New Jersey. They had heard about the jobs in New Jersey's factories. They had also heard about the good farmland in New Jersey.

Life was not easy at first for the immigrants. Most felt scared in a new and strange land. Many had to learn to speak English. Most had little or no money. Their only possessions were the things they had been able to carry on their backs.

Many immigrants came to live in the cities. Most had to learn new skills to work in the factories. The immigrants worked hard and saved money. Many of them lived in tenements. After a while, some were able to open their own businesses.

The immigrants wanted their children to get a good education. They sent their children to New Jersey's schools. A good education was very important. It would help their children to get ahead.

New Jersey — Home to All Most of the immigrants learned a new way of living and of doing things in America. But they also kept some of their own **customs.** A custom is a special way of doing things. Different groups of immigrants had different customs. There were customs for religion, for marriages, and for other celebrations and parts of family life.

Sometimes immigrants were not well liked in New Jersey. People al-

Many immigrants make New Jersey their home today. The people shown here are becoming American citizens.
■ What are they reading?
■ Why have they raised their hands?

ready living in New Jersey thought some of the immigrants' customs were strange. This way of thinking was very unfair. Even though the immigrants did keep some of their own ways of doing things, they also tried very hard to become good Americans. They worked hard and helped the state to grow and become strong.

CHECKUP

1. Where did many of the immigrants come from between the years 1840 and 1920?
2. How did the immigrants travel?
3. What were some of the problems the immigrants faced in starting a new life in America?

4. **Thinking Critically** Compare life in the immigrants' homelands with the immigrants' new life in the United States.

Changing Cities

What changes came to New Jersey's cities in the early 1900s?

VOCABULARY

sewer   trolley car

Cities Continue to Grow   By 1910, New Jersey's population had reached 2½ million. Much of the increase in population was because of immigration. Between 1900 and 1920, thousands of immigrants settled in New Jersey. This caused the state's population to grow very fast in a short number of years.

Immigrants continued to move to New Jersey's cities. Because of this, the cities grew larger. Newark was the largest city. Other big cities included Jersey City, Paterson, and Trenton. Passaic's population grew rapidly with the arrival of immigrants. In 1910 it had nearly nine times more people than in 1880.

As the cities grew more crowded, there were more problems. Streets became tied up with traffic. Water became polluted as more and more garbage was dumped into rivers and streams. City schools had problems. There were more students in the schools but not enough classroom space for them.

As the problems in the crowded cities got worse, it became clear that some changes had to be made. Life in New Jersey's cities would have to be improved if the state wished to keep the cities strong.

City Life Improves   Changes in the cities were made slowly. But changes did happen. For example, the city of Newark spent millions of dollars to build new **sewers.** A sewer is an underground pipe that carries away water and waste products. The new sewers helped to keep the city cleaner. Other new pipes brought fresh water into Newark. This fresh water came from reservoirs in the hills of Passaic County.

Other changes included new streets. These streets were paved with stones. New schools were built, too. This was important for New Jersey's young people. But even with more schools, most of the city's children left school before the eighth grade. Many of them left by the fifth grade to go to work in the factories.

Many schools built earlier in this century are still in use.
■ Compare this Paterson school with your school.

Fosterfields and Longstreet Farm

Fosterfields and Longstreet Farm are two places in our state that show farming as it was many years ago. Fosterfields is a living history farm near Morristown. Longstreet Farm is another farm, near Holmdel. Fosterfields shows what a New Jersey farm looked like around 1900. Longstreet Farm is a farm of about 1890.

Many New Jersey farms of the period 1890 to 1900 were general farms. General farms are farms that produce many different crops and farm animals. Visitors to these two farms will see cattle, horses, pigs, and chickens, and a variety of crops. Workers at the farms dress the way people dressed in 1890 or 1900. They work on the farms in the same way and with the same kinds of wagons, tools, and machines that were in use 80 to 90 years ago. Visitors can see cows being milked and horses pulling plows. You can also see horses being fitted with new iron horseshoes. In the farmhouse you will be able to see how your great grandparents and great-great grandparents might have lived on a farm. What you will probably remember best if you visit Fosterfields or Longstreet Farm is how hard people worked around the turn of the century. Many of the machines and helpful inventions that we use today did not exist then. But living on a farm in those days must have been fun. You may wish that you could go back in time if you have a chance to visit Fosterfields or Longstreet Farm.

This trolley car ran to the community of Englewood.
■ **In what county did the trolley run?**

Better Transportation Transportation in the cities also began to change. In 1889 the first **trolley cars,** or electric streetcars, had already begun to run in Atlantic City. Newark also had trolley cars by 1890. It took time for the trolley car to become popular. New tracks had to be built for the trolley cars. Poles and electric wires were also needed to make the electric cars run. But the trolley car was a success. By 1914, trolley cars ran in every big city and many towns.

Trolley cars were not the only new way to travel. By 1900 another invention in transportation appeared. This invention was the automobile. In 1900 very few New Jerseyans owned automobiles. Trains, horse-drawn cars, and trolley cars were the most popular ways to travel. But over the next 15 years, more and more automobiles were seen on the roadways of our state.

CHECKUP
1. What problems did New Jersey's cities face in the early 1900s?
2. Name two important changes in transportation by 1900.
3. **Thinking Critically** Why was it important for the state to make sure that the cities stayed strong?

193

A Time of Reform

In what areas did New Jerseyans work for reforms from 1900 to 1914?

Government Reform The years 1900–1914 were a time of **reform.** A reform is a change that makes something better. There were reforms in many areas. Many people believed that reforms in government were needed. They were not happy with the government. There were some dishonest people in the government. Often certain people were able to get special favors from some dishonest **public officials.** A public official is a

Today, voting machines are used widely instead of ballots and ballot boxes. The large handle (center) closes a curtain behind the voter.
■ How does the woman cast her vote?

person who holds a public office. The dishonest public officials did not care about what was best for the people. They worked to gain power or money for themselves.

Election reforms were needed. People did not like the way their votes were counted during an election. Many people wanted better state laws for workers in the factories and other businesses. Women wanted reforms in government, too. In 1900 they still did not have the right to vote.

Governor Murphy Many people worked hard to get the reforms in government that were needed. In 1902, New Jersey Governor Franklin Murphy began to make some important changes in government. One of the biggest changes was the way in which people voted. A law passed in 1903 gave voters in New Jersey official **ballots** and official boxes in which the ballots would be placed. A ballot is a piece of paper that is used for voting in secret. Ballots and ballot boxes helped make elections fairer in New Jersey.

Governor Murphy made other changes. He was concerned about the thousands of young children working in the factories. Sometimes these children were not treated well. They were often paid a great deal less than adults who did the same job. Governor Murphy got a law passed that

This photograph of Governor Woodrow Wilson was taken in 1912.
■ Who, do you think, are the other people in the photograph?

helped protect children in the factories. This new law allowed only children 14 years or older to work in the factories. Children under the age of 14 could work only on farms, in stores, or on streets.

Governor Wilson In 1910 the people of New Jersey elected a governor who promised to carry out more reforms. This new governor was Woodrow Wilson. Wilson had been born in Virginia. He had attended Princeton University and had taught history there. Later he became president of the university.

Governor Wilson fought for the **primary system.** This system allows voters to choose the people who run for public office. Wilson also got a law passed that gave the state some control over the prices companies charged people for electricity, telephones, and natural gas. With Governor Wilson's help, another law was passed for the good of all working people. This law protected workers who were injured while on the job. It made the employers responsible for injuries. This law pushed factory and other business owners to improve safety conditions for workers.

Women Work for Reforms A number of New Jersey women spent their lives trying to make life better for other people. They formed women's clubs to do this. These clubs worked for reforms in factories, prisons, and schools. A new law supported by the women's clubs said that young boys could not work at night in the glass factories. Women also fought for better education. They wanted schools to start kindergartens for very young children. They also wanted more training for teachers and better schools for them to work in. Mabel Smith Douglass of Jersey City fought hard to start a state college just for women. She was successful. In 1918 the New Jersey College for Women opened. Later the college was renamed Douglass College. It is now part of Rutgers, The State University. The women's clubs also worked to open a separate prison for women. In 1910 the women's prison was started in Clinton.

The Road to Women's Rights Women still did not have the right to vote. They also did not have some other rights that men had. These included the right to have the same job opportunities as men and the same pay as men for doing the same work.

In 1866 some women had already begun to work for women's rights. They began with one of the most important rights of all — the

A student reads in her room at the New Jersey College for Women in the 1920s.
■ Has anyone in your family attended a college in New Jersey?

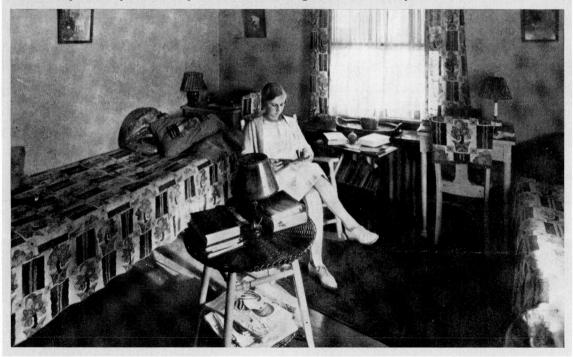

Women marched in Washington, D.C., to gain support for their cause.
■ Why, do you think, is Mary Philbrook shown at top left?

right to vote. Lucy Stone from Orange began a group called the New Jersey Suffrage League. Suffrage is the right to vote. Three years later a group called the National Suffrage League was started. Women from all over the country joined together to fight for the right to vote. Lucy Stone was one of the people who led this national group. She and many other women gave speeches and wrote articles about women's right to vote.

Slowly the National Suffrage League grew stronger. In New Jersey, women marched in parades or held **rallies** to support their ideas. A rally is a meeting of people for a special purpose or cause. In 1911 a woman named Mary Philbrook from Jersey City joined the fight for the right to vote. Philbrook was a well-known lawyer. Years earlier, Philbrook had fought the New Jersey government just to be allowed to practice law in the state. Now she worked very hard to help women get the right to vote. But this fight was a long and hard one. It was not until 1920 that American women gained the right to vote.

CHECKUP
1. What is a reform?
2. What were two important reforms that Governor Murphy made?
3. Who started New Jersey's first state college for women?
4. When did women get the right to vote?

5. **Thinking Critically** In what area, in your opinion, were the most important reforms made during the years 1900–1914?

Keeping a Diary

WHAT IS A DIARY?

A diary is a written record of what you do and how you feel about things that are important to you. Diaries can be important records of history. They can tell us how people in the past felt about events. Diaries can tell us about the daily lives of famous people or people who were not famous. They can give us a look at how life was in the past.

Here are some diary entries made by an immigrant named George. He left Greece to come to America in 1910.

July 14, 1910. Tomorrow the ship I am traveling on will reach America. I am very excited about starting my new life. I will also be glad to leave this ship. The trip has been long, and I have been seasick for many days. Other people on the ship are also excited. But some still feel a little sad about leaving their homes. I guess we are all a little scared about what we will find in America.

July 15. This morning I went up onto the top deck of the ship. It was crowded with people. We all watched as we passed by the Statue of Liberty. Finally the ship dropped anchor, and we all went down the gangplank onto Ellis Island. I had to wait in a long line so that I could get a medical examination. Finally the people at Ellis Island told me I could enter the United States. At first I wandered around the big brick building at Ellis Island. Then I saw the place where I could buy a ticket to New Jersey. My cousin John had written me a letter before I left Greece telling me to come to Newark, where he and his family already lived. He said I could live with him until I found a job and my own place to live.

July 16. My first morning in Newark, I woke up early and got dressed quickly. Mary, John, and their two children were still asleep in the small apartment. I decided to go out and look around the city by myself. As I walked out onto the street, people were already busy setting up vegetable and fruit stands for the day. Electric trains ran up and down the streets. I had never seen so many buildings in one place before.

SKILLS PRACTICE

Now use your imagination to write some diary entries. Imagine that you and your family are moving from Iowa to New Jersey. Your father will be working in a new office in Morristown. Write diary entries for your first 2 days in New Jersey. Tell how you traveled, what you did, and what you saw. Do not forget to write down a date for each diary entry. Anyone reading your diary in the future will be able to learn how you felt about moving to a new place in the 1980s.

CHAPTER 11 REVIEW

MAIN IDEAS

1. Immigrants came to New Jersey to find a new and better life. They had heard about the jobs in New Jersey's factories and other businesses and about the good farmland in the state.
2. The immigrants came to America from Ireland, Italy, Greece, Russia, and many other countries.
3. New sewers, water pipelines, streets, and schools were built in New Jersey's cities in the early 1900s. Trolley cars and automobiles became popular forms of transportation.
4. New Jerseyans worked for election and voting reforms and reforms in industry, education, and prisons.
5. Women won the right to vote in 1920.

VOCABULARY REVIEW

Write the word or words that best complete each sentence. Use a separate sheet of paper.

1. A person who comes to a country to make a home is an _____.
2. A _____ is a change that makes something better.
3. A special way of doing things is a _____.
4. A _____ is a piece of paper that is used for voting in secret.
5. The _____ allows voters to choose the people who run for public office.
6. The lowest-priced ticket on a ship is a _____.
7. An underground pipe that carries away water and waste products is a _____.
8. A _____ is a person who holds a public office.
9. A meeting of people for a special purpose or cause is a _____.
10. An electric streetcar is a _____.

CHAPTER CHECKUP

1. What is the Statue of Liberty?
2. What important reforms did New Jersey women work for?
3. **Thinking Critically** Do New Jersey's cities today face any of the same problems that they did in the early 1900s?
4. **Thinking Critically** Why were women not allowed to vote for such a long time?

APPLYING KNOWLEDGE

1. Immigrants coming to the United States in the early 1900s could not bring many of their belongings with them to their new home. As you read, they often could bring only what they could easily carry with them. Imagine that you are an immigrant. What possessions would you want to take to a new land? Explain why these belongings are important to you.
2. Take the part of Governor Franklin Murphy, Governor Woodrow Wilson, Mabel S. Douglass, or Mary Philbrook. Write a speech about a reform that you feel is needed. Your speech should explain why the reform is needed and who will be helped by it. Give your speech in class and try to win your classmates' support.

CHAPTER

12 New Jersey Through the World Wars and the 1950s

War, Good Times, and Bad Times

What was life like for New Jerseyans during World War I, the Twenties, and the Great Depression?

VOCABULARY

prosperity   stock

depression

A New Jerseyan Leads the Nation

As you learned in the last chapter, Governor Woodrow Wilson brought about important changes in our state.

Soon, people outside of New Jersey began to learn about Wilson's ideas. Many believed that he would make a good leader for the whole country. In 1912, Woodrow Wilson was elected President of the United States.

As President, Wilson wanted to work toward reforms, just as he had as governor of New Jersey. President Wilson worked for reforms in the areas of trade, banking, industry,

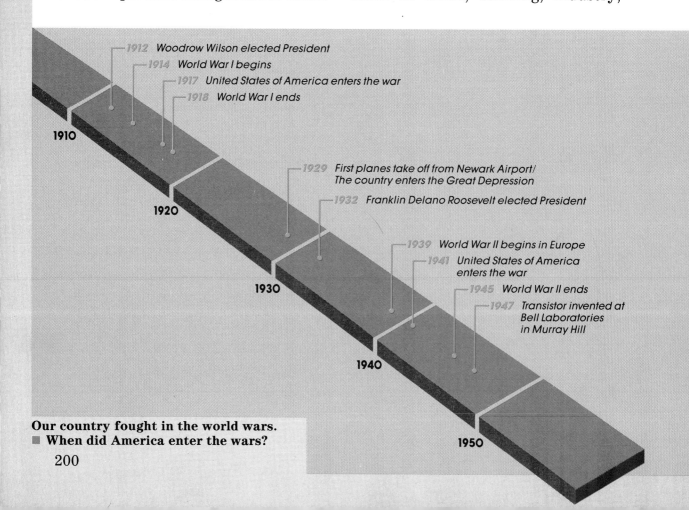

- 1912   Woodrow Wilson elected President
- 1914   World War I begins
- 1917   United States of America enters the war
- 1918   World War I ends

1910

- 1929   First planes take off from Newark Airport/ The country enters the Great Depression
- 1932   Franklin Delano Roosevelt elected President

1920

- 1939   World War II begins in Europe
- 1941   United States of America enters the war
- 1945   World War II ends
- 1947   Transistor invented at Bell Laboratories in Murray Hill

1930

1940

1950

Our country fought in the world wars.
■ **When did America enter the wars?**

200

agriculture, and child labor. But he never had a chance to work on all of his ideas for reforms, because a great war began in Europe in 1914.

New Jersey in World War I   The great war that began in 1914 became known as World War I. In 1917 the United States started fighting in that war. New Jersey helped the United States and its allies win the war. About 150,000 New Jerseyans helped fight the war. Over 3,000 died. New Jersey's 16 military bases trained many soldiers. Many of the soldiers sailed for Europe from the Hoboken docks.

Factories in New Jersey turned out many items that were needed for the war. These included guns, planes, trucks, tanks, tents, and blankets. Ammunition was also made in the state. Ammunition was made north of Dover at Picatinny Arsenal, which was owned by the United States Army. An ammunition factory for the war was built near Mays Landing. The over 6,500 workers at the factory lived in a town built especially for them by the government. The town was called Belcoville.

America needed a "bridge of ships" to send soldiers and supplies to Europe. Fast destroyers, transport ships, and great cargo ships were built at Camden. Shipyards in Newark, Kearny, and Elizabethport also put out many kinds of ships. New

hip-hip!

ANOTHER SHIP—
ANOTHER VICTORY

UNITED STATES SHIPPING BOARD ▩ EMERGENCY FLEET CORPORATION

BOYS and GIRLS!
You can Help your Uncle Sam
Win the War

W.S.S.

Save your Quarters
BUY WAR SAVINGS STAMPS

World War I posters raised spirits and asked for everyone's help.
■ How could children help?

Jersey-made submarines were also used in the war.

Only 19 months after America declared war, America and its allies won. World War I ended on November 11, 1918.

The Twenties New Jerseyans were glad when World War I ended. They wanted their country to be at peace. For most New Jerseyans the 1920s were a period of good times.

During World War I many people had grown tired of the old ways of doing things. They were ready for a change. There were many changes in the 1920s. There were new styles of clothing, new music, and new dances.

This 1926 magazine cover shows some of the new styles of the 1920s.
■ **What changes are shown?**

Industry, Skyscrapers, and Travel The 1920s saw the growth of some of the industries for which New Jersey is well known today. The chemical industry is one example. But it also saw the end of the important silk industry in Paterson. More than 30,000 people in the city of Paterson were left without work.

The other big cities in the state enjoyed some **prosperity** (prä sper′ ət ē). Prosperity is good times for the economy. In Trenton and Newark a number of skyscrapers were built. The port of Newark became more important. In 1928, work began on Newark Airport. A year later the airport saw thousands of planes take off. The airplane was still a somewhat new means of transportation. Buses, trolleys, and automobiles crowded city streets.

Traffic through the state was heavier than ever. New highways, bridges, and tunnels helped travelers in automobiles. The Pulaski Skyway was built between Newark and Jersey City. More and more means of transportation connected New Jersey to neighboring states. The Delaware River Bridge, between Camden and Philadelphia, was one of several bridges that opened in the 1920s. The Holland Tunnel, under the Hudson River between New York and New Jersey, had been completed a little earlier. It saw even greater traffic. Ferryboats, however, still carried most of the cars across the river.

202

The Great Depression Late in 1929 the United States entered a **depression** that lasted about 10 years. A depression is a time when many people have no jobs and very little money. The depression that began in 1929 was so terrible that it became known as the Great Depression. During the Great Depression many companies went out of business. Many banks closed, and some people lost their savings. Some people lost their jobs. Some people who still had jobs had their pay cut. People who were out of work did not have much money to spend, so they bought fewer goods. Factories had to close or make fewer products because stores were not able to sell their goods.

Hard Times for New Jersey The depression meant hard times for most Americans. Many New Jerseyans suffered. At one point, hundreds of thousands of New Jerseyans did not have jobs. Some families used up all their savings. Many people had to sell their homes and other things they owned just to get money to live on.

Some New Jerseyans did not have enough to eat. Churches and other organizations set up places to feed hungry people. Farmers received lower prices for their products. Many farmers had to sell their farms because they could not pay their bills. Americans wondered if good times would ever come again.

During the Great Depression, many New Jerseyans lost their jobs.
■ **What do these New Jerseyans want and whom do they blame?**

Fighting the Depression   In 1932, Franklin D. Roosevelt was elected President of the United States. As President, he started many programs to provide jobs to help fight the depression. One of these programs was the Civilian Conservation Corps (CCC). The CCC hired young men to work on conservation projects. They built wildlife shelters, **stocked** streams with fish, and planted trees. To stock is to provide with a supply of something. New Jerseyans in the CCC also helped to improve the state and county parks. For their work they received, in addition to room and meals, $30 a month.

Another program started by Roosevelt was the Works Progress Administration (WPA). The WPA gave jobs to more than 100,000 New Jerseyans who were out of work. WPA workers in New Jersey did many things. They put in sewer systems and built public schools, post offices, highways, and bridges. They built Roosevelt Stadium in Jersey City and a new boardwalk in Cape May, among other things.

Other programs started by President Roosevelt gave money to people out of work. They could use the money for food, clothing, and other items that they needed.

The Depression Begins to Lift   In the 1930s, war began in Europe and Asia. Many Americans were afraid that the United States would have to

The WPA provided jobs for many people during the depression.
■ What are these WPA workers doing?

enter the war. If war was coming, America would have to be prepared. That meant spending money for guns, planes, tanks, and other items needed for war. This created many new jobs. People went back to work. There was prosperity once again.

CHECKUP
1. What New Jersey governor became President of the United States of America?
2. Give two examples of the prosperity of the 1920s.
3. What was the purpose of the Civilian Conservation Corps (CCC)?
4. **Thinking Critically** Compare the 1920s to the depression years.

World War II

How did New Jerseyans help our nation during World War II?

The United States Enters World War II   The war that broke out in Europe and Asia in the 1930s became known as World War II. The United States entered World War II in 1941, when Japan attacked Pearl Harbor, in the Hawaiian Islands. Those Pacific islands were owned by the United States. Many American navy ships were sunk or damaged at Pearl Harbor. The United States declared war on Japan after the attack.

Japan had two allies—Germany and Italy. To help Japan, Germany and Italy declared war on the United States. The United States fought on the side of the United Kingdom of Great Britain and Northern Ireland, France, the Soviet Union, China, and some other countries.

New Jersey Lends a Hand   Over half a million men and women from New Jersey fought in World War II. Before the war was over, there were more than 13,000 dead from our state. Fort Dix, in the Pine Barrens, and Camp Kilmer, in Middlesex County, were important camps for the soldiers before they left to fight.

Once again New Jerseyans helped the war effort at home. New Jersey factories and businesses were very busy. A large number of women took many different kinds of jobs in the factories and other businesses. All kinds of ships were made in the shipyards of Camden, Kearny, and Newark. Airplane engines were made in Paterson. Factories in the state also made uniforms, radios, motors, and many other items.

Farmers were asked to raise more food. Food was needed for the soldiers. It was also needed to help feed people in Europe. The war caused a great deal of damage. It was hard for farmers in Europe to grow enough food.

During World War II, a large number of women worked at jobs that had before been closed to them.
- Where are these women working?
- What is their job?

Albert Einstein (1879 – 1955)

Albert Einstein was one of the world's greatest scientists. He was also an immigrant to the United States who made the state of New Jersey his home.

Germany was Einstein's birthplace. He was born in 1879. His parents moved to Switzerland when he was a child. Albert Einstein was what most people would call a genius. Yet when he was a boy, his teachers thought him backward and slow. He was not even very good in mathematics. All this changed as he got older.

Einstein moved back to Germany in 1914. By then he was a famous university professor. He left Germany in 1933, when Adolf Hitler and the Nazis came to power. Einstein was Jewish. The Nazis hated Jews. They had begun to take away most of the rights of German Jews. Einstein came to Princeton, where he had been invited to do research at the Institute for Advanced Study.

Albert Einstein was not the kind of scientist who works in a laboratory, surrounded by test tubes. He worked in a book-lined room, and pencils and paper were his tools. Einstein spent nearly all of his time thinking of theories, or explanations, of the ways that physical things in the universe work with or against each other. Einstein's work on atomic energy led to the development of the atomic bomb.

Einstein was happy living and working in Princeton. The community welcomed him not only as a world-famous scientist but as a neighbor and friend. In 1940, Einstein became an American citizen and a citizen of New Jersey.

Because our country was helping to feed soldiers and people in Europe, food was in short supply and expensive at home. To help grow more food, people who were not farmers planted **victory gardens.** These were small vegetable gardens. The vegetables were grown for family and friends. Young people about your age often took care of the gardens. That was how they helped to win the war.

Many goods, including some foods, were **rationed** during the war. To ration is to supply in a limited amount. Meat, sugar, butter, coffee, canned goods, shoes, tires, and gasoline were some of the things that people could buy only with ration stamps. Ration stamps were given to all families by the government. Every month these stamps could be picked up at the local post office. The number of stamps a family was given was determined by the size of the family. After a family used up its stamps, it could not get more until the next month.

The War Ends In 1945, World War II was over. Germany, Italy, and Japan had been defeated. The United States had the problem of changing from wartime to peacetime. Why was it a problem to change from war to peace? First, millions of men and women would be returning home from the war. These people would need jobs. Second, factories would have to change the kinds of goods

Ration stamps were printed in Hoboken and other places.
■ **Why were ration stamps used?**

they made. For example, the auto plants in Edgewater and Linden would start making automobiles again instead of parts for tanks and airplanes. There were many changes. In many ways, life was very different than it had been before the war.

CHECKUP

1. What countries were the United States' allies in World War II?
2. What is a victory garden?
3. What problem did New Jersey factories face after World War II?
4. **Thinking Critically** How was World War II good for the economy of our state and country?

207

The Years Following World War II

How was life in New Jersey different after World War II?

VOCABULARY

housing development	electronics
industrial park	satellite
public transportation	

More People Move to the Suburbs

Suburbs had begun to grow in the late 1800s. After World War II many more people began to move from the cities to the suburbs. People moved to the suburbs to get away from crowded cities. At first the suburbs had almost nothing but one-family houses. Often many houses were built on a piece of land all at the same time. This was called a **housing development.** Many places, such as Willingboro, grew from housing developments. Before long, many people were living in the suburbs and commuting to work in the cities.

Today many suburbs look much like cities. They do not have as many tall buildings as cities. But they do have apartment buildings. They also have large shopping centers. Some have **industrial parks.** These are large pieces of land that are set aside for factories, offices, and other buildings. In some places in New Jersey, it is hard to tell where the cities end and the suburbs begin.

Automobiles Help Suburbs to Grow

The automobile helped to make the

This housing development in New Jersey covers a lot of ground.
■ What besides houses is included in the housing development?

Subways are one form of public transportation. They are often found in large cities. The Newark subway helps people to get around the city of Newark.
■ Where and how do subways run?

move to the suburbs possible. Some people used **public transportation** to commute to the city. Buses, trains, and subways are public transportation. Most people drove their cars to and from work.

New Highways   Automobile commuters need more than just a car, though. They need good roads. Highways made it possible for New Jerseyans to live farther away from their jobs. Cars could travel at higher speeds on highways, making travel time shorter than on ordinary roads.

Both the New Jersey Turnpike and the Garden State Parkway were completed in the 1950s. The New Jersey Turnpike runs 141 miles (227 km) from the Delaware Memorial Bridge, at Deepwater in southwestern New Jersey, to Ridgefield Park, near the George Washington Bridge in the northeastern part of the state. The Garden State Parkway is a longer road. It runs 173 miles (278 km) from the southern tip of the state at Cape May to the New Jersey-New York border near Montvale.

Are either of these highways near you? The map on page 264 in the Atlas shows the major highways in New Jersey. These and other roads have helped to make travel easier.

209

Above is a model of *Telstar*, the first satellite to send television across the Atlantic Ocean.
■ **Why, do you think, is a transistor shown here?**

Space-age Industries Industry continued to grow in New Jersey after the war. New products began to appear. **Electronics** (i lek trän′ iks) was one industry that boomed. Electronics makes use of electricity to give us many wonderful things. Without electronics we would not have televisions, radios, or computers. An important part of many modern electronic devices is the transistor. The transistor was invented at Bell Laboratories in Murray Hill in 1947. The transistor is important in telephones, radios, space travel, and **satellites.** A satellite is a kind of spacecraft that moves around the earth. It can pick up telephone messages or television programs from stations on the earth. It sends these messages and programs to other parts of the earth. Some satellites gather information about the weather. The first weather satellite, *Tiros*, was made by RCA scientists in New Jersey.

The chemical industry also grew. Two products of this industry are medicines and vitamins. Certain vitamins were made first in New Jersey. Work on medicines and vitamins in New Jersey has helped improve the health of all Americans.

CHECKUP
1. Name two major highways in New Jersey that were built after World War II.
2. How has New Jersey been a leader in electronics and chemicals?
3. **Thinking Critically** Name three things that draw people from the cities to the suburbs.

Making an Outline for a Report

THE PURPOSE OF AN OUTLINE

A good report is well organized. The purpose of an outline is to help you organize your ideas. An outline is your plan for reporting. An outline may be written in question form. The answers to the questions will help you make your report.

OUTLINE

Below is an outline for a report. It is based on the sections about the 1920s and the Great Depression, on pages 202–204 of this chapter.

Read the outline below. Now read pages 202–204 again. Note how the outline follows the sections about the 1920s and the Great Depression.

The 1920s and the Great Depression
  I. What were the 1920s like?
 II. What happened in New Jersey during the 1920s?
III. What was the Great Depression?
 IV. How did New Jersey and New Jerseyans suffer during the depression?
  V. How did the United States fight the depression?
 VI. When and how did the Great Depression end?

SKILLS PRACTICE

Now try to write an outline on the topic of changes in America in the 1950s. Follow these steps in making your outline.

1. Ask yourself, "What do I want to know about my topic?"
2. Write down what you want to know in question form. Number your questions with Roman numerals.
3. Look for books or other materials that will help you answer your questions.
4. Under each question, write some information that will help you to answer the question.

Now you can make a well-organized report on your topic.

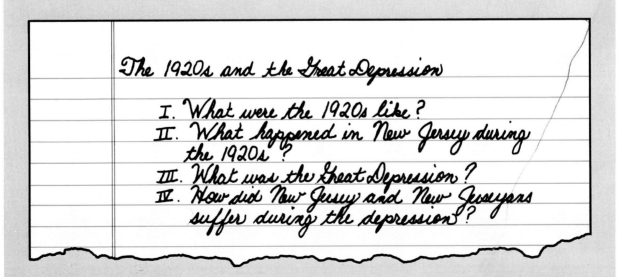

The 1920s and the Great Depression

  I. What were the 1920s like?
 II. What happened in New Jersey during the 1920s?
III. What was the Great Depression?
 IV. How did New Jersey and New Jerseyans suffer during the depression?

CHAPTER 12 REVIEW

MAIN IDEAS

1. New Jerseyans helped fight World War I and made many things needed for the war. The 1920s were a time of prosperity for most people. The years of the depression were hard times. Many people were out of work and had little or no money.
2. New Jerseyans fought in World War II. They also helped the war effort by making things for use in the war and raising food.
3. After World War II more people moved to the suburbs, where they could live in their own homes. The automobile made it possible for people to commute to work in the city. Major highways were built after the war, and industry became even more important in New Jersey.

VOCABULARY REVIEW

Write the word or words that best complete each sentence. Use a separate sheet of paper.

1. In a (housing development, depression), many houses are built on a piece of land at the same time.
2. A small vegetable garden planted for family and friends during World War II was a (satellite, victory garden).
3. A large piece of land used for factories, offices, and other buildings is an (electronic device, industrial park).

4. To provide with a supply of something is to (stock, ration).
5. (Prosperity, Public transportation) is good times for the economy.

CHAPTER CHECKUP

1. How did New Jersey help our country during World War I?
2. What were the two purposes of programs such as the Civilian Conservation Corps (CCC) and the Works Progress Administration (WPA)?
3. **Thinking Critically** Compare changes and growth in transportation in New Jersey before World War I and after World War II.
4. **Thinking Critically** Why are electronics and chemicals called space-age industries?

APPLYING KNOWLEDGE

1. Talk to your grandparents or older neighbors who lived during World War II. Ask what jobs they had, where they lived, what they did for entertainment, and similar questions. Using the information you gather, write a report that compares life in the United States during World War II with life in our country today.
2. Plan a victory garden. Draw a picture showing the size of your garden and the things you would plant.

SUMMARIZING UNIT 4

REVIEWING VOCABULARY

1. Immigrant   An immigrant is a person who comes to a country to make a home. Why did many people want to make a new home in the United States?

2. Custom   A custom is a special way of doing things. The different immigrants had different customs. Why, do you think, were customs important to the immigrants in their new home?

3. Reform   Many reforms, or changes that made life better, came about in the early twentieth century. What reforms in New Jersey directly affected children's lives?

4. Depression   Many people have no jobs and very little money during a depression. Why is the depression that began in 1929 in our country called the Great Depression?

5. Satellite   A satellite is a spacecraft that moves around the earth. What do satellites do? Name a satellite made or researched in New Jersey.

EXPRESSING YOURSELF

1. How Would You Feel?   Imagine that you are an immigrant to the United States. How would you feel when you saw the Statue of Liberty?

2. Who Would You Rather Be? If you were given the choice of being Governor Murphy, Mabel Smith Douglass, or Lucy Stone during the reform years 1900–1914, who would you choose to be? Explain your answer.

3. In What Ways?   Pretend that you are living during the Great Depression. You have just lost your job and have a large family to take care of. In what ways will life be different for you and your family?

4. What Would You Do?   The United States has entered World War II. Everyone is working hard to help the war effort. What would you do to help your country win the war?

5. What If?   After World War II many people left the cities for the suburbs. The suburbs began to grow and push into farmland and open space in New Jersey. If you were a farmer on a large farm that had been in your family for many years, would you sell your land for use as a housing development or industrial park? Why or why not?

New Jersey — Today and Tomorrow

In this unit you will learn about how New Jerseyans make things happen through the governments of their communities, state, and country. You will read about what life is like in the largest cities in our state. You will also learn about areas in which New Jersey is a leader and problems our state faces. This unit will give you ideas about your own future in New Jersey — what jobs you might like to have, places you might like to visit, and ways you might help to solve some of New Jersey's problems.

Laws for our state are made in Trenton by members of the state legislature. A meeting of the General Assembly is shown above.
■ How would you describe the meeting room of the General Assembly?

Boys and girls who take part in the Boys and Girls State
conventions each year learn about how government works.
■ Why, do you think, would such an experience be worthwhile?

You now know something about the land of our state, its people, and its history. The story of our state's past has taught you that people's actions make events happen. Today, New Jerseyans are still making things happen.

New Jersey is a major industrial state. Manufacturing is still strong in our state. Today, however, another industry is becoming larger and more important than ever before. This is the service industry. As you know, a service is something someone does for another person. Workers in the service industry do not make anything. They provide services other people want or need. New Jerseyans are

Charles Stansfield, Jr., an author of this book, teaches at Glassboro State College.
■ **What service does a teacher provide?**

served by salespeople, repair people, doctors, lawyers, nurses, social workers, librarians, teachers, firefighters, police, and other government workers.

Children and grandchildren are important members of family farms.
■ **What is this family group doing?**

Many farms in New Jersey today are still family farms. Farming is different than it used to be, though. Farmers must keep up on new ways of doing things on the farm and on new rules and laws that affect farming. They must also think about how they can market, or sell, their products.

216

Open space is important to the future of recreation in our state. People do not always agree about the use of open space. Some think open space should be used for recreation. These people want land to stay in its natural state. Others believe that open space should be used for housing and industry.

Some people wanted to turn the Great Swamp into a jetport. It is a wildlife refuge today.
■ What are these girls looking for?

Urban renewal projects have brought new life to many cities.
■ What are these workers doing to fix up this building?

The people of New Jersey's cities are working together to make their cities even better places to live. There are urban renewal projects in many New Jersey cities. The goal of these projects is to rebuild the cities. Sometimes urban renewal involves knocking down old buildings and putting up new ones. In some neighborhoods, people are fixing up old buildings for use as houses or offices. Sometimes the state or federal government gives money to cities to help urban renewal projects.

13 New Jersey's Government

State Government

What is state government?

Kinds of Government The **state government** of New Jersey is the government of all the people of New Jersey. Voters from all parts of the state elect people to make laws for them in Trenton, our state capital. A person must be a citizen of the United States, live in New Jersey, and be at least 18 years old to vote in New Jersey.

Voters in New Jersey also choose representatives to their **local governments.** County and city governments are two kinds of local government in New Jersey.

Our State Constitution A constitution is a set of laws by which a place is governed. The United States Constitution is the set of laws for our

The state capitol complex is made up of a number of buildings.
■ In what city is the capital located?

nation. Each of the 50 states also has its own constitution.

Over the years, New Jersey has had three constitutions. The first constitution for the state was written in 1776. New constitutions were written in 1844 and 1947. Each time our constitution was rewritten, it was changed to serve the people of New Jersey better. How long has our state had its present constitution?

The Capital City   Trenton was chosen as the capital of New Jersey in 1790. Before that, Burlington and Perth Amboy were both capitals of New Jersey. Between 1775 and 1790, however, no one place served as the capital of our state.

Once Trenton became New Jersey's capital, work began there on a special building called a **capitol.** *Capitol,* the word for the building where government leaders meet, sounds just like *capital,* the word for the special city where government leaders meet. You will notice, however, that the words *capitol* and *capital* are spelled differently.

The capitol is the most important building in Trenton. It is where our state leaders, including the governor, work. New Jersey's capitol is the second oldest state capitol in the United States. Work was started on the state capitol in 1792. The capitol has been added to over the years. After a fire in 1885, the capitol's present dome

Because of its round shape the room under a dome is called a rotunda. In our capitol this room is three stories high.
■ How is the rotunda decorated?

The capitol's dome is gilded.
■ What color is the dome?

was added. The top of the dome is gilded, or covered with a thin layer of real gold. Other major parts of the building were built between 1889 and 1907. The capitol's official name is the Statehouse.

CHECKUP

1. Who can vote in an election in the state of New Jersey?
2. Name two kinds of local government in our state.
3. How many constitutions has New Jersey had since the United States declared its independence from Great Britain in 1776?
4. Describe the history of and changes in the state capitol.
5. **Thinking Critically** What is the difference between state government and local government?

How New Jersey's State Government Works

What do the three branches of New Jersey's government do?

VOCABULARY

executive branch	bill
legislative branch	veto
judicial branch	justice
legislative district	

Branches of State Government
The state government has three branches, or parts. They are the **executive branch,** the **legislative branch,** and the **judicial branch.**

Executive Branch   The person who heads the executive branch of New Jersey's government is the governor.

The governor's job is to make sure that all of the state's laws are followed. The governor is the leader of the state.

The governor is elected for a 4-year term. He or she can be re-elected for a second 4-year term but cannot serve more than two terms in a row.

Legislative Branch   The laws of New Jersey are made by the legislative branch of the government. There are two parts to the legislative branch of the state government. They are the State Senate and the General Assembly.

The governor is the leader of the state of New Jersey.
■ What is the name of New Jersey's present governor?

HOW A BILL BECOMES A LAW

1. A member of the General Assembly or State Senate writes a bill.

2. The General Assembly and the State Senate approve the bill.

3. The governor signs the bill, and it becomes a law.

4. If the governor vetoes the bill, it goes back to the General Assembly and the State Senate.

5. The General Assembly and the State Senate vote again. If the bill gets 2/3 of the votes, it becomes a law.

The State Senate has 40 members, one for each **legislative district** in the state. A legislative district is a division of the state for the election of representatives to the state legislature. Each of the 40 districts in New Jersey has about the same number of people. The voters in each district elect one person to represent their district in the State Senate. These representatives are called senators. They serve a 4-year term.

The General Assembly has 80 members, two for each legislative district. Members of the General Assembly serve a 2-year term.

The job of the legislative branch is to make laws for New Jersey. To make a law, both the Senate and the General Assembly must approve a **bill**. A bill is a possible law. If a bill is approved, it is sent to the governor. If the governor also approves the bill, he or she signs it, and the bill becomes a law. But the governor may decide to **veto**, or turn down, the bill. When this happens, the legislature still has a chance to make the bill a law. If two thirds of the members of both the State Senate and the General Assembly approve the bill, it becomes a law. This means that 27 members of the State Senate and 54 members of the General Assembly must vote for the vetoed bill.

Judicial Branch   The branch of government that explains the laws is called the judicial branch. This branch makes certain that people

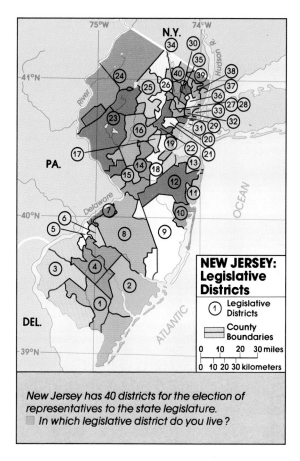

New Jersey has 40 districts for the election of representatives to the state legislature.
In which legislative district do you live?

who break the law are punished. The judicial branch is made up of a system of courts.

The state supreme court is the highest court in New Jersey. It is made up of a chief **justice**, or judge, and six associate justices. The governor appoints, or chooses, these seven judges. The State Senate must approve the governor's choices.

CHECKUP

1. Who is the leader of the state?
2. What are the two parts of the legislative branch?
3. What is the highest state court?
4. **Thinking Critically**   Compare the three branches of the government of New Jersey.

Local Government

What services do local governments in New Jersey provide?

VOCABULARY

county seat	board of chosen freeholders

County Government   As you know, New Jersey is divided into 21 counties. Each one has a **county seat**. A county seat is the town or city where the county government is located. The county courthouse and office buildings are found in the town or city that is the county seat.

Each county is governed by a **board of chosen freeholders**. The name *freeholder* comes from the days when New Jersey was a colony. At that time only freeholders, or property owners, could hold public office. Each county in the state has a board of three to nine freeholders. They are elected by the county's voters every 3 years. One of the freeholders on each board is elected director by the other freeholders on the board. It is the board's job to make the laws for the county. The board also sees that the laws are carried out.

The county government provides many other services. It keeps records of marriages, births, and deaths. It has a system of county courts and a police force. Can you name any other services a county government might provide?

This park ranger works for Morris County.
■ What, do you suppose, does her job involve?

The local government provides many services that are very important to the people in the community.
■ **What community services are shown here?**

Other Kinds of Local Government

There are cities, towns, townships, boroughs (bėr′ ōs), and villages in New Jersey. In which of these communities do you live?

Every city, town, township, borough, and village in New Jersey has a government. Like the government of a county, the government of a community provides many services. These services include police and fire protection. Other services provided by a community government may include schools, roads, libraries, and public health. The government of a community also decides where traffic lights will be placed. It may decide where and how trash will be picked up. It can also decide on the place to open a new park.

To provide services, local governments need money. People living in the community pay taxes on property they own. This money is used for community and county services.

CHECKUP

1. What is a county seat?
2. Explain the name *freeholder*.
3. What kinds of services do the governments of counties, cities, towns, townships, boroughs, and villages provide?
4. **Thinking Critically** Name an important service provided by the government of your community.

New Jersey and the Federal Government

Who represents New Jerseyans in Washington, D.C.?

VOCABULARY

congressional district

The Federal Government   Our nation is made up of separate states. Do you remember how many states there are? Each state can, as you have learned, govern itself in some ways. In other ways it is controlled by the federal government in Washington, D.C.

Electing Members of Congress   As citizens of the United States, New Jersey voters choose people to represent them in Congress. Congress is the legislative branch of the federal government. It meets in our nation's capital, Washington, D.C. The Congress of the United States is divided into two parts. One part is known as the Senate. The other part is the House of Representatives. You read in Chapter 9 that the two houses of Congress were the result of a compromise among the states.

Each state in the United States has two representatives in the United States Senate. These people are called senators. They are chosen for a 6-year term. Each senator represents his or her entire state.

The number of representatives from a state in the House of Representatives depends on how many people live in the state. States with

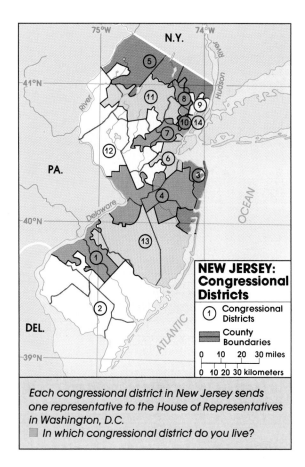

NEW JERSEY: Congressional Districts

- ① Congressional Districts
- ▬ County Boundaries

0   10   20   30 miles
0 10 20 30 kilometers

Each congressional district in New Jersey sends one representative to the House of Representatives in Washington, D.C.

▬ *In which congressional district do you live?*

large populations have more representatives. States with smaller populations have fewer representatives. New Jersey has 14 representatives in the House of Representatives. They serve 2-year terms.

New Jersey's representatives represent the people living in their **congressional districts**. A congressional district is a division of the state according to population for the election of representatives to Congress. Each of New Jersey's 14 congressional districts elects one person to serve in the House of Representatives in Washington, D.C.

226

SENATOR Bill Bradley

REPRESENTATIVE
Marge Roukema

SENATOR Frank Lautenberg

New Jersey sends 14 representatives and 2 senators to Congress. Marge Roukema is one of New Jersey's representatives.
■ **What are the names of New Jersey's senators?**

Electing the President New Jersey voters also help to choose the President of the United States. Presidential elections are held every 4 years, in the month of November. Any citizen of the United States 18 years or older may vote in a Presidential election.

CHECKUP

1. What is the legislative branch of the federal government called?
2. Whom does a senator represent?
3. How many representatives does New Jersey have in the House of Representatives of the Congress?
4. **Thinking Critically** How do senators and representatives differ?

227

Reading Pictures

PICTURES TELL STORIES

On pages 12–13 you can see some symbols of our state. You can see that our flower is the purple violet and our bird is the eastern goldfinch.

In 1982 the United States Postal Service issued 50 stamps showing state birds and state flowers. A different stamp for each state shows the official state bird and flower and gives their names. The name of the state, its bird, and its flower are given in the same places on each stamp. Twelve of these state stamps are shown at the bottom of this page. Find the 12 states on the map on pages 262–263.

SKILLS PRACTICE

Study the 12 stamps below and complete the following steps. Write your answers on a separate sheet of paper.

1. Make an alphabetical list of the states the stamps represent.
2. What are the state bird and state flower of Montana? Of Oregon?
3. Which state has the mountain laurel as its state flower?
4. Which state has the lilac as its state flower? Name the state that has a cardinal as its state bird. What color is the cardinal?
5. List the state birds of Rhode Island, Nevada, and Oklahoma.

CHAPTER 13 REVIEW

MAIN IDEAS

1. There are three levels of government — federal, state, and local.
2. The state government of New Jersey is the government of all the people of New Jersey.
3. New Jersey has had three constitutions. The latest was written in 1947.
4. There are three branches of state government. They are the executive branch, the legislative branch, and the judicial branch.
5. The legislative branch makes the laws. The executive branch carries out the laws. The judicial branch explains the laws.
6. The governor is the leader of the state.
7. Local governments provide police and fire protection, keep records, and take care of roads, among other things.
8. New Jerseyans elect 2 senators, 14 representatives, and the President to represent them in Washington, D.C.

VOCABULARY REVIEW

Match the terms with their definitions. Use a separate sheet of paper.

a. legislative branch
b. veto
c. capitol
d. bill
e. justice
f. legislative district
g. county seat
h. board of chosen freeholders
i. congressional district
j. state government

1. A judge
2. The government of all the people of New Jersey
3. A possible law
4. To turn down
5. The lawmaking part of government
6. The people who make laws for a county and see that the laws are carried out
7. The town or city where a county government is located
8. A division of the state according to population for the election of representatives to Congress
9. The building in which the governor and other state leaders work
10. A division of the state for the election of representatives to the State Senate and General Assembly

CHAPTER CHECKUP

1. Name the three different levels of government.
2. What can the State Senate and General Assembly do about a vetoed bill?
3. Would the state government work without the judicial branch?
4. What do senators and representatives in Washington, D.C., do?
5. **Thinking Critically** What level of government, do you think, affects you most directly?
6. **Thinking Critically** Why is it important to vote when you reach 18 years of age?

APPLYING KNOWLEDGE

Find out the names of the people who represent you in the United States Senate and the House of Representatives in Washington, D.C., and in the State Senate and the General Assembly in Trenton. Show the information you have found on a chart. Use the headings *United States Congress* and *New Jersey State Legislature* on your chart.

14 New Jersey's Cities

The Jersey City-Newark-Elizabeth Urban Area

What industries are important in this great urban area?

VOCABULARY

urban area	planetarium
Hispanic	container
ethnic	

Why People Live in Cities Where do you live? Do you live in a large city? Or do you live near a large city, in one of its suburbs? Do you live in an apartment or a house? Perhaps you live on a farm out in the country.

New Jersey has many kinds of places where people live. But most New Jerseyans live in cities or **urban areas.** An urban area can be made up of a large city and its suburbs or many separate cities and their suburbs. New Jersey is the second most urban state in the nation. About 89 percent of New Jerseyans live in urban areas. Only the state of California is more urban.

Can you think of reasons why people live in cities? If you said there

Journal Square Transportation Center is a landmark in Jersey City. The tall part of the building is shaped like a T. Commuters take trains and buses from the center.
■ **What else, do you think, do people do at the center?**

are many jobs in cities, you are right. But there are other reasons, too. In cities there are many things to do. You can visit museums, tall buildings, parks, and zoos. You can watch sports. You can see plays and hear concerts. You are close to shopping and schools.

A Trip Through New Jersey's Cities A car trip through some of New Jersey's cities would be interesting. We will start in the urban area formed by the cities of Jersey City, Newark, and Elizabeth.

Jersey City Jersey City is the easternmost city in the urban area formed by the three cities. This city is located on the Hudson River across from New York City. With a population of over 200,000, it is the second largest city in our state.

Jersey City has a busy port. It is also an important railroad center. Goods made in the city include chemicals, paper products, clothing, and toys. In addition to being a center for trade, transportation, and industry, Jersey City is the home of several colleges. St. Peter's College and Jersey City State College are two schools in Jersey City.

Jersey City is also the site of a beautiful park on the Hudson River. The park is called Liberty State Park. From Liberty State Park, visitors can see the Statue of Liberty as they fish,

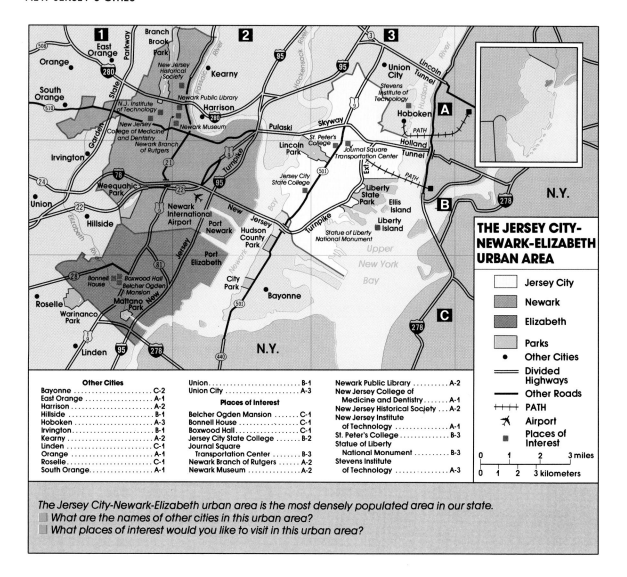

THE JERSEY CITY-NEWARK-ELIZABETH URBAN AREA

□	Jersey City
▨	Newark
▰	Elizabeth
▨	Parks
•	Other Cities
══	Divided Highways
—	Other Roads
┼┼┼┼	PATH
✈	Airport
▪	Places of Interest

0   1   2   3 miles
0   1   2   3 kilometers

Other Cities

Bayonne	C-2
East Orange	A-1
Harrison	A-2
Hillside	B-1
Hoboken	A-3
Irvington	B-1
Kearny	A-2
Linden	C-1
Orange	A-1
Roselle	C-1
South Orange	A-1
Union	B-1
Union City	A-3

Places of Interest

Belcher Ogden Mansion	C-1
Bonnell House	C-1
Boxwood Hall	C-1
Jersey City State College	B-2
Journal Square Transportation Center	B-3
Newark Branch of Rutgers	A-2
Newark Museum	A-2
Newark Public Library	A-2
New Jersey College of Medicine and Dentistry	A-1
New Jersey Historical Society	A-2
New Jersey Institute of Technology	A-1
St. Peter's College	B-3
Statue of Liberty National Monument	B-3
Stevens Institute of Technology	A-3

The Jersey City-Newark-Elizabeth urban area is the most densely populated area in our state.
▨ What are the names of other cities in this urban area?
▨ What places of interest would you like to visit in this urban area?

picnic, and play. It is also possible to take a ferry from the park to the Statue of Liberty or Ellis Island.

In recent years, block associations, or groups, have worked hard to make Jersey City neighborhoods pleasant places to live and visit. Their wish has brought old neighborhoods back to life. The Italian Village is one such "new" community.

To the north of Jersey City is Hoboken. Hoboken is also on the Hudson. It, too, is an important railroad center. Many people commute to Hoboken by train and then take PATH trains under the Hudson to New York City. Hoboken was once a major industrial port and shipping center. Today old houses and factories are being fixed up for use as homes and offices. We might stop at one of the popular good restaurants in Hoboken. Art exhibits, plays, concerts, and dance festivals also bring people to this city. It is also the home of Stevens Institute of Technology.

Just north of Hoboken is Union City. Union City is an industrial center. It has the largest percentage of **Hispanic** people of any city in our state. A Hispanic is a person with a Spanish language background. On our visit to Union City, we would see many shop signs in Spanish.

To the south of Jersey City is Bayonne. This city had one of the first oil refineries in America. It is still an important oil-refining center. There are many docks and shipyards in Bayonne.

Newark   If we travel across the Pulaski Skyway from Jersey City, we come to our state's largest city — Newark. Over 300,000 people live in Newark. The people of Newark have many different backgrounds. There are strong **ethnic** groups and neighborhoods in the city. *Ethnic* means "having to do with a group of people who share language, customs, and often the same religion and country of origin." Italian Americans, German Americans, and Portuguese Americans live in Newark. Other groups are also important. Blacks make up over half of Newark's population. A large number of Hispanics also live in the city.

Standing on the busiest street corner in Newark, we would see many tall buildings. Today, beautiful new office buildings tower above older skyscrapers. Many people work in these buildings. Newark is an insurance and banking center. Of-

Newark is an important insurance and banking center.
■ **What Newark businesses are shown in this photograph?**

fice workers in Newark also work for electric and telephone companies and for the government.

Many different kinds of things are manufactured in Newark. These include electrical equipment, paints, chemicals, machinery, and jewelry. Beverages and canned goods are other Newark products.

The city of Newark is also a port. Many goods from other countries, such as cars and lumber, enter our country at Port Newark. Goods from our state and country also leave the port for other parts of the world. Newark International Airport is also important to trade and travel. The airport was enlarged and rebuilt in the 1970s.

Newark is also the home of many schools. Both the New Jersey Institute of Technology and the University of Medicine and Dentistry of New Jersey are located in Newark. Rutgers, The State University, also has a branch in the city.

Newark Public Library is one of the largest libraries in the state. The nearby Newark Museum is well known for its collection of American art and its science and natural history exhibits. It also has a **planetarium.** This is a building that has a cameralike machine that shows how the planets and stars look in the sky. The New Jersey Historical Society is also in Newark. Historic objects are preserved in its museum.

Newark International Airport handles flights to and from other parts of our country and the world.
■ **What is the building shown at the right?**

Branch Brook Park in Newark covers 486 acres (197 ha) and has around 3,500 Japanese cherry trees.
■ **Why are parks important to families living in the city?**

Two parks in Newark also attract many people. They are Weequahic and Branch Brook parks. Branch Brook Park was the country's first county recreation area. It has thousands of Japanese cherry trees. When the trees bloom in April, the Cherry Blossom Festival is held. Cherry blossom time in Branch Brook Park is a beautiful sight.

For some years, many people have been leaving Newark to live somewhere else. The city has had its problems. Living conditions have been poor for many people. Housing programs have helped the city. Old buildings have been repaired and new housing has been built with state and federal money.

Elizabeth Just south of Newark is Elizabeth, New Jersey's fourth largest city. Elizabeth has a population of over 100,000.

There are many different industries in Elizabeth. Machinery, chemicals, mattresses, cookies, clothing, and other products are made in the city. There are also oil refineries, steelworks, and shipbuilding yards in Elizabeth.

The new port of Elizabeth opened in 1962. It includes piers for 30 ocean-going ships and many warehouses. Sea-Land Service, a large shipping firm, is based in Port Elizabeth. Port Elizabeth and Port Newark were the world's first **container** ports. Containers are large steel

Containers are stacked on a ship in Port Elizabeth.
■ Where are the cranes that lift the containers?

boxes that can be filled with goods. The containers are used for shipping. They are moved on and off container ships quickly by huge cranes. Elizabeth shares Newark Airport with Newark. Part of the airport is located within the city limits of Elizabeth.

Elizabeth's early history is sometimes said to be also that of New Jersey. That is because many important people and events in New Jersey history are connected with the city. Visitors to Elizabeth can trace the city's history in many old houses, churches, and graveyards. Some historic buildings are gone now, but historical markers stand at different sites. Many historic buildings and sites are found on Broad Street, East Jersey Street, West Jersey Street, and Rahway Avenue. Many people visit Boxwood Hall, Belcher Ogden Mansion, and Bonnell House each year. Elizabeth Avenue, an important street in the city, is probably the oldest highway in New Jersey.

There are many neighborhood parks in Elizabeth. Warinanco Park and Mattano Park are two larger parks enjoyed by the people of Elizabeth. The population of Elizabeth includes many recent immigrants. A large group of Cuban immigrants has settled in the city.

CHECKUP

1. What is an urban area?
2. What can people do at Liberty State Park in Jersey City?
3. What is the largest city in the state of New Jersey?
4. What is special about Port Elizabeth and Port Newark?

5. **Thinking Critically** How does the location of Jersey City, Newark, and Elizabeth affect industry in the three cities?

The Paterson-Clifton-Passaic Urban Area

How has the Passaic River been important to the three cities in this urban area?

VOCABULARY

historic district   textile
resident

Another Major Urban Area   Another urban area is formed by Paterson, Clifton, and Passaic. Paterson is the third largest city in our state. Its population is over 100,000. The urban area of Paterson, Clifton, and Passaic has over 400,000 people.

Paterson   You learned in Chapter 9 that Paterson began as a manufacturing center. Over the years, industry has changed in the city. At different times, Paterson was known for silk, locomotives, and airplane engines. Paterson's factories are still busy. Clothing, plastics, and machinery are some of the products made in Paterson.

In the 1960s and 1970s the people of Paterson became interested in preserving the history of industry in their city. They formed a group called the Great Falls Development Corporation. The group wanted to save the **historic district** around the Great Falls of the Passaic River. A historic district is an area of great historic interest. As you remember, the Great Falls was where the industrial center was started. In 1976 the Great Falls area was made a National Historic Landmark District. Visitors to this area today can see many different uses of the old mills. The Rogers Locomotive Erecting Shop,

This is the site of the Paterson Museum.
■ What can be seen in its yard?

1835
REBUILT. 1871.
ROGERS
LOCOMOTIVE
& M. WORKS.

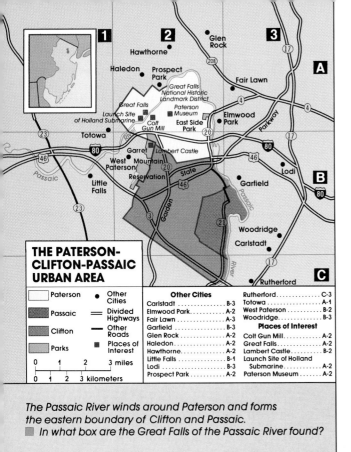

THE PATERSON-CLIFTON-PASSAIC URBAN AREA

Paterson		●	Other Cities
Passaic		=	Divided Highways
Clifton		—	Other Roads
Parks		■	Places of Interest

| 0 | 1 | 2 | 3 miles |
| 0 | 1 | 2 | 3 kilometers |

Other Cities
Carlstadt B-3
Elmwood Park........... A-2
Fair Lawn A-3
Garfield B-3
Glen Rock A-2
Haledon................. A-2
Hawthorne.............. A-2
Little Falls B-1
Lodi B-3
Prospect Park A-2

Rutherford............. C-3
Totowa A-1
West Paterson B-2
Woodridge.............. B-3

Places of Interest
Colt Gun Mill........... A-2
Great Falls.............. A-2
Lambert Castle.......... B-2
Launch Site of Holland
 Submarine............. A-2
Paterson Museum A-2

The Passaic River winds around Paterson and forms the eastern boundary of Clifton and Passaic.
■ *In what box are the Great Falls of the Passaic River found?*

which was rebuilt in 1871, is the home of the Paterson Museum. In the museum, tourists can learn about Paterson's growth. They can also see locomotives made in Paterson many years ago. Other mills in the district have been set aside for use as artists' lofts, art galleries, special shops, restaurants, and housing. The historic district has given jobs to many people living in Paterson.

Visitors and **residents** alike enjoy the Great Falls Festival. A resident is a person who lives in a place. The festival is held in the historic district each year on Labor Day weekend. There are tours of the historic area, rides, ethnic foods, and daredevil, or daring, acts above the Falls. At all times of year, people vis-

iting or living in Paterson enjoy the out-of-doors at Garret Mountain Reservation. Garret Mountain Reservation is a park on a rocky ridge overlooking Paterson. Lambert Castle is in the park and is a popular sight.

Clifton   Clifton has grown rapidly since World War II. Today it is a city of over 70,000 people. Like its neighbors to the north and south, Paterson and Passaic, it is on the Passaic River. It is an industrial city that manufactures **textiles,** steel, and chemicals. Textiles are woven fabrics or cloth.

Passaic   Just to the south of Clifton is the city of Passaic. Over 50,000 people live in Passaic. Immigrants from eastern Europe helped Passaic grow in the early part of this century. Today there are still many different ethnic groups in the city.

The waterpower of the Passaic River has also been important to the textile industry in Passaic. Other products manufactured in Passaic include chemicals, drugs, aircraft parts, electronic parts, plastics, and sporting goods.

CHECKUP
1. What can visitors see in the Great Falls Historic District?
2. About how many people live in the city of Clifton?
3. **Thinking Critically** Compare the industries, new and old, of Paterson, Clifton, and Passaic.

Trenton and Camden

Why is location important to both Trenton and Camden?

VOCABULARY

cable	cannery
ceramic	campus

Trenton   From the Jersey City-Newark-Elizabeth and Paterson-Clifton-Passaic urban areas, we travel southwest to Trenton, the capital of New Jersey. Have you ever thought about the best location for a state capital? State senators and assembly members must all travel frequently to the state capital. Citizens who need to visit state offices in the capital come from all parts of the state. For this reason the best location for a state capital is in the center of the state. Trenton is located on the Delaware River just west of the center of New Jersey. Most New Jerseyans can reach the city of Trenton by car in 2 hours or less.

As you read in Chapter 13, Trenton has served as our state's capital since 1790. Today over 50,000 people in Trenton work for the state government. The state capitol complex is where many state offices, including the governor's office, are located. As you remember, it is also where the state legislature meets. Also part of the complex are the State Library and the State Museum. Members of the state government and many other New Jerseyans use the State Library. The State Library has large

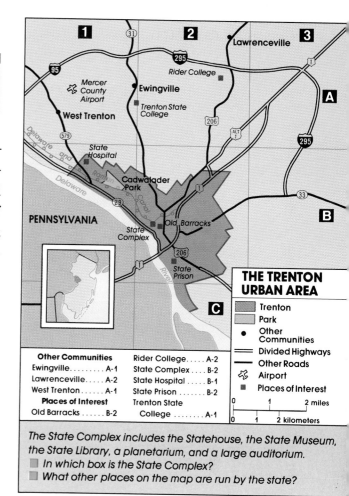

THE TRENTON URBAN AREA

Legend:
- Trenton
- Park
- • Other Communities
- ═ Divided Highways
- ── Other Roads
- Airport
- ■ Places of Interest

0 — 1 — 2 miles
0 — 1 — 2 kilometers

Other Communities
Ewingville.........A-1
Lawrenceville.....A-2
West Trenton......A-1

Places of Interest
Old Barracks......B-2

Rider College.....A-2
State Complex....B-2
State Hospital.....B-1
State Prison.......B-2
Trenton State College........A-1

The State Complex includes the Statehouse, the State Museum, the State Library, a planetarium, and a large auditorium.
■ In which box is the State Complex?
■ What other places on the map are run by the state?

law and reference collections. The State Museum has fine art, historical, and natural history exhibits. Nearby are a large auditorium and a planetarium for public use.

Trenton is also an important manufacturing center. Just outside the city, on a bridge over the Delaware River, is a sign that says "Trenton makes, the world takes." The sign tells of the importance of Trenton's industry to the rest of the world. Wire ropes, or **cables,** are one Trenton product.   Trenton-made

239

cables support many bridges, including the Brooklyn Bridge and the George Washington Bridge. **Ceramic** (sə ram′ ik) goods are also made in the city. Ceramic products are made out of minerals that are not metals, such as clay. These nonmetal materials are baked at very high temperatures. Ceramic goods made in Trenton include tile and decorative porcelain, such as figurines.

Jobs in Trenton's factories have brought people to the city over the years. Today, Trenton is New Jersey's fifth largest city, with a population of around 90,000. Trenton is also home to students at Trenton State College and Rider College.

Camden   On the Delaware River south of Trenton and across from Philadelphia is Camden, New Jersey's sixth largest city. Over 80,000 people live in Camden.

Camden is the most important port in southern New Jersey. Over 2 million tons (1,814,000 t) of goods are handled at the Port of Camden each year. There are busy factories in Camden that produce electronic items, chemicals, and auto parts. There are also **canneries**, or food-processing plants, in Camden.

The Campbell Museum in Camden has a large collection of soup bowls and ladles, or serving spoons, from all ages. Residents and visitors

The ceramic industry has been important to Trenton for many years. This woman is working on a porcelain figurine.
■ What is she doing to the figurine?

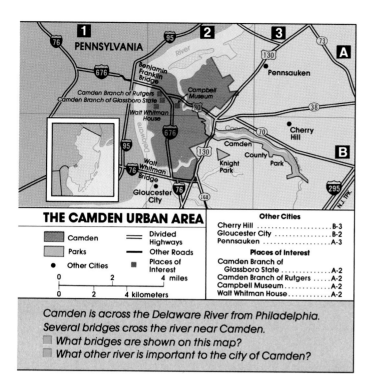

THE CAMDEN URBAN AREA

▧ Camden		═══ Divided Highways	
▢ Parks		── Other Roads	
● Other Cities		■ Places of Interest	

0 — 2 — 4 miles
0 — 2 — 4 kilometers

Other Cities
Cherry Hill B-3
Gloucester City B-2
Pennsauken A-3

Places of Interest
Camden Branch of
　Glassboro State A-2
Camden Branch of Rutgers A-2
Campbell Museum A-2
Walt Whitman House A-2

Camden is across the Delaware River from Philadelphia.
Several bridges cross the river near Camden.
▢ What bridges are shown on this map?
▢ What other river is important to the city of Camden?

can enjoy a new waterfront park where ferries from Philadelphia once landed. Today, people can relax under trees in the park, enjoy the cool breezes, and watch ships go by on the Delaware River.

Two state schools, Rutgers and Glassboro State College, have branch **campuses** in Camden. A campus is a group of school buildings in a park-like setting. These branches allow Camden residents to take college courses without leaving their city.

Tour's End　Our journey through some of New Jersey's cities is at an end. There are many other cities and towns in the state that are well worth visiting and knowing. As we said at the beginning of the chapter, New Jersey is very urban. It is a land of cities.

The Rutgers campus in Camden is like a park.
■ Why is this good for studying?

CHECKUP

1. About how many people in the city of Trenton work for the state government?
2. What can be found at the State Library in Trenton?
3. What sights bring visitors to the city of Camden?
4. **Thinking Critically** Why, do you think, is Camden the most important port in southern New Jersey?

Reading a Mileage Table

WHAT IS A MILEAGE TABLE?

As you know, a table is a good way to organize facts. The table below shows the distance between some cities in New Jersey. It is called a mileage table.

Suppose you wanted to go from Trenton to Newark. Put a finger on Trenton in the left column. Put a finger of your other hand on Newark in the top row. Now move both fingers, one across and one down, until they meet. They should meet at 49. It is 49 miles (79 km) between the two cities.

SKILLS PRACTICE

It takes a little practice to read a mileage table. Soon it will be easy for you. Practice your table-reading skills by reading the table and answering these questions.
1. How many miles is it from Jersey City to Cape May?
2. Which two cities are the farthest apart? Look for the largest number on the table, and then move one finger up to the name of the second city.
3. How far is it from Paterson to Clifton? From Clifton to Salem?

MILEAGE TABLE	Asbury Park	Atlantic City	Camden	Cape May	Clifton	Elizabeth	Flemington	Hackensack	Jersey City	Long Branch	Morristown	Newark	New Brunswick	Paterson	Phillipsburg	Salem	Trenton	Vineland
Atlantic City	78		59	40	118	103	98	123	112	82	126	108	93	121	124	63	75	35
Camden	76	59		80	93	79	57	98	90	69	74	83	58	90	83	35	34	33
Cape May	111	40	80		165	150	123	159	148	115	161	155	125	169	149	69	100	48
Clifton	55	118	93	165		16	53	6	13	54	20	10	36	4	72	127	61	130
Elizabeth	40	103	79	150	16		37	21	16	40	16	5	20	19	59	112	44	109
Flemington	63	98	57	123	53	37		57	47	54	31	41	25	55	25	90	23	84
Hackensack	60	123	98	159	6	21	57		15	55	32	15	40	8	77	132	61	129
Jersey City	51	112	90	148	13	16	47	15		46	22	6	31	22	68	123	55	120
Long Branch	9	82	69	115	54	40	54	55	46		56	45	34	59	70	135	46	68
Morristown	71	126	74	161	20	16	31	32	22	56		16	33	24	42	121	51	121
Newark	45	108	83	155	10	5	41	15	6	45	16		25	14	62	117	49	114
New Brunswick	38	93	58	125	36	20	25	40	31	34	33	25		41	47	92	25	89
Paterson	59	121	90	169	4	19	55	8	22	59	24	14	41		59	131	67	120
Phillipsburg	88	124	83	149	72	59	25	77	68	70	42	62	47	59		116	49	110
Salem	126	63	35	69	127	112	90	132	123	135	121	117	92	131	116		67	28
Trenton	42	75	34	100	61	44	23	61	55	46	51	49	25	67	49	67		61
Vineland	104	35	33	48	130	109	84	129	120	68	121	114	89	120	110	28	61	

CHAPTER 14 REVIEW

MAIN IDEAS

1. New Jersey is the second most urban state in the United States. About 89 percent of New Jerseyans live in urban areas.
2. In order of size from largest to smallest, the six largest cities in New Jersey are Newark, Jersey City, Paterson, Elizabeth, Trenton, and Camden.
3. Shipping, oil-refining, and chemical, machinery, and clothing manufacturing are some of the important industries in the Jersey City-Newark-Elizabeth urban area.
4. The Passaic River has offered waterpower to industry in the Paterson-Clifton-Passaic urban area. This power has been very useful for textile manufacturing in the three cities.
5. Trenton's location near the center of the state is important to that city as the state capital. Camden's location on the Delaware River across from Philadelphia has made it a strong industrial center and the most important port in southern New Jersey.

VOCABULARY REVIEW

Fill in each blank with the word or words that best complete each sentence. Use a separate sheet of paper.

1. A _____ is a large steel box that can be filled with goods for shipping.
2. An _____ can be made up of a large city and its suburbs or many separate cities and their suburbs.
3. An area of great historic interest is a _____ .
4. A _____ is a factory where food is processed.
5. A _____ is a person with a Spanish language background.

CHAPTER CHECKUP

1. Explain why many people like to live in cities.
2. What is an ethnic neighborhood?
3. Describe what happens at the container port of Elizabeth.
4. **Thinking Critically** Why would the Great Falls historic district be of interest to people who are from states other than New Jersey?
5. **Thinking Critically** Why is a city like Camden a good location for a branch campus of Rutgers?
6. **Thinking Critically** What other cities or towns in our state would you like to learn more about?

APPLYING KNOWLEDGE

1. Find out about the city or town in which you live. If you do not live in a city or town, find out about one near you. Write a brief report. Your report should (1) locate the city or town on a map of New Jersey, (2) list the cities and other landmarks around it, and (3) briefly tell some important things about the city or town.
2. Pretend that you have been asked to design a city. Your plan or map should include the following: (1) a business center, (2) a transportation system, (3) parks, (4) neighborhoods of houses, (5) schools, and (6) museums, theaters, and concert halls. Draw your city plan on a large piece of paper for posting.

15 New Jersey: A Leader Among the States

A National Leader

In what areas is New Jersey a national leader?

VOCABULARY

Megalopolis	foreign trade
specialize	import
commerce	export

Location Is Important As you have read, New Jersey has been called a crossroads and a corridor. Our state has been a busy place from early times. It has been the scene of many important events in our country's history. The location of our state was important in the past. It is still important today.

New Jersey belongs to the Middle Atlantic Region. This region is made up of the states in the middle of the east coast of our country. As the map on page 246 shows, these states lie between the northeastern states

and the southeastern states. Most of the Middle Atlantic states, including New Jersey, are near the Atlantic Ocean. New Jersey lies at the center of the region. It is a busy and prosperous member of the Middle Atlantic Region. *Prosperous* means "enjoying healthy growth."

New Jersey belongs to another region on the east coast. This region is known as **Megalopolis**. A megalopolis is a supercity. It is the word used for the region of big cities, smaller cities, towns, and other communities from Boston, Massachusetts, to Washington, D. C. The big cities of Newark, Jersey City, Elizabeth, Paterson, Trenton, and Camden, and other communities in our state are part of the chain of cities that make up Megalopolis.

As the map on page 246 shows, New Jersey has a good location in Megalopolis. It is located in the middle of the region. It also lies between New York City and Philadelphia. Nearly one fifth of all the people in the United States live within a day's drive of our state. People can get to New Jersey quickly by car, bus, and train. Some people come from other states each day to work in New Jersey. Others come to visit our state and see its sights.

New Jersey's location has helped make it one of the leading states in our country. It is a leader in many ways.

New Jersey's busy highways have earned it the name Corridor State.
■ What kinds of vehicles use our state's highways?

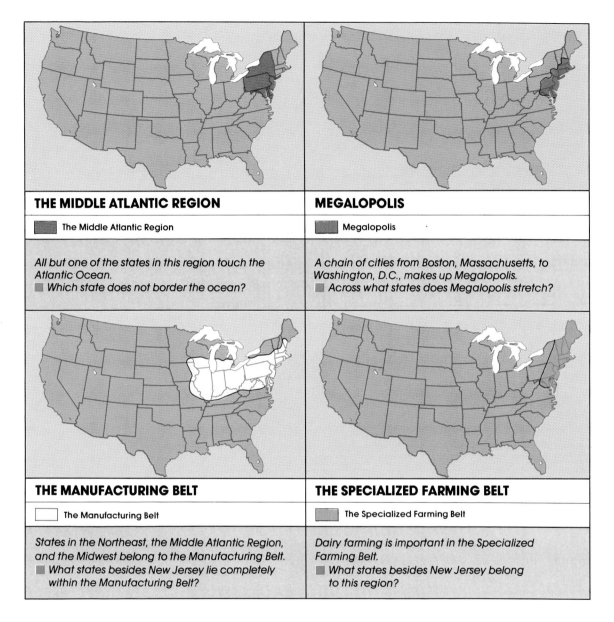

THE MIDDLE ATLANTIC REGION

⬛ The Middle Atlantic Region

All but one of the states in this region touch the Atlantic Ocean.
⬛ *Which state does not border the ocean?*

MEGALOPOLIS

⬛ Megalopolis

A chain of cities from Boston, Massachusetts, to Washington, D.C., makes up Megalopolis.
⬛ *Across what states does Megalopolis stretch?*

THE MANUFACTURING BELT

⬜ The Manufacturing Belt

States in the Northeast, the Middle Atlantic Region, and the Midwest belong to the Manufacturing Belt.
⬛ *What states besides New Jersey lie completely within the Manufacturing Belt?*

THE SPECIALIZED FARMING BELT

⬛ The Specialized Farming Belt

Dairy farming is important in the Specialized Farming Belt.
⬛ *What states besides New Jersey belong to this region?*

Manufacturing New Jersey is a leading manufacturing state. New Jersey's factories make many kinds of goods. These goods include chemicals, plastics, rubber, canned foods, and electrical products. More people in New Jersey work in manufacturing than at any other job.

New Jersey's location and good transportation system have helped it become a manufacturing center. New Jersey is an important member of the Manufacturing Belt. This region is shown on the map above.

Farming New Jersey is also a farming state. Because our state has so many cities and towns, land is expensive. New Jersey farmers must find the best use for their land. Many farmers in our state **specialize**. That means that they grow only one or two crops or raise a certain kind of animal. They do not try to produce everything that can grow or live on a farm. Look at the map on the opposite page. New Jersey is one of a number of states that belong to the Specialized Farming Belt. Many of our state's farmers raise dairy cattle. Other New Jersey farmers grow certain fruits or vegetables, such as blueberries, cranberries, peaches, tomatoes, potatoes, and corn.

Commerce and Foreign Trade The buying and selling of goods is known as **commerce**, or trade. New Jersey is a center for commerce. Much of New Jersey's commerce goes through the ports of Newark, Elizabeth, and Camden. These ports handle goods coming from and going to other parts of the United States. They are also important ports for **foreign trade**. Foreign trade is the buying and selling of products between countries. Products bought from other countries are **imports**. Products sold to other countries are **exports**.

Transportation New Jersey has an excellent transportation system. There are over 33,000 miles (53,000 km) of roads and highways in our state. People use these to commute to work and to visit other parts of the state. Manufactured goods and farm products are carried on our state's roads and highways by trucks. Railroads also serve the state in

New Jersey ranks third in cranberry production after Massachusetts and Wisconsin.
■ On what kind of land are cranberries grown?

many ways. They run on about 1,650 miles (2,655 km) of track. Passenger trains serve about 100 cities in our state. Trains are used by New Jerseyans who work in New York and Philadelphia. Rail lines also carry goods in New Jersey.

New Jersey also has over 250 airports. Newark International Airport is one of the United States' major airports.

CHECKUP
1. What is Megalopolis?
2. Why do many of the farmers in our state specialize?
3. Name three uses of roads and highways in our state.
4. **Thinking Critically** Compare the location of the state of New Jersey with that of other states in the Middle Atlantic Region.

A Leader in Many Other Ways

How do people enjoy themselves in New Jersey?

The Tourist Industry Every year millions of people come to New Jersey for pleasure. These people are **tourists**. They spend money for meals, places to stay, and sightseeing. Taking care of visitors makes jobs for New Jerseyans. The tourist industry is the second largest industry in the state, after manufacturing. It brings in about $8 billion a year. New Jersey is one of the top five tourist states.

Sports New Jerseyans are very active in sports. These sports range from boating and bowling to skiing and surfing.

New Jerseyans also enjoy watching team sports and horse racing. A number of professional sports teams play at the Meadowlands Sports Complex. Sports played include basketball, football, hockey, and soccer. Horse racing is also popular at the Meadowlands and other places in New Jersey.

Recreational Areas There are 40 state parks and 11 state forests in New Jersey. Some of the parks are historical, such as Princeton Battlefield State Park. Others offer good

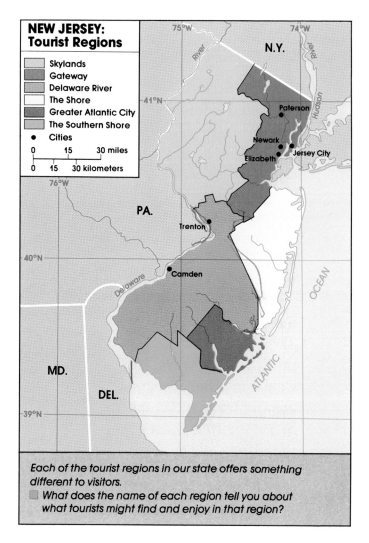

NEW JERSEY: Tourist Regions

- Skylands
- Gateway
- Delaware River
- The Shore
- Greater Atlantic City
- The Southern Shore
- • Cities

Each of the tourist regions in our state offers something different to visitors.
■ What does the name of each region tell you about what tourists might find and enjoy in that region?

hiking and camping, such as Wharton State Forest. There is good picnicking and fishing and a nature area at Island Beach State Park on the shore. Find these state parks and forests on the map on page 40.

There are also a number of national parklands in New Jersey. These include Gateway National Recreation Area, Statue of Liberty National Monument, and Brigantine National Wildlife Refuge.

The Rutgers women's basketball team is one of the top teams in the country.
■ **Whom are they playing against?**

The New Jersey Symphony often performs at the Garden State Arts Center in Holmdel.
■ **What instruments can you identify?**

The Arts New Jersey has many museums, theaters, and concert halls. They are found in communities of all sizes. The Papermill Playhouse in Millburn is the home of the State Theatre of New Jersey. The New Jersey Symphony Orchestra and the Garden State Chamber Orchestra are two well-known musical groups.

Colleges and Universities New Jersey has over 30 colleges and universities, both public and private schools. Princeton University, founded in 1746, and Rutgers, The State University, founded in 1766, are among the oldest universities in our country.

CHECKUP

1. Give two reasons why the tourist industry is important to our state.
2. What New Jersey sport do you enjoy the most?
3. **Thinking Critically** Who runs the national parklands in New Jersey?

New Jersey's Problems

What are some problems New Jersey faces today?

Air, Water, and Soil Pollution

Making the earth's air, water, and soil dirty is called **pollution**. Air pollution is a problem in most states, especially in urban areas. In many parts of New Jersey, the air is polluted by wastes from factories and cars, trucks, and buses. Waste is material that is of no use. The air is also polluted by smoke and gases from open fires.

People have begun to discuss how to clean up the air. One way has been to check cars each year for the amount of bad smoke and gases they send out into the air. If a car gives off too much, it must be fixed.

Water pollution comes about when waste gets into the ocean, lakes, rivers, and streams. Waste from businesses and factories has polluted water in our state. Other waste products also find their way into New Jersey waters. Water pollution kills fish and does not allow people to enjoy the ocean, lakes, rivers, and streams as they might. Today, people are learning how to stop water pollution and treat wastes that get into the water.

A third kind of pollution is soil pollution. Each year, cities and towns have to find a way to get rid of the thousands of tons of garbage and trash they collect. The usual way is to bury it in places called **landfills**. The garbage and trash is put into

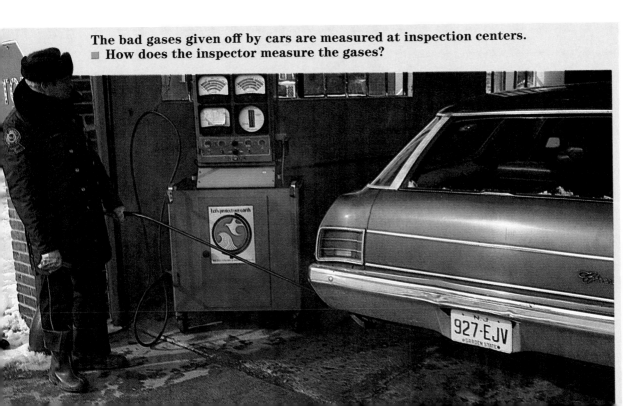

The bad gases given off by cars are measured at inspection centers.
■ How does the inspector measure the gases?

long ditches and covered with soil. Soil can be polluted by garbage and trash. Other ways of getting rid of garbage and trash must be found. If garbage and trash were burnt, the energy given off could be used for heat or power.

Toxic Waste and Acid Rain   The most serious type of soil pollution is **toxic waste**. Toxic waste is very dangerous chemicals and special waste products from factories. Toxic waste is buried or stored in the soil. How to store toxic waste safely is the number one problem in soil conservation today. Some toxic waste sites are being cleaned up in New Jersey. Our state is also studying new ways of storing toxic waste.

Acid rain is another serious pollution problem. This kind of pollution comes from factories in the Midwest. Clouds above the factories become filled with pollution. The clouds move east. When rain falls from the clouds, it is called acid rain. Acid rain pollutes both the soil and water when it falls to earth. Acid rain is a problem many eastern states are working on.

Social Problems   New Jersey has most of the same **social problems** that other states have. Social problems are people problems. They come up when people live close together. When people live close together, they must think not only of their own

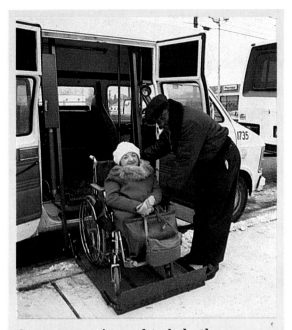

State money is used to help the handicapped.
■ **How is this person being helped?**

well-being but also of the well-being of others. Here are some questions about social problems:

1. How can New Jersey provide equality in schooling, in jobs, and in protection under the law?
2. How can New Jersey best help those out of work, the ill, and the handicapped?
3. How can New Jersey cut crime and protect its citizens?
4. How can New Jersey raise money to pay for social services?

CHECKUP

1. What is being done to help clean up the air?
2. What are social problems?
3. **Thinking Critically** How can you help to solve our state's problems?

The People of New Jersey

Who are some well-known people from New Jersey?

VOCABULARY

playwright

New Jerseyans Help Shape American History   People from New Jersey have helped make the United States a great country. People such as Molly Pitcher, William Paterson, James Still, George McClellan, John Stevens, Mary Philbrook, and Woodrow Wilson all shaped American history. Today, New Jerseyans from all different fields are still helping our state and country grow.

New Jerseyans in Space   New Jerseyans have helped to explore outer space. Walter M. Schirra, Jr., of Hackensack, led the Apollo 7 mission in 1968. Edwin E. ("Buzz") Aldrin, Jr., from Montclair, was lunar module pilot on the first manned landing on the moon, Apollo 11. Terry Hart of Morris Plains flew on the space shuttle *Challenger* in 1984.

New Jerseyans in Art and Literature   More than 30,000 artists make New Jersey their home. George Segal is a world-famous sculptor who

Buzz Aldrin tests his equipment.
■ **What is he holding?**

This Segal sculpture is in Princeton.
■ **What is it a sculpture of?**

Millicent H. Fenwick
(1910 —   )

One New Jerseyan who has made contributions on many levels is Millicent Fenwick. Fenwick was born in New York City in 1910. She later moved to Bernardsville, New Jersey, where she raised a family while working as a magazine editor. Fenwick became interested in politics in the 1930s, just before the beginning of World War II. Politics is the art or science of government. Worried by the rise of the Nazi party in Germany and "by what governments could do," she joined the National Conference of Christians and Jews.

In the 1950s, Fenwick served her community of Bernardsville as a member of the borough council. In 1969 she was elected to the New Jersey General Assembly, where she served two terms. Fenwick went to the House of Representatives in Washington, D.C., in 1975 as representative from the Fifth Congressional District. She was a member of the House until 1982, when she ran for the Senate against Frank Lautenberg, and lost.

Although interested and later involved in politics, Fenwick does not consider herself a politician but a public servant. Her concern has not been her own career and image but the protection and good of the people. In her 70s, Millicent Fenwick is still an active public servant. Today she lives and works in Rome, Italy. Fenwick is the head American delegate to the United Nations Food and Agriculture Organization (FAO). Through the group, she is working on the problems of hunger and crop production in needy countries.

lives in South Brunswick. Segal creates plaster and bronze people. Segal has said that New Jersey's highways and cities have given him ideas for his works. Today his figures form parts of the collections of New Jersey museums and the Museum of Modern Art and the Guggenheim Museum in New York City.

New Jersey is also the home of many writers. Peter Benchley of Princeton wrote *Jaws*, which was later made into a movie. Mary Higgins Clark of Washington Township writes mysteries. The poet and **playwright** Amiri (Le Roi Jones) Baraka lives in Newark. A playwright is a person who writes plays. Baraka wrote the play *The Slave*.

Perhaps you have read books in the Nancy Drew series. Harriet Adams of Maplewood wrote these stories under the pen name of Carolyn Keene. Another New Jersey author you might know is Judy Blume of Elizabeth. Have you read Judy Blume's books *Tales of a Fourth Grade Nothing* and *Are You There God? It's Me Margaret*.

New Jersey Sports Figures New Jerseyans can also be proud of the many sports stars from their state. Among those well-known today are Carl Lewis of Willingboro and Elaine Zayak of Paramus. Carl Lewis won gold medals in four events at the 1984 Los Angeles Olympic Games. In 1982, Elaine Zayak won the world

Judy Blume (top) has written children's books. Doug Heir (bottom) of Cherry Hill set records in the Wheelchair Division of the Olympics. ■ What was one of Heir's events?

figure-skating championship. She is famous for her triple jumps. Top tennis players from our state include Peter Fleming of Chatham and Pam Casale of Fairfield.

Drew Pearson, formerly of the Dallas Cowboys, and Joe Theisman of the Washington Redskins both played football at South River High School. Baseball's Larry Doby is from Paterson. He was the first black to play in the American League. Other baseball players from New Jersey include Don Newcombe of Elizabeth and Monte Irvin of East Orange.

Entertainers from New Jersey
Many musical entertainers live or were born in New Jersey. They in-clude Dionne Warwick and Eddie Rabbitt from East Orange, George Benson of Englewood Cliffs, Gloria Gayner and Connie Francis from Newark, and the Isley Brothers and Phoebe Snow of Teaneck. Their styles range from that of Frank Sinatra to that of Bruce Springsteen.

Bruce Springsteen's music may be familiar to you. Springsteen grew up in Freehold. He played in local bands in clubs in and around Asbury Park. Since his first album in 1973, he has had many hit songs. Many of his songs tell about real life and what he calls "the runaway American dream." These themes have won Springsteen fans all over our country and the world.

Monte Irvin (left) and Larry Doby (right) were elected to the Baseball Hall of Fame.
■ What is a hall of fame?

Bruce Springsteen is a popular New Jersey-born musician.
■ Why, do you think, do people like his songs?

Jerry Lewis and Meryl Streep are actors from New Jersey.
■ **Who is posing with Jerry Lewis in this photograph?**

Jerry Lewis and Meryl Streep are two well-known actors from New Jersey. Jerry Lewis went to Irvington High School. He began his career as a comic entertainer at a resort in the Catskill Mountains of New York. He first starred in films in the 1950s. Some of his films are *Sad Sack*, *Cinderfella*, and *The King of Comedy*. Jerry Lewis is also known for his work for the Muscular Dystrophy Association. Meryl Streep of Bernardsville is considered a fine serious actress. She studied acting at Yale University. Her films include *The Deer Hunter*, *Kramer* vs. *Kramer*, and *Out of Africa*. She won an Academy Award for Best Actress in *Sophie's Choice*.

New Jersey and You You are also part of the story of New Jersey. You are our state's future. You will make important decisions that will affect life in our state. You will work with others to solve our state's problems. Your study of New Jersey's history and geography will help you to be a better New Jerseyan.

CHECKUP

1. Name three astronauts from the state of New Jersey.
2. Name two New Jersey writers of children's books.
3. **Thinking Critically** In what area, in your opinion, has a person from New Jersey made the greatest contribution to the happiness of other people?

Writing a Dialogue

WHAT IS A DIALOGUE?

Do you know what a dialogue is? It is when two or more people talk with each other. Dialogues can be written. When a dialogue is written, a new paragraph is begun for each speaker. The first word is indented. A speaker's words are enclosed in quotation marks.

The following dialogue is between Brenda, who lives outside of Salem, New Jersey, and her friend Sandy from Camden. Sandy's family is visiting Brenda's family for part of the summer. On a hot day in late August, Brenda and Sandy are sitting on the back steps of Brenda's house husking corn they have just picked in the vegetable garden.

A DIALOGUE

"Isn't it great to have corn fresh from the garden?" said Brenda.

"It sure is!" agreed Sandy. "Farmers have it so easy."

"Why do you think farmers have it easy?" asked Brenda. "My family works hard in the garden. Who do you think plants and takes care of the vegetables?"

"Oh," answered Sandy, "I thought that the vegetables grew without any help."

"We have to give our vegetable garden a lot of attention," said Brenda. "We have to weed and water the garden. We have to tie up the tomato plants and protect the corn from birds."

"I guess I have a lot to learn about farming," said Sandy.

"Let's go in and put the water on for the corn," said Brenda. "You haven't had real corn on the cob until you've tasted freshly picked corn."

SKILLS PRACTICE

Note where quotation marks are placed in the dialogue. Now, on a sheet of paper, copy the sentences below and place quotation marks in the right places.

Would you like to go to the seashore tomorrow? asked Brenda.

Oh, I'd love to, replied Sandy. I brought my new bathing suit and I love the ocean.

The beach we go to has big waves, said Brenda. Maybe we'll see some people surfing today.

That will be fun. I've never seen anyone surf before, said Sandy.

Now write a dialogue of your own in which two people are talking. They are talking about living in New Jersey. Before you start writing, read the first paragraph in column 1 again. Follow the directions given in that paragraph.

You may want to start your dialogue with one of the following.

a. "My favorite part of New Jersey is the mountains," said Juan to his friend.

b. "My mom really has an exciting job," said Alice to her friend Susie.

c. "We're going to see the Giants play at the Meadowlands," Don told his cousin Chet. "Would you like to come with us?"

CHAPTER 15 REVIEW

MAIN IDEAS

1. New Jersey is a national leader in manufacturing, farming, commerce, and transportation.
2. New Jersey is one of the top five tourist states in the United States.
3. People enjoy sightseeing; watching sports; hiking; picnicking; camping; and going to concerts, plays, and museums in New Jersey.
4. Pollution of various kinds and social problems are problems faced by New Jersey today.
5. Some well-known New Jerseyans are Terry Hart, Millicent Fenwick, George Segal, Judy Blume, Larry Doby, Bruce Springsteen, and Meryl Streep.

VOCABULARY REVIEW

Match the words with their definitions. Use a separate sheet of paper.

a. specialize
b. tourist
c. landfill
d. pollution
e. playwright

1. Making the air, water, and soil dirty
2. A person who writes plays
3. Long ditches covered with soil, where garbage and trash are buried
4. A person who travels for pleasure
5. To do one or two things instead of many things

CHAPTER CHECKUP

1. How does New Jersey's location help manufacturing and transportation in the state?
2. Why is land expensive in New Jersey?
3. How do social problems arise?
4. **Thinking Critically** Why are colleges and universities important to the state of New Jersey?
5. **Thinking Critically** What can you do now to help solve the problem of pollution in our state?
6. **Thinking Critically** Which of the New Jerseyans named in the last lesson would you like to be and why?

APPLYING KNOWLEDGE

1. Pretend that you have been hired to gather information for the "New Jersey & You . . . Perfect Together" campaign. Make a list of sights in New Jersey that everyone should see. Then make a poster advertising one of these places. Using your poster, give a brief talk about the sight you chose. In your talk try to persuade others to visit the sight.
2. At the top of a sheet of paper, write the words *New Jersey Products*. Under this title make two columns. Label the columns *Farm Products* and *Factory Products*. In each column list as many products as you can.

SUMMARIZING UNIT 5

REVIEWING VOCABULARY

1. Capitol The state capitol is the building where government leaders for our state meet. Where is New Jersey's capitol located? When was it built?

2. Bill A bill is a possible law. Describe how a bill becomes a law in the New Jersey state legislature.

3. Urban Area New Jersey's urban areas are made up of a large city and its suburbs or many separate cities and their suburbs. Name two important urban areas in our state.

4. Pollution Making the earth's air, water, and soil dirty is called pollution. Explain how the air, water, or soil can be polluted. Then discuss how the pollution problem you have chosen can be solved.

5. Social Problem Social problems come about when people live close together. Name two social problems New Jersey faces. Who can solve our state's social problems?

EXPRESSING YOURSELF

1. Who Would You Rather Be? If you were old enough to run for mayor, governor, or President, which would you rather be? Explain your answer.

2. What Would You Do? Imagine that your class is going to visit a city near your school. Your teacher has given you a chance to choose what you would like to do on your field trip. What can people do in cities? What would you do?

3. What If? Most cities have parks where residents can play or relax in green surroundings. What if cities did not have parks? Do you think that city residents would miss having a bit of the country in the city?

4. You Make the Decision Pretend that you are a local government leader. There are a number of social problems in your community. There is crime. Some people are without jobs. Handicapped people do not have the services they need. You will only receive enough money from the state and federal governments this year to work on one of these problems. You have a hard decision to make. Which problem would you choose to work on? Why?

5. In What Ways? Pretend that you are one of the well-known New Jerseyans named in the last chapter of this unit. In what ways would your life be different? In what ways would your life be the same?

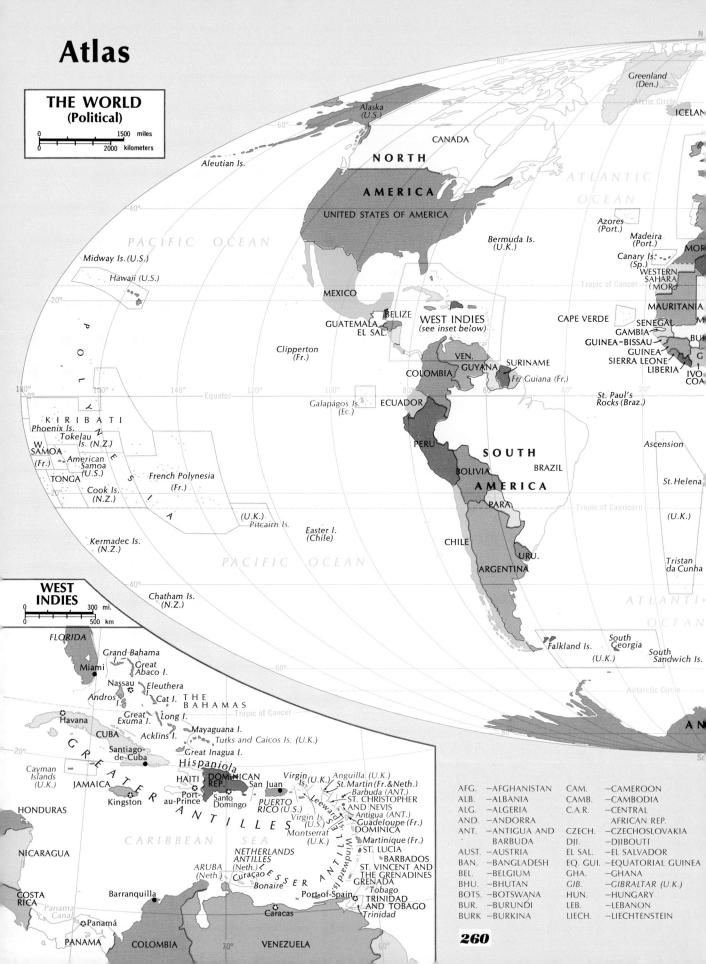

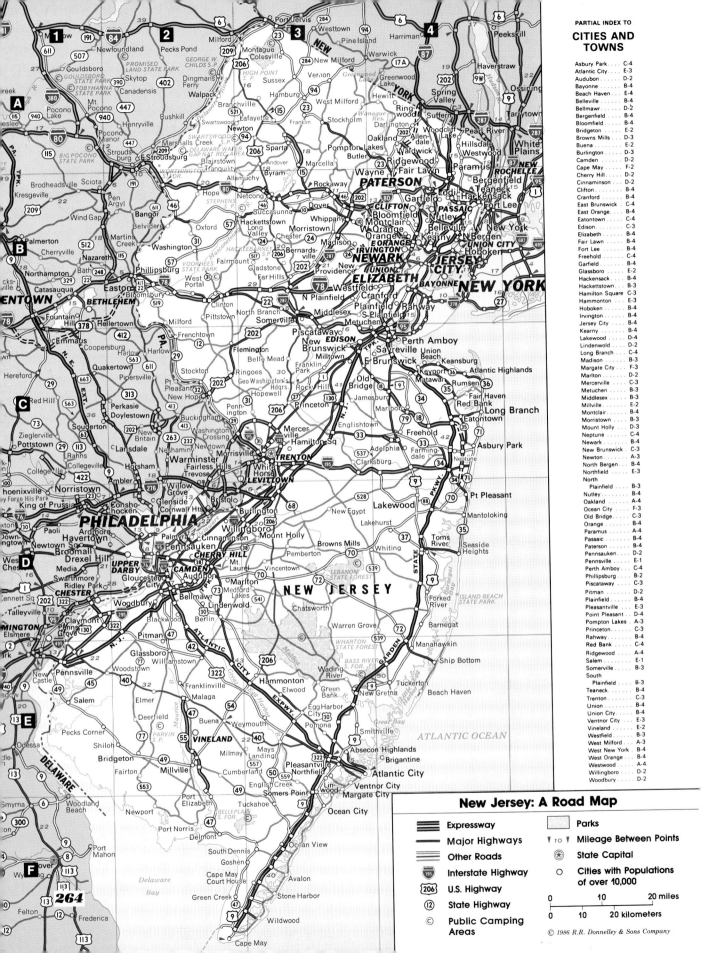

New Jersey: A Road Map

Expressway		Parks	
Major Highways		Mileage Between Points	
Other Roads		State Capital	
Interstate Highway		Cities with Populations of over 10,000	
U.S. Highway			
State Highway			
Public Camping Areas			

0   10   20 miles

0   10   20 kilometers

© 1986 R.R. Donnelley & Sons Company

264

GAZETTEER

The Gazetteer is a geographical dictionary. It shows latitude and longitude for cities and certain other places. Latitude and longitude are shown in this form: (41°N/74°W). This means "41 degrees north latitude and 74 degrees west longitude." The page reference tells where each entry may be found on a map.

Africa (af′ ri kə). The earth's second largest continent. p. 33.

Antarctica (ant ärk′ ti kə). The earth's third smallest continent. p. 33.

Appalachian Mountains (ap ə lā′ chən moun′ tənz). Mountain range extending northeast and southwest between eastern Canada and Alabama. p. 79.

Arctic Ocean (ärk′ tik ō′ shən). Large body of salt water north of the Arctic Circle. p. 33.

Asia (ā′ zhə). The earth's largest continent. p. 33.

Atlantic City (at lan′ tik sit′ ē). City on the Atlantic Ocean in Atlantic County. The most popular resort in America. (39°N/74°W). p. 63.

Atlantic Coastal Plain (at lan′ tik kōs′ təl plān). Strip of low, almost flat land lying next to the Atlantic Ocean. The plain stretches from Georgia to New Jersey. More than half of New Jersey lies on the Atlantic Coastal Plain. p. 71.

Atlantic Ocean (at lan′ tik ō′ shən). Large body of salt water separating North America and South America from Europe and Africa. p. 33.

Australia (ô strāl′ yə). The earth's smallest continent. Also the name of the country that covers the whole continent. p. 33.

Belvidere (bel′ və dēr). County seat of Warren County. (41°N/75°W). p. 79.

Bergen (bėr′ gən). First planned, walled village in New Jersey. Built by the Dutch in 1660 near what is now Jersey City. (41°N/74°W). p. 123.

Blairstown (blãr′ stoun). Town in Warren County. (41°N/75°W). p. 79.

Bordentown (bôrd′ ən toun). City in Burlington County. Located on the Delaware River below Trenton. (40°N/75°W). p. 161.

Boston (bô′ stən). Capital of Massachusetts. Seaport city on Massachusetts Bay. (42°N/71°W). pp. 262–263.

Branchville (branch′ vil). Borough in Sussex County. (41°N/75°W). p. 79.

Bridgeton (brij′ tən). County seat of Cumberland County. (39°N/75°W). p. 71.

Brotherton (brŦH′ ər tən). Indian reservation founded in New Jersey in 1758. Closed in 1802. Location of present-day Indian Mills in Burlington County. (40°N/75°W). p. 88.

Budd Lake (bud lāk). Lake in Morris County. (41°N/75°W). p. 77.

Burlington (bėr′ ling tən). City in Burlington County, on the Delaware River. Capital of West New Jersey. (40°N/75°W). p. 123.

Camden (kam′ dən). County seat of Camden County, and New Jersey's sixth largest city. Important port and manufacturing center on the Delaware River, across from Philadelphia. (40°N/75°W). p. 40.

Cape May (kāp mā). **1.** Southernmost point in New Jersey, jutting out into the Atlantic Ocean. (39°N/75°W). p. 107. **2.** City in Cape May County. One of America's oldest seaside resorts. (39°N/75°W). p. 71.

Clifton (klif′ tən). City in Passaic County. Industrial center on the Passaic River, between Paterson and Passaic. (41°N/74°W). p. 40.

Connecticut Farms (kə net′ i kət färmz). Now Union in Union County. Location of Revolutionary War battle. (41°N/74°W). p. 139.

Culvers Lake (kəl′ vərz lāk). Lake in Sussex County, near Branchville. (41°N/75°W). p. 70.

Delaware River (del′ ə wär riv′ ər). River that starts in the Catskill Mountains in New York. Flows into the Atlantic Ocean at Delaware Bay. Forms the boundary between New Jersey and Pennsylvania and Delaware. p. 40.

Delaware Water Gap (del′ ə wär wôt′ ər gap). Great opening cut through Kittatinny Mountain by the Delaware River. On the New Jersey-Pennsylvania border. (41°N/75°W). p. 79.

Dover (dō′ vər). Fast-growing town in Morris County. Location of iron mills during Revolutionary War. (41°N/75°W). p. 77.

Eastern Hemisphere (ēs′ tərn hem′ ə sfir). The half of the earth east of the Prime Meridian. Australia and most of Europe, Africa, and Asia are in the Eastern Hemisphere. p. 39.

Elizabeth (i liz′ ə bəth). Fourth largest city in New Jersey. County seat of Union County and important port and industrial city. (41°N/74°W). p. 40.

Ellis Island (el′ əs ī′ lənd). Island in New York Harbor off Jersey City on which an immigrant center was located. (41°N/74°W). p. 232.

Equator (i kwā′ tər). On a map, the line that circles the earth halfway between the two poles. It is labeled 0° latitude. p. 38.

Europe (yür′ əp). The earth's second smallest continent. p. 33.

Flatbrookville (flat′ brük vil). Town in Sussex County. (41°N/75°W). p. 79.

Fort Christina (fôrt kris tē′ nə). Swedish fort near present-day Wilmington, Delaware. (40°N/76°W). p. 107.

Fort Elfsborg (fôrt elfs′ bôrg). Swedish fort built on the Delaware River in present-day Salem County. (40°N/75°W). p. 107.

Fort Nassau (fôrt nas′ ô). Dutch trading post near present-day Gloucester City in Camden County. (40°N/75°W). p. 107.

Freehold (frē′ hōld). County seat of Monmouth County. Founded in 1715 as Monmouth Court House. (40°N/74°W). p. 55.

Great Falls (grāt fôls). Waterfall on the Passaic River at Paterson. (41°N/74°N). p. 238.

Great Swamp (grāt swämp). Large swamp in Morris County, now a National Wildlife Refuge. Formed from Glacial Lake Passaic. (41°N/74°W). p. 70.

Greenwich 1. (gren′ ich). Place in London, England, designated as 0° longitude. The Prime Meridian runs from the North Pole through Greenwich to the South Pole. (52°N/0°long.). p. 39. **2.** (grēn′ wich). Community in Cumberland County, on the Cohansey River. Founded by Quakers. Site of the Greenwich Tea Party in 1774. (39°N/75°W). p. 123.

Greenwood Lake (grēn′ wúd lāk). Large lake partly in Passaic County and partly in New York State. (41°N/74°W). p. 70.

Hackensack (hak′ ən sak). County seat of Bergen County. Industrial center. (41°N/74°W). p. 55.

Hackensack Meadows (hak′ ən sak med′ ōz). Marshlands at the head of Newark Bay, partly drained and filled for building the Meadowlands Sports Complex. Formed from Glacial Lake Hackensack. (41°N/74°W). p. 70.

Hackensack River (hak′ ən sak riv′ ər). River flowing south from New York State through Bergen County. Forms part of border between Bergen and Hudson counties. Empties into Newark Bay. p. 70.

Hackettstown (hak′ ət stoun). Town in Warren County. (41°N/75°W). p. 77.

Hammonton (ham′ ən tən). Town in Atlantic County. Farm service center and market. (40°N/75°W). p. 264.

High Point (hī point). The highest point in New Jersey, 1,803 feet (550 m) above sea level. Located on Kittatinny Mountain in Sussex County. (41°N/75°W). p. 68.

Highlands (hī′ lənds). One of the physical regions of New Jersey. The hills of the region belong to the Appalachian mountain chain. p. 77.

Hoboken (hō′ bō kən). City in Hudson County. A port and a railroad and industrial center on the Hudson River. (41°N/74°W). p. 232.

Hopatcong (hə pat′ kän). Borough in Sussex County. Resort on Lake Hopatcong. (41°N/75°W). p. 77.

Hudson River (hud′ sən riv′ ər). River that starts in Adirondack Mountains in New York. Flows into Upper New York Bay. The southernmost part of the river forms part of the boundary between New Jersey and New York. p. 40.

Indian Mills (in′ dē ən mils). Community in Burlington County. Once called Brotherton, it was

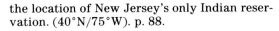
the location of New Jersey's only Indian reservation. (40°N/75°W). p. 88.

Indian Ocean (in′ dē ən ō′ shən). Large body of salt water between Africa and Australia. p. 33.

Jersey City (jer′ zē sit′ ē). Second largest city in New Jersey. County seat of Hudson County. Trade, transportation, and industrial center. (41°N/74°W). p. 40.

Kearny (kär′ nē). Town in Hudson County. Manufacturing center. Named for Philip Kearny, a Civil War general. (41°N/74°W). p. 264.

Kittatinny Mountain (kit ə tin′ ē moun′ tən). Ridge of the Appalachian Mountains running through New Jersey. The mountain is about 36 miles (58 km) long. It is cut by the Delaware Water Gap. p. 68.

Lake Hopatcong (lāk hə pat′ kän). Largest lake in New Jersey. Important resort in Morris County. (41°N/75°W). p. 40.

Lake Mohawk (lāk mō′ hôk). Lake near Sparta in Sussex County. (41°N/75°W). p. 77.

Leningrad (len′ ən grad). Second most populated city in the Soviet Union. Located on the Gulf of Finland. (60°N/30°E). p. 38.

Liberty Island (lib′ ərt ē ī′ lənd). Formerly Bedloe's Island. The home of the Statue of Liberty, in New Jersey waters of Upper New York Bay. (41°N/74°W). p. 232.

Long Branch (lông branch). City on the Atlantic Ocean in Monmouth County. One of the oldest seaside resorts in America. (40°N/74°W). p. 71.

Menlo Park (men′ lō pärk). Community in Middlesex County. Location of Thomas Edison's laboratory. (41°N/74°W). p. 74.

Middlebrook (mid′ əl brùk). Winter camp for General Washington and the Continental army during 1778–1779. In present-day Somerset County. (41°N/75°W). p. 139.

Middletown (mid′ əl toun). Community in Monmouth County. Founded by English settlers from Long Island. (40°N/74°W). p. 123.

Millville (mil′ vil). City in Cumberland County. (39°N/75°W). p. 71.

Monmouth (män′ məth). Now the borough of Freehold in Monmouth County. Location of important battle in the American Revolution. (40°N/74°W). p. 139.

Morristown (môr′ ə stoun). County seat of Morris County. Fast-growing office center. An early iron-making center, Morristown was twice winter headquarters (1777–1778 and 1779–1780) for General Washington and the Continental army. (41°N/74°W). p. 77.

New Amsterdam (nü am′ stər dam). Dutch trading post and settlement on Manhattan Island. (41°N/74°W). p. 107.

Newark (nü′ ərk). The largest city in New Jersey. County seat of Essex County. Located on Newark Bay. Founded in 1666 by English settlers from Connecticut. Major industrial and business center. (41°N/74°W). p. 40.

New Brunswick (nü brənz′ wik). County seat of Middlesex County. Location of Rutgers, The State University, and an important industrial and office center on the Raritan River. (40°N/74°W). p. 139.

New Netherland (nü nᴇтн′ ər lənd). Dutch colony that included parts of what are now New Jersey and New York. p. 107.

New Sweden (nü swē′ dən). Swedish colony on the lower Delaware River in present-day Gloucester and Salem counties and in northern Delaware. p. 107.

Newton (nüt′ ən). County seat of Sussex County. (41°N/75°W). p. 79.

New York City (nü yôrk sit′ ē). Most populated city in the United States. Located at the mouth of the Hudson River. Across the Hudson River from Jersey City, Hoboken, West New York, and Fort Lee. (41°N/74°W). pp. 262–263.

North America (nôrth ə mär′ ə kə). The earth's third largest continent. The United States is in North America. p. 33.

North Pole (nôrth pōl). The most northern place on the earth. p. 37.

Northern Hemisphere (nôr′ тнərn hem′ ə sfir). The half of the earth that is north of the Equator. p. 38.

Pacific Ocean (pə sif′ ik ō′ shən). Earth's largest body of water. Extends from the Arctic Circle to Antarctica and separates North America and South America from Asia and Australia. p. 33.

Palisades (pal ə sādz′). A line of high cliffs of rock rising to over 500 feet (152 m) on the west bank of the Hudson River. p. 74.

Paramus (pə ram′ əs). Borough in Bergen County. An industrial and office center. (41°N/74°W). p. 74.

Passaic (pə sā′ ik). City in Passaic County. Manufacturing center. (41°N/74°W). p. 40.

Passaic River (pə sā′ ik riv′ ər). River in northern New Jersey. Flows over the 70-foot (21-m) Great Falls at Paterson, past Newark, and into Newark Bay. p. 40.

Paterson (pat′ ər sən). The first planned industrial town in America, now New Jersey's third largest city. County seat of Passaic County. Located at the Great Falls of the Passaic River. (41°N/74°W). p. 40.

Pavonia (pə vō′ nē ə). Dutch patroonship near present-day Jersey City. First permanent settlement in New Jersey. (41°N/74°W). p. 107.

Perth Amboy (pər tham′ boi). City in Middlesex County. Port and industrial center on Raritan Bay. Capital of East New Jersey. (41°N/74°W). p. 70.

Philadelphia (fil ə del′ fē ə). City in Pennsylvania. Located at the point where the Delaware and Schuylkill rivers join. One of six cities in the United States with more than one million people. (40°N/75°W). p. 38.

Phillipsburg (fil′ əps bərg). Town in Warren County. Old metalworking center on the Delaware River. (41°N/75°W). p. 77.

Piedmont (pēd′ mänt). One of the physical regions of New Jersey. Also known as the Newark Basin. p. 74.

Piscataway (pis kat′ ə wā). Community in Middlesex County. Founded by English settlers from New England. (41°N/74°W). p. 123.

Prime Meridian (prīm mə rid′ ē ən). 0° line of longitude. It divides the earth into the Eastern and Western hemispheres. p. 39.

Princeton (prin′ stən). Borough in Mercer County. Scene of important Revolutionary War battle. Home of Princeton University. (40°N/75°W). p. 139.

Raritan River (rar′ ət ən riv′ ər). The longest river completely within New Jersey. The river is 75 miles (121 km) long. p. 40.

Red Bank (red bangk). Location of an important Revolutionary War battle. On the banks of the Delaware River in Gloucester County. (40°N/75°W). p. 139.

Ridge and Valley Region (rij ənd val′ ē rē′ jən). One of the physical regions of New Jersey. Its mountains are part of the Appalachian mountain chain. p. 79.

Ringwood (ring′ wůd). Borough in Passaic County. Old iron town. (41°N/74°W). p. 139.

Salem (sāl′ əm). County seat of Salem County.

Founded by Quakers. (40°N/75°W). p. 123.

Sandy Hook (san′ dē hůk). A narrow strip of land in northern Monmouth County. It extends 5 miles (8 km) into the Atlantic Ocean. (40°N/74°W). p. 71.

Shrewsbury (shrüz′ ber ē). Borough in Monmouth County. Founded by English settlers from Long Island. (40°N/74°W). p. 123.

South America (south ə mãr′ ə kə). The earth's fourth largest continent. p. 33.

South Orange (south ôrinj). Community in Essex County. (41°N/74°W). p. 232.

South Pole (south pōl). The most southern place on the earth. p. 37.

Southern Hemisphere (suᴛH′ ərn hem′ ə sfir). The half of the earth south of the Equator. p. 38.

Springfield (spring′ fēld). Township in Union County. Location of Revolutionary War battle. (41°N/74°W). p. 139.

Succasunna (sək ə sə′ nə). Community in Morris County. (41°N/75°W). p. 264.

Swartswood (swôrtz′ wůd). Community in Sussex County. (41°N/75°W). p. 79.

Teaneck (tē′ nek). Community in Bergen County. Early suburb. (41°N/74°W). p. 264.

Trenton (trent′ ən). The fifth largest city in New Jersey. The state capital and the county seat of Mercer County. Scene of one of the most important battles of the American Revolution. (40°N/75°W). p. 40.

Union City (yün′ yən sit′ ē). City in Hudson County. (41°N/74°W). p. 74.

Vineland (vīn′ lənd). City in Cumberland County. New Jersey's largest city in area. Important farming center. (39°N/75°W). p. 71.

Washington, D.C. (wash′ ing tən dē sē). Capital of the United States of America. On the Potomac River. (39°N/77°W). pp. 262–263.

Watchung Ridges (wäch′ ung rij′ əs). Steep hills in the Piedmont. p. 74.

Western Hemisphere (wes′ tərn hem′ ə sfir). The half of the earth west of the Prime Meridian. Includes all of North America and South America. p. 33.

Woodbridge (wůd′ brij). State's largest township, in Middlesex County. Founded by English settlers from New England. (41°N/74°W). p. 40.

GLOSSARY

The page reference in each entry tells where the term is first used in the text.

abolitionist (ab ə lish′ə nist). A person who wanted to put an end to slavery. p. 164.

account book (ə kount′ buk). A record kept by a store, telling what goods were sold and how much they cost. p. 23.

acid rain (as′ id rān). Rain that has a high amount of certain acids due to air pollution. p. 251.

agriculture (ag′ ri kəl chər). Farming; the growing of crops and raising of animals. p. 60.

ally (al′ ī) A friend or helper. p. 143.

ancestor (an′ ses tər). A family member who lived long ago. p. 16.

apprentice (ə prent′ əs). A person who works for a certain amount of time while learning a trade. p. 127.

archaeology (är kē äl′ ə jē). The science of digging up artifacts and studying them. p. 25.

artifact (är′ tə fakt). An object that was made and used by people in the past. p. 24.

assembly (ə sem′ blē). A lawmaking group of elected people. p. 119.

astronaut (as′ trə nôt). A person who travels in outer space. p. 32.

asylum (ə sī′ ləm). A home for the mentally ill. p. 163.

ballot (bal′ ət). A piece of paper that is used for voting in secret. p. 194.

barrack (bar′ ək). A large building or group of buildings in which soldiers live. p. 129.

bill (bil). A possible law. p. 223.

board of chosen freeholders (bôrd ov chōz′ ən frē′ hōl dərz). A group of three to nine people who make and carry out laws for a county. p. 224.

border (bôr′ dər). To touch; an outer edge or boundary. p. 35.

boundary (boun′ dər ē). A line that separates one state or country from another; a border. p. 35.

cable (kā′ bəl). A wire rope. p. 239.

campus (kam′ pəs). A group of school buildings in a parklike setting. p. 241.

canal (kə nal′). A deep, water-filled ditch built to connect other waterways. p. 160.

cannery (kan′ ə rē). A food-processing plant. p. 240.

capital (kap′ ə təl). A city that is the seat of government of a country or state. p. 75.

capitol (kap′ ə təl). The building where government leaders meet. p. 219.

celt (selt). A large, sharpened stone with a wooden handle, used by the Lenape to cut down saplings. p. 91.

ceramic (sə ram′ ik). Of or relating to the making of any product from a nonmetal material baked at very high temperatures. p. 240.

Civil War (siv′ əl wôr). A war fought between people of the same country. The American *Civil War* was fought between the North and the South from 1861 to 1865. p. 169.

climate (klī′ mət). The kind of weather a place has over a long period of time. p. 63.

colony (kol′ ə nē). A place that is settled at a distance from the country that rules it. p. 105.

commerce (käm′ ərs). Trade. p. 247.

community (kə myü′ nət ē). The place where people live. p. 17.

commute (kə myüt′). To travel back and forth regularly. p. 18.

compass rose (kum′ pəs rōz). A drawing that shows where north, south, east, and west are on a map. p. 37.

compromise (käm′ prə mīz). A decision that gives each side something. p. 154.

congressional district (kən gresh′ ə nəl dis′ trikt). A division of the state according to population for the election of representatives to Congress. p. 226.

conservation (kän sər vā′ shən). The careful use and protection of something, especially natural resources. p. 73.

container (kən tā′ nər). A large steel box that can be filled with goods for shipping. p. 235.

continent (kän′ tə nənt). A very large body of land. There are seven *continents*. They are Asia, Australia, Africa, Europe, Antarctica, South America, and North America. p. 33.

Continental army (kän′ ti nen təl är′ mē). A group of soldiers from the colonies, led by George Washington. p. 136.

contour line (kon′ tür līn). On a map, a line that separates the colors used to show elevation of the land. p. 69.

county (koun′ tē). The largest division of local government within a state. p. 54.

county seat (koun′ tē sēt). The town or city where the county government is located. p. 224.

currency (kər′ ən sē). Coins and paper money. p. 153.

custom (kus′ təm). A special way of doing things. p. 190.

dairy farm (dār′ ē färm). A place where cows are raised to produce milk. p. 80.

dam (dam). A wall-like structure that holds back a flow of water. p. 77.

Declaration of Independence (dek lə rā′ shən ov in də pen′ dəns). A document explaining why the American colonists were breaking away from Great Britain. p. 137.

Delaware Water Gap (del′ ə wār wôt′ ər gap). An opening cut through Kittatinny Mountain by the Delaware River. p. 79.

269

delegate (del′ ə git). A person who acts or speaks for other people. p. 134.

depression (di presh′ ən). A time when many people have no jobs and very little money. p. 203.

dialect (dī′ ə lekt). A variety, or form, of a language. p. 88.

east (ēst). A direction word. If one faces north, *east* will be on one's right. p. 36.

economy (i kän′ ə mē). The making and selling of goods and services. p. 172.

electronics (i lek trän′ iks). An area of study from which television, radio, computers, and other devices using electricity have developed. p. 210.

elevation (el ə vā′ shən). Distance above sea level. A mountain that has an *elevation* of 5,000 feet (1,500 m) is 5,000 feet (1,500 m) above sea level. p. 69.

Equator (i kwā′ tər). The imaginary line on the earth that is halfway between the North Pole and the South Pole. The *Equator* is shown on a map or globe by the latitude line numbered 0° p. 38.

estimate (es′ ti māt). To judge or figure out something, such as distance or location on a map or globe. p. 41.

ethnic (eth′ nik). Having to do with a group of people who share language, customs, and often the same religion and country of origin. p. 233.

executive branch (eg zek′ yə tiv branch). The part of government that carries out the laws. p. 221.

explorer (ik splōr′ ər). Someone who searches for new places and things. p. 95.

export (ek′ spôrt). A product sold to another country. p. 247.

Fall Line (fôl līn). A line of small waterfalls and rapids. The *Fall Line* in New Jersey separates the Atlantic Coastal Plain from the Piedmont. p. 75.

federal (fed′ ər əl). National. p. 153.

First Continental Congress (fərst kän tə nen′ təl kän′ grəs). The first meeting of delegates from each of the 13 colonies. p. 134.

food processing (füd prä′ ses ing). Preparing, freezing, or canning food to be sold. p. 73.

foreign trade (fôr′ ən trād). The buying and selling of products between countries. p. 247.

fort (fôrt). A place built to protect people. p. 110.

fuel (fyül). Something that can be burned to produce heat or power. p. 59.

genealogy (jē nē äl′ ə jē). A written history of a family. p. 26.

geography (jē og′ rə fē). The study of the earth and how people use it. p. 16.

glacier (glā′ sher). A thick sheet of ice and snow. p. 70.

globe (glōb). A model of the earth. p. 33.

govern (gəv′ ərn). To rule. p. 110.

government (gəv′ ərn mənt). A group of men and women who make laws and see that they are carried out. p. 17.

graph (graf). A special kind of a drawing that uses pictures, circles, bars, and lines to give facts and compare things. p. 56.

grid (grid). A system of crossing lines that form boxes on a map or globe. Crossing latitude and longitude lines form a *grid*. p. 41.

growing season (grō′ ing sēz′ ən). The period when crops can grow. p. 64.

headquarters (hed′ kwôrt ərz). The business center of a company; the place where the head or heads of a company work. p. 78.

hemisphere (hem′ ə sfir). Half of a sphere, or ball; half of the earth. p. 38.

heritage (her′ ət ij). Ways and beliefs handed down from one generation to the next. p. 99.

Hessian (hesh′ ən). A German soldier who was paid by the British to fight the Americans. p. 139.

Hispanic (his pan′ ik). A person with a Spanish language background. p. 233.

historical document (his tôr′ ə kəl dok′ yə mənt). A written record from the past, such as a letter or an account book. p. 23.

historical marker (his tôr′ ə kəl mär′ kər). A sign that tells about something important in history. p. 20.

historical source (his tôr′ ə kəl sôrs). Something or someone that tells us about the past. p. 23.

historic district (his tôr′ ik dis′ trikt). An area of great historic interest. p. 237.

historic house (his tôr′ ik hous). A house that looks the way it did many years ago. p. 29.

history (his′ tər ē). The story of what happened in the past. p. 16.

housing development (hou′ zing di vel′ əp mənt). Many houses built on a piece of land all at the same time. p. 208.

immigrant (im′ ə grənt). A person who comes to a country to make a home. p. 186.

import (im′ pôrt). A product bought from another country. p. 247.

indentured servant (in den′ chərd sər′ vənt). A person who sold his or her services for a certain period of time in exchange for free passage to America. p. 126.

independence (in də pen′ dəns). Freedom. p. 136.

industrial park (in dus′ trē əl pärk). A large piece of land set aside for factories, offices, and other buildings. p. 208.

judicial branch (jü dish′ əl branch). The part of government that interprets, or explains, the laws. p. 221.

justice (jəs′ təs). A judge. p. 223.

key (kē). The place on a map where symbols are explained. p. 42.

labor union (lā′ bər yün′ yən). A group of workers who try to get employers to improve working conditions and pay. p. 173.

landfill (land′ fil). Long ditches covered with soil, where garbage and trash are buried. p. 250.

latitude (lat′ ə tüd). Distance north or south of the earth's Equator, measured in degrees. The lines that measure *latitude* run from east to west on a map or globe. p. 38.

legislative branch (lej′ is lā tiv branch). The part of government that makes the laws. p. 221.

legislative district (lej′ is lā tiv dis′ trikt). A division of the state for the election of representatives to the state legislature. p. 223.

legislature (lej′ ə slā chər). A lawmaking body, or group. p. 156.

local government (lō′ kəl gəv′ ərn mənt). The men and women who make and enforce the laws and provide services in a county, city, town, township, borough, or village. p. 218.

local historian (lō′ kəl his tôr′ ē ən). A person who works at finding out about a community's history. p. 28.

local history (lō′ kəl his′ tər ē). The history of a community. p. 19.

locomotive (lō kə mōt′ iv). An engine that moves on its own power. p. 162.

longhouse (lông′ hous). The kind of house built by the Lenape Indians. Some *longhouses* were up to 60 feet (18 m) long. A number of families lived in each longhouse. p. 91.

longitude (lon′ jə tüd). Distance east or west of the Prime Meridian, measured in degrees. Lines of *longitude* on a map or globe run from the North Pole to the South Pole. p. 39.

Loyalist (loi′ ə list). An American colonist who remained loyal to the British king and government. p. 135.

maize (māz). Indian corn. p. 93.

manufacturing (man yə fak′ chər ing). The making of goods by hand or machine, especially in large quantities. p. 158.

map (map). A special kind of drawing that can show different parts of the earth. p. 33.

Megalopolis (meg ə läp′ ə ləs). A supercity. p. 245.

merchant (mər′ chənt). A person who buys and sells goods to make money. p. 120.

militia (mə lish′ ə). An army of local citizens. p. 144.

mineral (min′ ər əl). A thing found in the earth. A *mineral* is neither plant nor animal. p. 58.

monument (mon′ yə mənt). Something that is built to honor a person or event. p. 20.

moraine (mə rān′). A ridge of rocks, sand, and soil left by a glacier. p. 70.

mountain chain (mount′ ən chān). A long, unbroken line of mountains. p. 74.

Native American (nā′ tiv ə mer′ ə kən). One of any group of American Indians; people whose ancestors came to America long before anyone else. p. 88.

natural resource (nach′ ər əl rē′ sôrs). Something provided by nature that is useful to people. Minerals, forests, soil, and water are all *natural resources*. p. 58.

New Jersey Plan (nü jər′ sē plan). An idea put forth by William Paterson of New Jersey, at the Constitutional Convention in 1787. Paterson suggested that there be one house of Congress in which all states would have the same number of representatives. p. 154.

New World (nü wėrld). Another name for the Western Hemisphere. It includes the continents of North America and South America. p. 104.

north (nôrth). A direction word. *North* is the direction toward the North Pole. p. 36.

North Pole (nôrth pōl). The most northern place on the earth; the northern end of the earth's axis. The *North Pole* is located in the Arctic Ocean. p. 36.

nursery (nərs′ rē). A place where plants are grown for sale. p. 60.

ocean (ō′ shən). A large body of water. There are four *oceans*. They are the Arctic, Atlantic, Pacific, and Indian oceans. p. 33.

oil refinery (oiəl ri fīn′ rē). A plant where gasoline and other products are made from oil. p. 76.

open space (ō′ pən spās). Unsettled or undeveloped land. p. 73.

oral history (ôr′ əl his′ tər ē). Information about the past that is gathered by talking with people who remember events in the past. p. 25.

ore (ôr). A mineral that is mined because it contains something that can be used, such as a metal like iron. p. 58.

Parliament (pär′ lə mənt). The part of the British government that makes laws. p. 133.

patent (pat′ ənt). A paper that gives only the person who invented a thing the right to make, use, or sell the invention. p. 51.

Patriot (pā′ trē ət). A person who loves and supports his or her country. Colonists who wanted to break away from Great Britain were *Patriots*. p. 135.

patroon (pə trün′). The person to whom land was given under the patroon system. p. 108.

patroon system (pə trün′ sis′ təm). A plan to get more people to move to New Netherland. A patroon was given a large piece of land and had to bring or send 50 settlers to New Netherland. p. 108.

patroonship (pə trün′ ship). The land given to a person under the patroon system. p. 108.

phonograph (fō nə graf). A machine that produces sounds; known today as a record player. p. 176.

phratry (frā′ trē). A group of two or more smaller Indian family groups known as clans. p. 96.

Piedmont (pēd′ mänt). A region of flat land and hills in the United States. The Italian word *piedmont* means "the land at the foot of the mountains." p. 74.

Pine Barrens (pīn bar′ ənz). An area of pine forests and sandy soil in southern New Jersey. p. 73.

plain (plān). A broad strip of low, flat land. p. 71.

planetarium (plan ə tār′ ē əm). A building that has a cameralike machine that shows how the planets and stars look in the sky. p. 234.

playwright (plā′ rīt). A person who writes plays. p. 254.

pollution (pə lü′ shən). Making the earth's air, water, and soil dirty. p. 250.

population density (pop yə lā′ shən den′ sə tē). How crowded a place is; the number of people per unit of area such as square mile or square kilometer. p. 52.

precipitation (pri sip ə tā′ shən). Any form of water that falls to earth. Rain, snow, sleet, and hail are kinds of *precipitation*. p. 63.

preserve (pri zerv′). To keep safe and unchanged. p. 28.

primary system (prī′ mär ē sis′ təm). A plan that allows voters to choose the people who run for public office. p. 195.

Prime Meridian (prīm mə rid′ ē ən). The line of longitude from which other lines of longitude are measured. The *Prime Meridian* is numbered 0°. It passes through Greenwich, England. p. 39.

proprietor (prə prī′ ə tər). An owner. p. 118.

prosperity (prä sper′ ə tē). Good times for the economy. p. 202.

public official (pub′ lik ə fish′ əl). A person who holds a public office. p. 194.

public transportation (pub′ lik trans pər tā′ shən). Buses, trains, and subways that carry passengers from one place to another. p. 209.

rally (ral′ ē). A meeting of people for a special purpose or cause. p. 197.

ratify (rat′ ə fī). To approve. p. 155.

ration (rash′ ən). To supply in a limited amount. p. 207.

redcoat (red′ kōt). A British soldier. p. 139.

reform (ri fôrm′). A change that makes something better. p. 194.

region (rē′ jən). An area that has something special about it that makes it different from other areas. p. 68.

religious freedom (ri lij′ əs frēd′ əm). The freedom to follow one's own religion. p. 119.

research (ri sərch′). To search for facts about something. p. 28.

reservation (rez ər vā′ shən). Land that has been set aside, or reserved, for the Indians by the government. p. 99.

reservoir (rez′ ər vwär). A place where water can be collected and stored for use. p. 61.

resident (rez′ ə dənt). A person who lives in a place. p. 238.

resort (ri zôrt′). A place that people visit for fun. p. 73.

revolution (rev ə lü′ shən). A complete and often violent change of government. p. 135.

royal colony (roi′ əl kol′ ə nē). A colony governed by the king or queen of England. p. 123.

sachem (sā′ chəm). The male leader, or chief, of a phratry. *Sachem* means "powerful one" or "one above all others." p. 96.

satellite (sat′ əl īt). A kind of spacecraft that moves around the earth. p. 210.

scale (skāl). A way of showing size or distance on a map. p. 42.

secede (si sēd′). To withdraw from. p. 169.

sewer (sü′ ər). An underground pipe that carries away waste and waste products. p. 191.

slash and burn (slash and bərn). The clearing of land for farming by cutting trees and burning them. The ashes from the burnt trees help to make the soil better for growing crops. p. 93.

slave (slāv). A person who is owned by another person. p. 126.

social problem (sō′ shəl präb′ ləm). A people problem; a problem that arises when people live close together. p. 251.

Sons of Liberty (sunz ov lib′ er tē). A group of colonists who led the fight against tax stamps. p. 133.

south (south). A direction word. *South* is the direction toward the South Pole. p. 36.

South Pole (south pōl). The most southern place on the earth; the southern end of the earth's axis. The *South Pole* is located on the continent of Antarctica. p. 36.

specialize (spesh′ ə līz). To do one or two things instead of many things. p. 246.

sphere (sfir). An object that is round like a ball. The earth is a *sphere*. p. 33.

state government (stāt gəv′ ərn mənt). The men and women who make and carry out the laws of a state. p. 218.

states' rights (stāts rīts). Rights that do not belong to the federal government but that can be exercised by the separate states, according to the Constitution. p. 168.

steamboat (stēm′ bōt). A boat moved by steam power. p. 161.

steerage ticket (stir′ ij tik′ ət). The lowest-priced ticket on a passenger ship. p. 187.

stock (stäk). To provide with a supply of something. p. 204.

strike (strīk). To stop working until certain changes are made. p. 173.

suburb (sub′ ərb). A smaller town or community near a large city. p. 76.

surrender (sə ren′ dər). To give up. p. 111.

symbol (sim′ bəl). On a map, something that stands for a real place or thing on the earth's surface. p. 42.

tax (taks). Money paid to a government or to the people who rule the land. p. 119.

temperature (tem′ pər ə chər). Degree of hot or cold, such as of the air. p. 64.

tenement (ten′ ə mənt). A large, crowded apartment building. p. 177.

textile (teks′ təl). A woven fabric or cloth. p. 238.

thatched roof (thacht rüf). A house covering made of straw or other plant matter. p. 108.

toll (tōl). Money paid for travel on a turnpike. The *toll* helps to pay for the road and its care. p. 158.

tourist (túr′ əst). A person who travels for pleasure. p. 248.

toxic waste (tok′ sik wāst). Very dangerous chemicals and special waste products from factories. p. 251.

trading post (trād′ ing pōst). A place where things can be bought, sold, or traded. p. 107.

transportation (trans pər tā′ shən). The moving of people and goods from one place to another. p. 18.

trolley car (trol′ ē kär). An electric streetcar. p. 193.

turnpike (tərn′ pīk). A kind of road at different places on which travelers had to pass through a turning pike, or gate, where they paid a toll. p. 158.

Underground Railroad (ən′ dər ground rāl′ rōd). A system of secret escape paths that slaves could take to freedom. There were safe resting stops for the slaves on the paths. p. 164.

urban (ėr′ bən). Of or relating to a city. p. 177.

urban area (ėr′ bən âr′ ē ə). A large city and its suburbs or many separate cities and their suburbs. p. 230.

veto (vē′ tō). To turn down. p. 223.

victory garden (vik′ tər ē gär′ dən). A small vegetable garden grown for family and friends during World War II. p. 207.

weather (weᴛʜ′ ər). The way the air is at a certain time in a given place. p. 62.

weir (war). A dam made from sticks or fences set in the water to trap fish. p. 94.

west (west). A direction word. If one faces north, *west* will be on one's left. p. 36.

BIOGRAPHICAL DICTIONARY

The page reference in each entry tells where each person is first mentioned in the text.

Aldrin, Edwin E. "Buzz", Jr. (äl' drin, ed' win ē buz jün' yər) (1930–). New Jersey–born astronaut. Lunar module pilot on Apollo 11, the first manned landing on the moon. p. 252.

Anne (an) (1665–1714). British queen during New Jersey's days as a royal colony. p. 123.

Berkeley, John (bèrk' lē, jon) (?–1678). One of the first proprietors, along with George Carteret, of New Jersey. p. 118.

Blume, Judy (blüm, jü' dē) (1938–). New Jersey–born author of many popular children's books. p. 254.

Bradley, Bill (brad' lē, bil) (1943–). United States senator from New Jersey since 1979. Basketball player with the New York Knickerbockers from 1967 to 1977. p. 227.

Brearley, David (brēr' lē, dā'vid) (1745–1790). A New Jersey delegate to the Constitutional Convention in 1787. p. 153.

Brown, Tom, Jr. (broun, tom jün'yər) (1950–). Tracker who runs a survival school in Asbury. p. 72.

Cabot, John (kab' ət, jon) (1450–1498). Italian ship captain who sailed to North America for the country of England in 1497 and explored the eastern coast of Canada. p. 104.

Caldwell, Hannah (kôl' dwel, han' ä) (1738–1780). Wife of a New Jersey minister. Mistakenly killed by the British during the battle of Connecticut Farms. p. 144.

Carteret, George (kär' tèr et, jôrj) (1610?–1680). One of the first proprietors, along with Lord Berkeley, of New Jersey. p. 118.

Carteret, Philip (kär' tèr et, fil' ip) (1639–1682). Nephew of George Carteret. Became governor of New Jersey in 1665. p. 118.

Clark, Abraham (klärk, ā' brä ham) (1726–1794). New Jersey lawyer and one of the five delegates from New Jersey to the Second Continental Congress. Signed the Declaration of Independence. p. 136.

Cleveland, Grover (klēv' lənd, grō' vèr). (1837–1908). Twenty-second and twenty-fourth President of the United States. Only person born in New Jersey who became President. He officially accepted the gift of the Statue of Liberty from France. p. 188.

Clinton, Henry (klin' tən, hen' rē) (1738–1795). British general of the Revolutionary War who replaced General William Howe. p. 143.

Colt, Samuel (kōlt, sam' ü əl) (1814–1862). Inventor of the revolver. p. 51.

Columbus, Christopher (kō lum' bəs, kris' tō fèr) (1451–1506). Italian explorer who sailed for the country of Spain. In 1492, while searching for a water route to the Indies, Columbus discovered the New World. p. 103.

Crane, Stephen (krān, stēv' ən) (1709–1780). A New Jersey delegate to the First Continental Congress. p. 135.

Dayton, Jonathan (dā' tən, jon' ə thən) (1760–1824). A New Jersey delegate to the Constitutional Convention in 1787. p. 153.

De Hart, John (də härt, jon) (1728–1795). A New Jersey delegate to the First Continental Congress. p. 135.

Dix, Dorothea (diks, dôr ō thē' ə) (1802–1887). Massachusetts reformer who spoke out in 1843 against bad living conditions in New Jersey's prisons, poorhouses, and mental asylums. p. 163.

Doby, Larry (dō' bē, lär' ē) (1924–). Former baseball player from New Jersey. First black to play in the American League. Elected to the Baseball Hall of Fame in 1977. p. 255.

Douglass, Mabel Smith (dug' ləs, mā' bəl smith) (1877–1933). New Jersey woman who worked to start a state college for women. p. 196.

Edison, Thomas (ed' i sən, tom' əs) (1847–1931). Inventor of the phonograph, an electric lamp that could last for many hours, and a new way to make movies, as well as hundreds of other devices. p. 176.

Einstein, Albert (īn' stīn, al' bèrt) (1879–1955). Scientist whose work in the area of atomic energy led to the invention of the atomic bomb. p. 206.

Fenwick, Millicent H. (fen′ wik, mil′ə cent āch) (1910–). Head American delegate to the United Nations Food and Agriculture Organization (FAO) in Rome, Italy. Representative from the Fifth Congressional District in New Jersey from 1975 to 1982. p. 253.

Fitch, John (fich, jon) (1743–1798). Inventor who ran a steamboat service on the Delaware River between Philadelphia and New Jersey in the 1780s. p. 161.

Franklin, William (frangk′ lin, wil′ yəm) (1731–1813). Son of Patriot Benjamin Franklin. Loyalist who became the royal governor of New Jersey in 1775. p. 136.

George III (jôrj ҭHə thérd) (1738–1820). British king who made the American colonists pay heavy taxes in the 1700s. p. 132.

Goodwin, Hannibal (gùd′ win, han′ ə bəl) (1822–1900). Minister and inventor of the first plastic film, which was used in cameras and in making movies. p. 175.

Hamilton, Alexander (ham′ əl tən, al eg zan′ dər) (1757–1804). Statesman from New York who had the idea to start a manufacturing center at the Great Falls of the Passaic River. p. 158.

Hart, John (härt, jon) (1711?–1779). One of the five delegates from New Jersey to the Second Continental Congress. Oldest signer of the Declaration of Independence. p. 136.

Hays, Mary Ludwig (hāz, mãr′ē lùd′ wig) (1754?–1832). Woman who took her husband's place at the battle of Monmouth during the Revolutionary War. Because she brought pitchers of water to the soldiers during the battle, she was called Molly Pitcher. p. 140.

Heir, Doug (hãr, dug) (1960–). Record-setting New Jersey athlete in the Wheelchair Division of the 1984 Olympics. p. 254.

Hitler, Adolf (hit′ lér, ad′ olf) (1889–1945). Nazi and German leader during World War II. p. 206.

Holland, John (hol′ ənd, jon) (1840–1914). Teacher from Paterson who built the first submarine, later used by the United States Navy. p. 175.

Hopkinson, Francis (häp′ kin sən, fran′ sis) (1737–1791). Artist and writer who was one of the five New Jersey signers of the Declaration of Independence. Helped to design the American flag and the Great Seal of the State of New Jersey. p. 136.

Houston, William Churchill (hüs′ tən, wil′ yəm chérch′ hil) (1746–1788). A New Jersey delegate to the Constitutional Convention in 1787. p. 153.

Howe, William (hou, wil′ yəm) (1729–1814). British general during the Revolutionary War. Sent troops to attack the Continental army in Princeton in 1777. p. 139.

Hudson, Henry (hud′ sən, hen′ rē) (?–1611). English ship captain who explored for Holland. In 1609, Hudson sailed along the southern coast of New Jersey to Sandy Hook and continued north into a large inland river. This river is known today as the Hudson River. p. 106.

Hyatt, John (hī′ ət, jon) (1837–1920). Inventor of the world's first plastic. Hyatt's plastic factory was located in Newark. p. 175.

Irvin, Monte (ér′ vin, män′ tē) (1919–). Former baseball player from New Jersey. Elected to the Baseball Hall of Fame in 1973. p. 255.

James, Duke of York (jāmz, dük ov yôrk) (1633–1701). Also known as the Duke of Albany. Brother of King Charles II of England. Sent Richard Nicolls to take control of New Netherland to establish English rule of the colony. p. 112.

Jefferson, Thomas (jef′ ér sən, tom′ əs) (1743–1826). Third President of the United States and main writer of the Declaration of Independence. p. 137.

Kean, Thomas (kān, tom′ əs) (1935–). Governor of New Jersey since 1982. p. 221.

Kearny, Philip (kär′ nē, fil′ ip) (1814–1862). General who led New Jersey troops during the Civil War. p. 171.

Kinsey, James (kin′ sē, jāmz) (1731–1803). A New Jersey delegate to the First Continental Congress. p. 135.

Kraft, Herbert C. (kraft, hər′ bért sē) (1927–). New Jersey archaeologist who studies and writes about the Lenape Indians. p. 98.

Lautenberg, Frank (lout′ ən bərg, frangk) (1924–). United States senator from New

Jersey since 1982. In business in Clifton before being elected to the Senate. p. 227.

Lewis, Jerry (lü′ is, jär′ ē) (1926–). New Jersey–born actor. National chairman of the Muscular Dystrophy Association. p. 256.

Lincoln, Abraham (ling′ kən, ā′ brä ham) (1809–1865). Sixteenth President of the United States and President during the Civil War. p. 169.

Livingston, William (liv′ ing stən, wil′ yəm) (1723–1790). A New Jersey delegate to the First Continental Congress. First governor of the state of New Jersey. p. 157.

Maass, Clara (mäs, klar′ ä) (1876–1901). New Jersey nurse who gave her life to find a cure for malaria and for whom a hospital in Belleville is named. p. 22.

McClellan, George (mä kləl′ ən, jôrj) (1826–1885). Northern general during the Civil War who became governor of New Jersey in 1878. p. 171.

Mercer, Hugh (mér′ sér, hü) (1721?–1777). American general who fought against the British during the battle of Princeton, in which he was killed. p. 140.

Morris, Lewis (mor′ is, lü′ is) (1671–1746). First New Jersey–born governor of the New Jersey colony. Took office in 1738. p. 123.

Morse, Samuel (môrs, sam′ ü əl) (1791–1872). Artist and inventor of the telegraph. p. 51.

Murphy, Franklin (mér′ fē, frangk′ lin) (1846–1920). Governor of New Jersey from 1902 to 1905. Responsible for important reforms during these years. p. 194.

Nicolls, Richard (nik′ əlz, rich′ érd) (1624–1672). English governor of New Jersey in 1664. Took the colony of New Netherland away from Peter Stuyvesant and the Dutch. p. 112.

Paterson, William (pat′ ər sən, wil′ yəm) (1745–1806). Author of the New Jersey Plan and governor of New Jersey from 1790 to 1793. p. 154.

Philbrook, Mary (fil′ brùk, mãr′ ē) (1872–1958). First woman lawyer in New Jersey. Worked for women's right to vote. p. 197.

Printz, Johan (prints, yō′ hän) (1592–1663). Governor of the New Sweden colony from 1643 to 1653. p. 110.

Roosevelt, Franklin D. (rō′ ze vəlt, frangk′ lin dē) (1882–1945). Thirty-second President of the United States. President Roosevelt led the nation during the Great Depression and World War II. p. 204.

Roukema, Marge (rou kə mə, märj) (1929–). United States representative from the Fifth Congressional District in New Jersey. p. 227.

Segal, George (sē′ gəl, jôrj) (1924–). New Jersey sculptor of plaster and bronze figures. p. 252.

Smith, Richard (smith, rich′ érd) (1735–1803). A New Jersey delegate to the First Continental Congress. p. 135.

Springsteen, Bruce (spring′ stēn, brüs) (1949–). New Jersey–born popular musician. p. 255.

Stevens, John (stē′ vəns, jon) (1749–1838). Inventor who developed steamboats. Also builder of the first railroad locomotive in America in 1825. p. 162.

Still, James (stil, jämz) (1812–1885). Self-taught doctor who treated sick people living in the Pine Barrens. p. 170.

Stockton, Richard (stok′ tən, rich′ érd) (1730–1781). New Jersey lawyer from Princeton who was one of the five New Jersey delegates to the Second Continental Congress and a signer of the Declaration of Independence. p. 137.

Stone, Lucy (stōn, lü′ sē) (1818–1893). New Jersey woman who helped to begin the New Jersey Suffrage League, which worked to help women gain the right to vote. p. 197.

Streep, Meryl (strēp, mãr′ əl) (1949–). New Jersey–born actress. p. 256.

Stuyvesant, Peter (stī′ və sənt, pē′ tər) (1610?–1672). Dutch governor of New Netherland. Gained control of New Sweden and established the strength of the Dutch in New Jersey and New York. p. 111.

Tubman, Harriet (tub′ mən, hãr′ ē ət) (1820?–1913). Former Maryland slave who worked on the Underground Railroad, guiding hundreds of slaves to freedom. p. 165.

Vail, Alfred (vāl, al′ fred) (1807–1859). Morris-

town-born telegrapher who gave Samuel Morse money for his work on the telegraph. p. 51.

Verrazano, Giovanni da (vär rä tsä nō, jō vän′ nē dä) (1485?–?1528). Italian explorer who sailed for France. In 1524, Verrazano sailed into New York Bay and along the coast of New Jersey. The Verrazano Bridge, connecting Staten Island to Long Island, now bears his name. p. 105.

Washington, George (wäsh′ ing tən, jôrj) (1732–1799). First President of the United States and commander in chief of the Continental army during the American Revolution. p. 136.

Whitman, Walt (whit′ mən, wôlt) (1819–1892).

Poet whose home in Camden is now a historic house. p. 29.

Wilson, Woodrow (wil′ sən, wŭd′ rō) (1856–1924). Twenty-eighth President of the United States. President of Princeton University from 1902 to 1910 and governor of New Jersey from 1911 to 1913. p. 195.

Witherspoon, John (wiŦH′ ėr spün, jon) (1723–1794). Minister and president of the College of New Jersey, now Princeton University. A New Jersey delegate to the Second Continental Congress and the only member of the clergy to sign the Declaration of Independence. p. 22.

Woolman, John (wŭl′ mən, jon) (1720–1772). New Jersey Quaker preacher and abolitionist. p. 130.

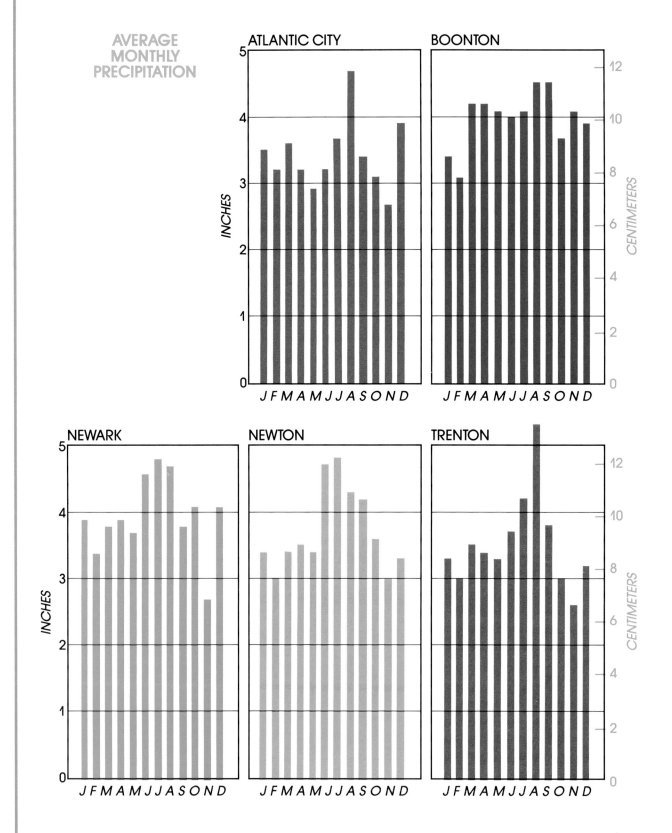

AVERAGE
MONTHLY
PRECIPITATION

ATLANTIC CITY

BOONTON

NEWARK

NEWTON

TRENTON

278

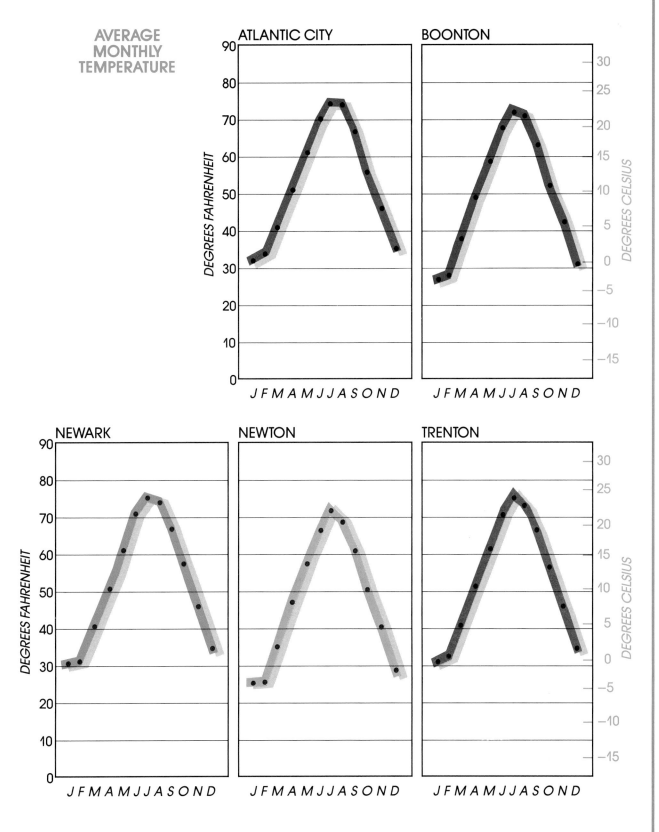

AVERAGE
MONTHLY
TEMPERATURE

ATLANTIC CITY

BOONTON

NEWARK

NEWTON

TRENTON

279

FACTS ABOUT NEW JERSEY'S COUNTIES

County Name	County Seat	County Population	Population Rank	Area in Square Miles (Square Kilometers)	Area Rank
Atlantic	Mays Landing	201,300	15	568 (1,471)	3
Bergen	Hackensack	844,300	1	237 (613)	15
Burlington	Mount Holly	378,800	10	808 (2,093)	1
Camden	Camden	482,000	7	223 (578)	17
Cape May	Cape May Court House	89,100	19	263 (680)	14
Cumberland	Bridgeton	133,500	16	498 (1,290)	5
Essex	Newark	831,800	2	127 (329)	19
Gloucester	Woodbury	207,300	14	327 (848)	11
Hudson	Jersey City	559,900	4	46 (120)	21
Hunterdon	Flemington	92,600	18	427 (1,105)	8
Mercer	Trenton	313,800	12	227 (587)	16
Middlesex	New Brunswick	618,400	3	316 (819)	12
Monmouth	Freehold	525,300	5	472 (1,223)	6
Morris	Morristown	417,900	9	471 (1,219)	7
Ocean	Toms River	375,200	11	641 (1,661)	2
Passaic	Paterson	455,200	8	187 (485)	18
Salem	Salem	66,500	21	338 (875)	10
Somerset	Somerville	210,900	13	305 (789)	13
Sussex	Newton	120,200	17	525 (1,361)	4
Union	Elizabeth	505,500	6	103 (267)	20
Warren	Belvidere	85,400	20	359 (930)	9

GOVERNORS OF THE STATE OF NEW JERSEY

1. William Livingston	1776–1790
2. Elisha Lawrence	1790
3. William Paterson	1790–1793
4. Elisha Lawrence	1793
5. Richard Howell	1793–1801
6. Joseph Bloomfield	1801–1802
7. John Lambert	1802–1803
8. Joseph Bloomfield	1803–1812
9. Charles Clark	1812
10. Aaron Ogden	1812–1813
11. William S. Pennington	1813–1815
12. William Kennedy	1815
13. Mahlon Dickerson	1815–1817
14. Jesse Upson	1817
15. Isaac H. Williamson	1817–1829
16. Peter D. Vroom	1829–1832
17. Samuel L. Southard	1832–1833
18. Elias P. Seeley	1833
19. Peter D. Vroom	1833–1836
20. Philemon Dickerson	1836–1837
21. William Pennington	1837–1843
22. Daniel Haines	1843–1845
23. Charles C. Stratton	1845–1848
24. Daniel Haines	1848–1851
25. George F. Fort	1851–1854
26. Rodman M. Price	1854–1857
27. William A. Newell	1857–1860
28. Charles S. Olden	1860–1863
29. Joel Parker	1863–1866
30. Marcus L. Ward	1866–1869
31. Theodore F. Randolph	1869–1872
32. Joel Parker	1872–1875
33. Joseph D. Bedle	1875–1878
34. George B. McClellan	1878–1881
35. George C. Ludlow	1881–1884
36. Leon Abbett	1884–1887
37. Robert S. Green	1887–1890
38. Leon Abbett	1890–1893
39. George T. Werts	1893–1896
40. John W. Griggs	1896–1898
41. Foster M. Voorhees	1898
42. David O. Watkins	1898–1899
43. Foster M. Voorhees	1899–1902
44. Franklin Murphy	1902–1905
45. Edward C. Stokes	1905–1908
46. John Franklin Fort	1908–1911
47. Woodrow Wilson	1911–1913
48. James E. Fielder	1913
49. Leon R. Taylor	1913–1914
50. James E. Fielder	1914–1917
51. Walter E. Edge	1917–1919
52. William N. Runyon	1919–1920
53. Edward I. Edwards	1920–1923
54. George S. Silzer	1923–1926
55. A. Harry Moore	1926–1929
56. Morgan F. Larson	1929–1932
57. A. Harry Moore	1932–1935
58. Clifford R. Powell	1935
59. Horace G. Prall	1935
60. Harold G. Hoffman	1935–1938
61. A. Harry Moore	1938–1941
62. Charles Edison	1941–1944
63. Walter E. Edge	1944–1947
64. Alfred E. Driscoll	1947–1954
65. Robert B. Meyner	1954–1962
66. Richard J. Hughes	1962–1970
67. William T. Cahill	1970–1974
68. Brendan T. Byrne	1974–1982
69. Thomas H. Kean	1982–

100 MOST POPULATED PLACES IN NEW JERSEY

Place	Population	Rank	Place	Population	Rank
Newark	329,248	1	Long Branch	29,819	53
Jersey City	223,532	2	Pemberton Twp.	29,720	54
Paterson	137,970	3	Bridgewater Twp.	29,175	55
Elizabeth	106,201	4	Nutley	28,998	56
Trenton	92,124	5	Neptune Twp.	28,366	57
Woodbridge Twp.	90,074	6	Livingston Twp.	28,040	58
Camden	84,910	7	Manchester Twp.	27,987	59
Hamilton Twp. (Mercer)	82,801	8	Washington Twp.	27,878	60
East Orange	77,690	9	Garfield	26,803	61
Clifton	74,388	10	Rahway	26,723	62
Edison Twp.	70,193	11	Paramus	26,474	63
Cherry Hill Twp.	68,785	12	Jackson Twp.	25,644	64
Bayonne	65,047	13	Bergenfield	25,568	65
Dover Twp.	64,455	14	Ridgewood	25,208	66
Middletown Twp.	62,574	15	Howell Twp.	25,065	67
Irvington	61,493	16	Millville	24,815	68
Union City	55,593	17	Cranford Twp.	24,573	69
Vineland	53,753	18	Lodi	23,956	70
Brick Twp.	53,629	19	Englewood	23,701	71
Passaic	52,463	20	Ocean Twp. (Monmouth)	23,570	72
Old Bridge Twp.	51,515	21	Deptford Twp.	23,473	73
Union Twp. (Union)	50,184	22	Berkeley Twp.	23,151	74
Parsippany-Troy Hills Twp.	49,868	23	Hazlet Twp.	23,013	75
Bloomfield	47,792	24	Maplewood Twp.	22,950	76
North Bergen Twp.	47,019	25	West Milford Twp.	22,750	77
Wayne Twp.	46,474	26	North Brunswick Twp.	22,220	78
Plainfield	45,555	27	Monroe Twp.	21,639	79
Gloucester Twp.	45,156	28	Evesham Twp.	21,508	80
Hoboken	42,460	29	Cliffside Park	21,464	81
Piscataway Twp.	42,223	30	Hillside Twp.	21,440	82
New Brunswick	41,442	31	Summit	21,071	83
Atlantic City	40,199	32	East Windsor Twp.	21,041	84
Willingboro Twp.	39,912	33	Scotch Plains Twp.	20,774	85
West Orange	39,510	34	Roselle	20,641	86
West New York	39,194	35	Carteret	20,598	87
Teaneck Twp.	39,007	36	Maple Shade Twp.	20,525	88
Perth Amboy	38,951	37	South Plainfield	20,521	89
Lakewood Twp.	38,464	38	Lyndhurst Twp.	20,326	90
Montclair	38,321	39	Winslow Twp.	20,034	91
Linden	37,836	40	Rockaway Twp.	19,850	92
East Brunswick Twp.	37,711	41	Lawrence Twp.	19,724	93
Hackensack	36,039	42	Millburn Twp.	19,543	94
Kearny	35,735	43	Egg Harbor Twp.	19,381	95
Belleville	35,367	44	Freehold Twp.	19,202	96
Ewing Twp.	34,842	45	North Plainfield	19,108	97
Pennsauken Twp.	33,775	46	Rutherford	19,068	98
Fort Lee	32,449	47	Hillsborough Twp.	19,061	99
Fair Lawn	32,229	48	Wall Twp.	18,952	100
Franklin Twp. (Somerset)	31,358	49			
Orange	31,136	50			
Westfield	30,447	51			
Sayreville	29,969	52			

Twp. is the abbreviaton for "Township."

The county is shown in parentheses when there is more than one place in New Jersey with the same name.

INDEX

CREDITS

Cover: Ralph Krubner

Graphs and time lines: Laura Shallop

Maps: General Drafting Co., Inc.; R. R. Donnelley Cartographic Services

Contributing artist: Michael Adams

Unit 1 10: © 1987 Mike Yamashita/Woodfin Camp & Associates. 11: *t.* Gene Ahrens/Shostal Associates; *b.l., r.* Walter Choroszewski. 12: *t.* New Jersey Department of Defense; *m.* no credit; *b.* Wayne Laniken/Bruce Coleman. 13: *t.* W.H. Hodge/Peter Arnold, Inc.; *inset* Derek Fell; *b.* E.R. Degginger. 14: *t.* Silver Burdett & Ginn; *b.* Rob Clark for Silver Burdett & Ginn. 15: *t.* Rhoda Sidney; *b.* Peter Byron for Silver Burdett & Ginn.

Chapter 1 16: Newark Public Library. 17: Rhoda Sidney. 18: Imagery. 19: Rhoda Sidney. 20: *l.* © Linda Bartlett/Photo Researchers, Inc.; *m.* Leo deWys, Inc.; *t.r., b.r.* Rhoda Sidney. 21: Rhoda Sidney; *inset* The Bettmann Archive. 22: David T. Gamble; *inset* Raymond Ross. 23: courtesy Press Journal, Englewood, N.J. 24: *t.* Paterson Museum; *b.* Collection of Leonard Hanson. 25: Rhoda Sidney, courtesy Von Steuben House, River Edge, N.J. 26: Jim Cesta/Freelance Photographers Guild. 28: Rhoda Sidney. 29: Silver Burdett & Ginn.

Chapter 2 32: *b.l.* NASA; *b.r.* Silver Burdett & Ginn. 36: Silver Burdett & Ginn. 41: J. Blank/Freelance Photographers Guild. 43: *t. left to right* Silver Burdett & Ginn; Silver Burdett & Ginn; © C. Vergara/Photo Researchers, Inc.; *b. left to right* Chris Sorensen; Vince Streano/Streano Havens; Silver Burdett & Ginn; Walter Chandoha. 44: *t.r.* Russell Dian for Silver Burdett & Ginn. 46: *t.* Silver Burdett & Ginn. 47: *t.* Silver Burdett & Ginn.

Chapter 3 50: *t.l.* The Granger Collection; *b.l.* National Portrait Gallery, Smithsonian Institution; *t.r.* Museum of the City of New York; *b.r.* Rutgers University. 51: Bob Krist/Leo deWys, Inc.; *inset* Bob Krist. 54: © C. Vergara/Photo Researchers, Inc. 57: *t.r.* Camerique/H. Armstrong Roberts. 58: Silver Burdett & Ginn. 60: Walter Choroszewski. 61: Rocky Weldon/Leo deWys, Inc. 65: Renate Miller/Monkmeyer Press.

Chapter 4 69: Eric Carle/Shostal Associates. 72: Rhoda Sidney. 73: E.R. Degginger. 75: Bob Krist. 76: Bob Krist/Leo deWys, Inc. 77: Walter Choroszewski. 78: Bob Krist/Leo deWys, Inc. 79: Walter Choroszewski.

Unit 2 85: The Granger Collection. 86: *l.* Seton Hall University Museum; *r.* The Granger Collection. 87: *t.* The Granger Collection; *b.* Culver Pictures.

Chapter 5 89: George C. Page Museum. 90–97: Seton Hall University Museum. 98: Carol Koeck. 99: Museum of the American Indian, Heye Foundation.

Chapter 6 102: The Bettmann Archive. 103: The Granger Collection. 105: Culver Pictures. 106: © J.G.L. Ferris, Archives of 76, Bay Village, Ohio. 108: Jersey City Public Library. 109: Ralph Krubner. 110: American Swedish Historical Museum. 111: Newark Public Library. 112: The Granger Collection. 113: Don Hulshizer.

Chapter 7 117: © Van Bucher/Photo Researchers, Inc.; *inset* The Granger Collection. 118: British Tourist Authority. 119: Delaware Art Museum. 120: The Granger Collection. 121: Silver Burdett & Ginn. 122: Northwind. 124: Newark Public Library. 125: courtesy Miller Cory House. 126, 127: The Granger Collection. 128: Walter Choroszewski. 130: Haverford College Library — Quaker Collection.

Chapter 8 133: Rhoda Sidney. 134: Gary Cooper. 136: The Granger Collection. 137: The United States Capitol. 138: Old Barracks Museum, Trenton. 140, 141: The Bettmann Archive. 142: Silver Burdett & Ginn. 143: National Park Service.

Unit 3 149: *t.* Paterson Museum; *b.* courtesy Dover Publications. 150: The Granger Collection. 151: *l.* courtesy The Campbell Soup Company; *r.* Northwind.

Chapter 9 153: American Numismatic Society. 154, 155: The Granger Collection. 156: New Jersey Historical Society. 157: The Granger Collection. 158: de Gregory/Leo deWys, Inc. 159: Ralph Krubner. 160: Boro of Wharton, photo Silver Burdett & Ginn. 161: The Granger Collection. 163: New Jersey Psychiatric Hospital; *inset* Historical Pictures Service, Chicago. 164: Silver Burdett & Ginn.

Chapter 10 170, 171: New Jersey Historical Society. 172: Billy Bafdeye/Leo deWys, Inc. 173: Culver Pictures. 174: New Jersey Historical Society. 175: Culver Pictures. 176: The Granger Collection. 177: The Bettmann Archive. 178: Culver Pictures.

Unit 4 183: *t.* The Granger Collection; *b.* Michael Spozarsky. 184: Brown Brothers. 185: *t.* Michael Spozarsky; *b.* AT&T Bell Laboratories.

Chapter 11 187: The Granger Collection. 188: *t.* Michael Spozarsky; *b.* The Granger Collection. 189: Brown Brothers. 190: Silver Burdett & Ginn. 191: Michael Spozarsky. 192: Breck Kent. 193: The Bettmann Archive. 194: Silver Burdett & Ginn. 195: Library of Congress. 196: Rutgers University Library. 197: The Bettmann Archive; *inset* New Jersey Historical Society.

Chapter 12 201, 202: The Granger Collection. 203: Wide World Photos. 204: The Bettmann Archive. 205: United States Army. 206: The Granger Collection. 207: Magnum; *inset* no credit. 208: Bob Krist. 209: New Jersey Transit. 210: AT&T Bell Laboratories.

Unit 5 214: E.R. Degginger. 215: Louis Backus. 216: *t.* Walter Choroszewski; *b.* Imagery. 217: *t.* Imagery; *b.* Sanford Burstein.

Chapter 13 218–219: New Jersey Office of Public Communications. 220, 221: Walter Choroszewski. 224: E.R. Degginger. 225: Silver Burdett & Ginn. 227: *t.* © 1987 Mike Yamashita/Woodfin Camp & Associates; *b.l.* Alyce Parseghian; *b.r.* Frank Lautenberg. 228: United States Postal Service.

Chapter 14: 230, 231, 233: Ralph Krubner. 234, 235: Michael Spozarsky. 236: George Goodwin/Monkmeyer Press. 237: Ralph Krubner; *inset* © George E. Jones/Photo Researchers, Inc. 240: Klaus Schnitzer. 241: Walter Choroszewski.

Chapter 15 244–245: Mike Yamashita/The Stock Shop. 247: J.T. Miller/The Stock Shop. 249: *l.* Silver Burdett & Ginn; *r.* Arthur Paxton/New Jersey Symphony. 250: Silver Burdett & Ginn. 251: New Jersey Transit. 252: *l.* NASA; *r.* Mike Yamashita; *inset* Michael Spozarsky. 253: Wide World Photos. 254: *t.* Thomas Victor/Putnam Publishing Company; *b.* Walter Choroszewski. 255: *l.* courtesy Larry Doby; *r.* Sygma. 256: *l.* Muscular Dystrophy Association; *r.* Theo Westerberg/Sygma.

2 3 4 5 6 7 8 9 10—KP—95 94 93 92 91 90 89 88 87